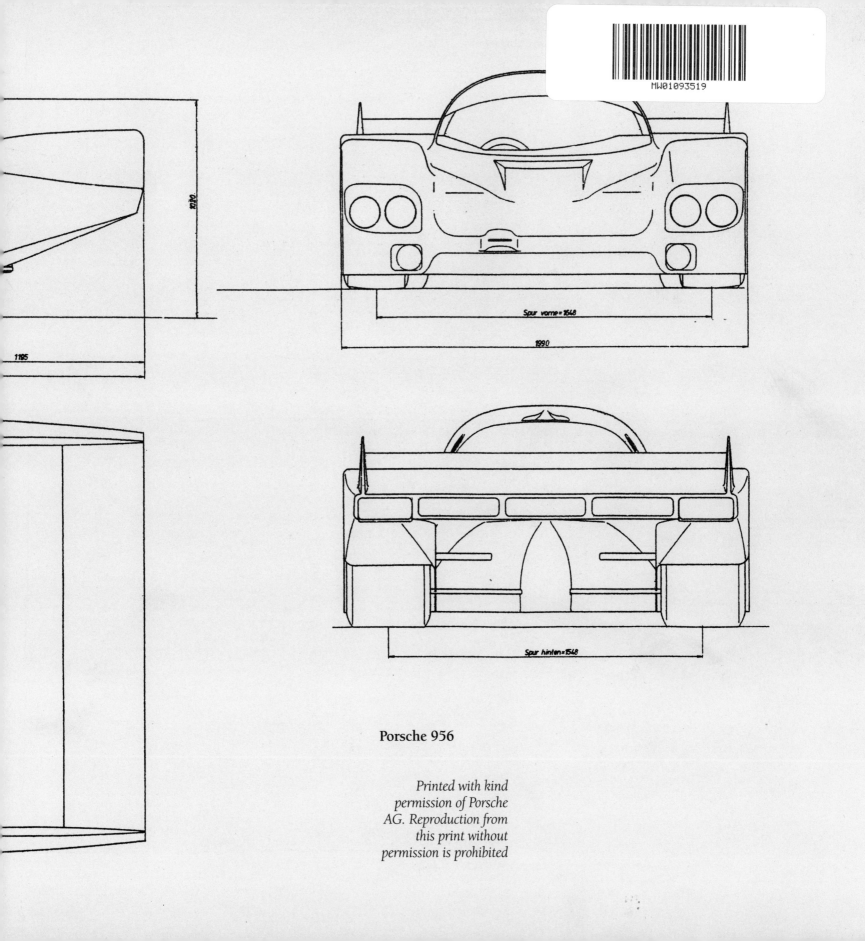

Spur vorne=1648

1990

1185

1020

Spur hinten=1548

Porsche 956

Porsche 956/962

Porsche 956/962
The enduring champions

Peter Morgan Foreword by Dipl. Ing. Peter Falk

First published in 2003

A catalogue record for this book is available from the British Library

ISBN 1 85960 951 1

Library of Congress catalog card no. 2003104828

Published by Haynes Publishing, Sparkford, Yeovil, Somerset, BA22 7JJ, UK

Tel: 01963 442030
Fax: 01963 440001
Int. tel: +44 1963 442030
Int. fax: +44 1963 440001
E-mail: sales@haynes.co.uk
Website: www.haynes.co.uk

Haynes North America, Inc.,
861 Lawrence Drive, Newbury Park,
California 91320, USA

Printed and bound in England by
J. H. Haynes & Co. Ltd, Sparkford

CONTENTS

FOREWORD

Dipl. Ing. Peter Falk

EVER SINCE Porsche was founded, it has always built sports cars and prototypes that were entered into races and rallies. To name just a few of the famous ones, these were the 550 Spyder, the 908/3, the 917 and the 936. So when FISA announced the regulations for a new World Endurance Championship at the start of the 1980s, it was inevitable Porsche should construct a new car to meet these rules.

Peter Falk

The regulations allowed a free engine, but only a certain amount of fuel per race. It was a tremendous challenge for our engineers and technicians to find the right engine/car combination with the highest possible power and the lowest possible fuel consumption. But within eight months, the first 956 was built in the workshops and later, this was followed by the 962C and the 962 for the American IMSA series.

The incredible number of victories all around the world that followed was only made possible as a result of the intensive co-operation between all the engineers, technicians, mechanics and drivers who were involved in the continuous development, both at the factory and on the racetracks. We had excellent specialists. They were real, lifetime Porsche people who came together as one team to do a fantastic job. In addition, we also had the world's best endurance drivers.

It was a fine time, but it was also a hard time. Fine, because the paddocks were still open and there was a sense of fair play among the rival manufacturers like Lancia, Jaguar, Sauber and Porsche. It was hard because in the later years, the power differences became smaller and the long-distance races gave way more and more to sprint races. The competition became very tough.

Peter Morgan has told the story of the 956/962 in an unbelievably precise manner, including the politics and the evolution of the regulations, the technical developments and the races. His interviews with team managers, engineers and drivers make the reading come alive and the brilliant pictures stir many memories.

This is a quite extraordinary book for all friends of race-car technology, endurance racing and – last but not least – the Porsche 956/962.

INTRODUCTION AND ACKNOWLEDGEMENTS

N O OTHER RACING CAR has been as successful as the Porsche 956/962. For a full 13 seasons during the 1980s and early 1990s, this family of racing cars formed the foundation of international sports car racing, bringing pleasure to countless tens of thousands of fans across the world.

These spectacular Porsches (and their direct derivatives) broke every endurance (and many short-distance) record for sports-prototype achievement, including winning the classic Le Mans event seven times, Daytona six times and at Sebring on four occasions.

Even before the 956, Porsche had a reputation as the builders of the best endurance racing cars, but what made this one special was the way in which the Stuttgart company shared its success.

With the right budget, a professional racing team could buy a proven Le Mans winner and have an excellent chance of repeating that success at any one of the blue-riband classics. Reinhold Joest did, so did Al Holbert, Bruce Leven, Preston Henn, Bob Akin and Jim Busby. As Joest confirms today, 'it was a case of buy this car and win'.

There is an easy tendency to glorify the cold statistics surrounding the 956 and 962 – to dwell on the race victories and the chassis numbers. But in writing the story of these cars, I wanted to touch the passion and the determination of the people – the racers – involved. It is their efforts that turned these carefully crafted sculptures of metal, rubber and plastic into winners.

It may be the drivers' adventures that normally capture the headlines, but the real story lays with the ability of the whole team to outsmart the competition. Look beneath the surface and you'll find the guy who designed the paint scheme, wrote the sponsor's press-copy or the doctor who prepared the energy drinks at Le Mans. It is the efforts of individuals like these that turned the 956 and 962 story into one of legend and made all the race victories look easy.

And behind it all was the power house that is Weissach. Porsche's Research and Development Centre, some 15 miles west of Stuttgart, was the pumping heart of the sports car world in the 1970s and 1980s.

What Weissach had in those years was key people. Any one of them would have made a difference in any business, but together and in motorsport, they formed an unstoppable team.

At their head was a natural leader – a vocational engineer who was revered as much for his experience as for his paternal leadership. Professor Dr Helmuth Bott was the focus of the entire Porsche engineering operation.

Manfred Jantke, former sports and public relations head at Porsche and himself one of the success factors, gives us an idea of the calibre of Bott's team. 'They were so good – fantastic people like Falk, Singer, Hensler and Mezger. They were all alike. They were giants in their qualities, but (most importantly) they weren't people with big egos, so it worked perfectly.'

Even today, the 956 and 962 are racing cars that generate huge enthusiasm wherever they are mentioned. To tell this story, I have talked to, corresponded with or referred to many individuals. So many people were involved in some way or another with the 956 and 962 programmes that it would be an impossible task to talk to everyone and mention every person whose lives were touched by these great racing cars. I apologise in advance to those I have missed – my story is the poorer for it.

I spent many hours in the Porsche Archiv, blowing the dust off Norbert Singer's engineering notes, looking at Peter Falk's detailed files and unearthing photographs that I hope will inform and entertain you. I could not have done this without the enthusiastic and material help of those custodians of Porsche's heritage: Klaus Parr, Jens Torner, Dieter Gross and the other enthusiastic staff in Zuffenhausen.

Photographs are a vital ingredient in this story and I have been fortunate to have access to several excellent libraries. The Porsche Archiv and Peter Falk supplied many invaluable images of the Weissach and aerodynamics development, together with many of the personnel shots you see here. Geoffrey Hewitt followed the IMSA scene from the late 1970s to the 1990s driving to the races in a 1974 Carrera and working freelance for most of the major manufacturers and suppliers. His superb photo art is regularly featured in *Racer, Autoweek, Car and Driver, Panorama* and many other historic racing publications.

I have also used images from the photo libraries of Rothmans International, LAT (with thanks to Kathy Agar), John Hearn and myself.

In the preparation of the manuscript, I would like to thank Peter Falk and Vern Schuppan for reading the

The Jochen Mass, Bob Wollek Rothmans-Porsche 962C at Monza in 1986.

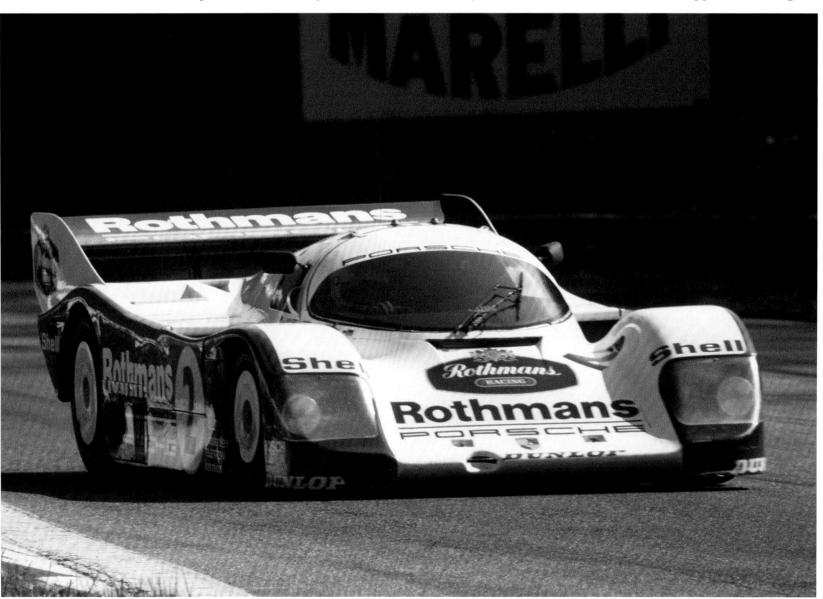

final version and supplying valuable inputs. I received help from many sources, but would particularly like to acknowledge the help (directly or indirectly) I have received from the following:

Jürgen Barth, Derek Bell, Klaus Bischoff, Siggi Brunn, Jim Busby, Bob Carlson, Paul Davies, Peter Falk, Paul Frère, Hurley Haywood, Preston Henn, Chris Horton, Clive Househam, Jacky Ickx, Manfred Jantke, Kevin Jeannette, Reinhold Joest, Ralf Juettner, Sigrun Eith-Juettner, Richard Lloyd, Sigrid Mauz, Moto Moriwaki, Jürgen Pippig, Sean Roberts, Graham Robson, Michael Schimpke, Andy Schupak, Vern Schuppan, Jeremy Shaw, Norbert Singer, Bob Snodgrass, Alwin Springer and Hans-Joachim Stuck.

At Haynes Publishing, I would like to thank Mark Hughes, Alison Roelich, Patrick Stephens and Steve Rendle for their invaluable support.

Few activities in my writing career have given me more enjoyment than talking to the racers involved with the 956 and 962. Many are still deeply involved in racing today, but all recall their years with the most successful of racing Porsches with pleasure. This then, is their story.

Peter Morgan, Marlborough, England

A static view of a Rothmans car at Weissach.

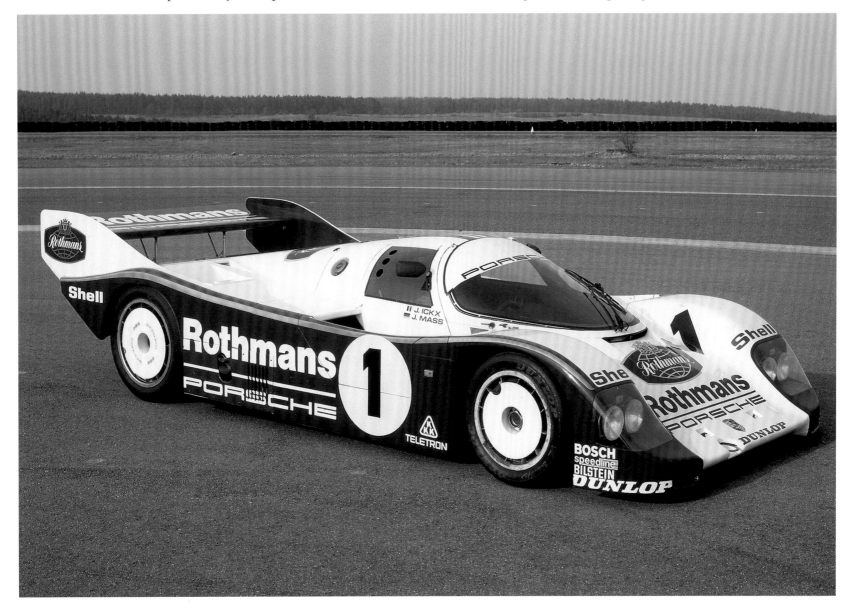

FUELLING THE ARGUMENT 1

The golden days of the 5-litre sports cars were sorely missed in the late 1970s. This is the first lap of the 1971 Le Mans 24 Hours with Porsche leading Ferrari, Ferrari, another Porsche and another Ferrari.

THE TROUBLE WITH sports car racing is that we tend to remember only the good parts. We remember Jacky Ickx outfoxing Hans Hermann to the chequered flag at Le Mans in 1969, or Mario bearing down on Steve McQueen and Peter Revson at Sebring in 1970. But the story of sports car racing has been like a roller-coaster ride – afterwards you tend to forget the moments of sheer panic.

Sports car racing was ready to panic in 1980. The distress was the end-result of an illness that began when the industry had been starved temporarily of its lifeblood – petrol – in 1974. The Middle East oil producers' embargo had brought industry, and particularly the automobile industry, to its knees.

The impact on the car makers was far-reaching. In a post-war climate of cheap fuel, the motoring world had previously thought little about the consequences of cars that only did a few miles to the gallon. However, as a direct consequence of the fuel shortage, gas-guzzling cars (often the sports or prestige models) became taboo. Almost overnight, customer attitudes towards the automobile changed and popular demand shifted towards fuel-efficient cars.

The effect on the motorsports industry (within

Europe in particular) was more fundamental. Racing suffered immediately as the major manufacturers that had been involved in racing beat a hasty retreat in search of lost revenue. The sport's changing circumstances triggered a far-reaching review of its administration.

World motorsport at that time was broadly governed by the Commission Sportive Internationale (the CSI), a branch of the Fédération Internationale de L'Automobile (the FIA).

Organisations such as the FIA and its committees were still run by elected individuals with almost no professional structure behind their best efforts.

The result was that everybody whose livelihoods depended on racing were trying to go their own way, including the circuit owners, promoters and the race teams. In short, the FIA wasn't on top of the ever-increasing professional demands of the sport or its publicity-hungry commercial backers. And the lean times around 1974 and 1975 highlighted these deficiencies.

The CSI had already been canvassing interest for a regulation change for sports car racing from 1975. They wanted to open up the technical challenge from being centred on the expensive sports prototypes, to a

After 1973, Porsche focused its race development on the 911. Two of these 2.1-litre turbocharged monsters were entered in the 1974 Le Mans 24 Hours. This car, driven by Gijs van Lennep and Gerhard Müller, finished second.

formula that included production-based grand touring cars. This, they reasoned, would attract greater manufacturer interest – their main priority.

The CSI's proposals painted a broad brush across all the non-single-seater classes. They defined a new Appendix J to their general motorsport regulations that divided sports and saloon competition into groups ranging from standard production (Group 1) through to full prototype (Group 6).

Nonetheless, the organisers of the most important race on the CSI's calendar, the Le Mans 24 Hours, were not impressed by the new regulations.

The Automobile Club de l'Ouest, (the ACO) felt that since virtually every manufacturer was having to re-invent its product range to include fuel-efficient cars, motorsport should take a responsible lead position and promote the research.

The ACO acted unilaterally and not for the first (or last!) time, they drafted their own rules. For the 1975 24 Hours they introduced a fuel consumption restriction on all entries. Every car had to run 20 laps between fuel stops and they defined a maximum fuel tank size.

In principle, it wasn't a bad idea. The CSI's only problem with the matter seems to have been that they

By 1976, the race 911 had evolved into the 935. This car, says Paul Frère, was exactly what the spirit of the Group 5 rules intended. With Norbert Singer's assistance, the 935 did not remain like this for too much longer . . .

The 936 was a last-minute prototype development in 1976 to counter the Alpine-Renaults at Le Mans. The car used parts from the 917 and 908 parts bins and won that year and again in 1977.

had not thought of it first. On hearing of the ACO's independent action, they threw Le Mans out of the FIA championships.

The intentions had been good, but as has happened so many times in sports car racing, the relevant parties were unable to agree on a common way forward. But it was the FIA's championships that suffered. Both headline sports car classes failed to attract consistent support from any more than a pair of manufacturers apiece, and so both Groups 5 and 6 became Porsche benefits. By 1978, Porsche had also withdrawn because of lack of competition. So it is not difficult to

see the reasons why the FIA's world championships were looking very sorry indeed by 1980.

North America, geographically and in spirit a million miles from the FIA in Paris, also found itself in a transition period. A new race promoter had emerged in the early 1970s alongside the established Sports Car Club of America and was developing professional sports car racing.

The emergent International Motor Sports Association (IMSA) promoted a mixed GT championship, but in the post-oil crisis environment, found it hard to attract the interest of North American manufacturers.

Everybody involved in framing the new regulations agreed that cars like the 1978 935/78 – tagged 'Moby Dick' for its flowing white bodywork – should not be permitted. This astonishing car was faster (at 226mph/ 364kph) than either the 936 or the winning Renault A442 prototypes

The 1970s FIA and IMSA series appeared quite similar at first look, but in reality they were very different. IMSA was very much commercially run and spectator-orientated, whereas the FIA championships were manufacturer-orientated with little concession to the 'show'.

The IMSA series was also tightly defined from a technical viewpoint to restrict costs, whereas the FIA championships wanted to encourage technical innovation by the big manufacturers. IMSA's main problem was that it was overrun by Porsches, and seeking some variation from the Stuttgart cars by the end of the 1970s, it was looking for a new direction.

As if to throw more pepper in the boiling pot, by this time all three blue-riband endurance classics – Le Mans, Sebring and Daytona – had excused themselves from the restrictions of the various championships.

In 1978, Jean-Marie Balestre, who at that time was president of the FFSA (Fédération Français du Sport Automobile) and a serving member of the CSI, proposed that it was time to act. The result was the replacement of the CSI with the Fédération Internationale du Sport Automobile (FISA), and Balestre (not surprisingly) was elected president.

Reporting to the FISA Plenary council were several commissions, including those covering technical regulations, medical and safety issues, Formula One and Sports Prototype racing.

Paul Frère had become a member of the CSI technical committee in 1972 and later became a vice-president. He was deeply involved in the formation of the sports car championship regulations through the 1970s and into the 1980s. He explains the rulemaker's view of why Groups 5 and 6 didn't turn out quite the way they had been intended.

'Originally, the World Championship for Manufacturers was to be for Group 5 cars – cars developed from homologated production GT models. This seemed logical because some of us, including me, thought that the cars competing in a manufacturers' championship must be representative of what those manufacturers produced.

'The problem was that the formula proved to be a Porsche benefit and that to allow front-engined cars to be more competitive, several amendments soon had to be made to the rules. The sort of car we wanted was the 1976 Porsche 935. But when we allowed the floor to be raised to accommodate the exhaust system of the front-engine cars – mainly the BMW 635 – we ended up with the 'Moby Dick', which really had very little in common with a 911!'

'Moby Dick' – the nickname given to the 1978 version of the 935 – astonished everyone at Le Mans that year when its maximum speed of 226mph (364kph) topped that of the winning Renault A442 and Porsche's own 936 prototypes.

'Long before that, loopholes in the regulations had already begun to defeat our efforts to keep the cars as near-standard looking as possible. We wanted that so they were immediately identifiable by the public.

"Moby Dick" really spelled the end of Group 5 [as a championship]. After 1978, Porsche left the private teams to fight it out with the works Lancias. When Lancia [with the Beta Monte Carlo] eventually won the championship, Porsche owners lost interest, and that was the end of Group 5.

'By this time, there was no championship for Group 6 cars either. After Renault beat the Porsches in 1978, they retired. That left Porsche virtually alone.'

Without serious manufacturer competition – and this says a lot for the culture of the company at that time – Porsche had to search hard to find a reason to race.

Poachers and game-keeper confer: from left to right are Porsche's Manfred Jantke, Norbert Singer, Peter Falk and Paul Frère. Taken in late 1982, Frère had come to Hockenheim to try the 956. (Peter Falk collection)

Dr Ernst Fuhrmann backed an entry of production-based cars for the 1980 Le Mans 24 Hours. The strategy of racing modified 924 Carrera GTs was sound when viewed as a development of the road cars, but stood no chance of overall victory. This is the Al Holbert/Derek Bell car that finished in 13th place.

The 936 received a suitably adapted 2.65-litre IndyCar engine for the 1981 Le Mans 24 Hours. Jacky Ickx (driving the car here) and Derek Bell enjoyed a straightforward run to win.

Ernst Fuhrmann, the boss, came up with a suggestion that, if not addressing the overall problem of the prototype championship, took Porsche in a different direction. He wanted to develop the minnow of the Porsche model range – the 924 – for racing. Actually, he wanted to do a lot more than that. He wanted to develop the 924 to race at Le Mans.

With no other factory competition at Le Mans in 1980, Fuhrmann decided to keep the 1976 and 1977 winners locked up in the factory museum and show the world that he was serious about the 924 being a real Porsche.

Each of the three cars entered was around 50mph slower than either the handful of other prototypes that were entered, or the Group 5 cars. So down-market (in Le Mans terms) were the 924s, that the best drivers saw little point in being seen in such a car. But in truth, the 924 Carrera GT programme was successful. Those who did drive them put in a sterling performance and, seasoned with various dramas, finished in the bottom half of the top ten or thereabouts. Meanwhile a 936 nearly won . . .

Reinhold Joest, the enterprising owner of the car, takes up this amusing sidebar to the main story. 'The problem was that Dr Fuhrmann was the boss at this time. Now Mr Bott and Mr Falk, they were racers.'

The Weissach men knew that the Carrera GTs wouldn't have the speed to win the 24 Hours. But nonetheless they wanted Porsche to win – and in the 936 they knew they had the car to do the job. 'The trouble was that Dr Fuhrmann thought racing meant a 924! But I said: "No, no. I want a sports car! I need a chassis."

'So Mr Bott said: "Do me a favour. Porsche will build you a new chassis – a 908 you know".' At this point you can imagine that Bott could have given Joest a mischievous wink.

'So when I got the chassis it was a 936, and I built the car from that. I bought all the spare parts. It was just playing politics, but it was the biggest deal. It cost a lot of money then. When you build a car by buying the spare parts, it's expensive! We built the bodywork – we rented a set from Porsche(!) and that was a very long process for us. But we did it and the car was fantastic. It was the best car that I have ever driven.'

Fuhrmann must have seen through the game at some point, but presented with the completed car (named a '908/80') at Le Mans, he could lodge little objection – except perhaps to make a note for Herr Bott's annual appraisal on the importance of sharing all information with all the Board.

Armed with the prospect of having the best car in the race, Reinhold Joest lined up Count Rossi of Martini as principal sponsor, and Jacky Ickx as his driving partner.

The 908/80 took on six Cosworth-powered French prototypes. With Jacky Ickx at the wheel, Joest's Porsche was the fastest thing at Le Mans that year, but the race didn't go according to plan.

'The start was terrible', continues Joest. 'It was raining and Jacky was driving. On the first lap, the fuel injection pump drive belt went. Jacky fitted a new one – that bodywork is very difficult to lift by yourself, and we restarted the race from last place. By midnight, or 2 o'clock, we had first place. Then around 6.30 we had this gearbox problem. We repaired it, but it wasn't the only thing. The shifting was hard – there was some metal (swarf) in there and sometimes it blocked the shift. But then we had a second problem. The reserve fuel pump stopped working. We had a normal tank capacity of 160-litres, but we were having to come in with only 85-litres used. The problem killed us in the end, and we lost the race by about two minutes (to Jean Rondeau's Cosworth-powered car). That was after 24 hours of racing with just two drivers – and 24 hours of rain. After that I said "good-bye racing" and that I'd never touch a steering wheel again! OK, I was racing again within two months!'

Looking at the 1980 Le Mans 24 Hours, Joest's battle against the race and Jean Rondeau – in that order – is the essence of what makes the French event (and the other classic endurance races) so magical to competitors and spectators alike. Today, with our feet firmly planted on the ground, it is difficult not to comment on the complete lack of top-level manufacturer teams in the prestige Group 6 class.

Le Mans in 1980 (and Daytona and Sebring) reflected the stagnation in which sports car racing found itself at the end of the 1970s. It was a good time for Porsche's customers who ran countless Group 5 935K3s – and who often found themselves on the top step of the podium. Something else was needed though to inject new life into a patient that seemed to have given up on living.

A new prototype formula was needed that would

bring back the manufacturers and entertain the crowds with the sight and sound of exciting racing cars.

Having experienced the unpredictable highs and lows of the 1970s regulations, as vice-president of FISA's technical committee Paul Frère became instrumental in proposing the new direction.

'The FISA president, Switzerland's Curt Schild, proposed a framework, but there was little enthusiasm from the major manufacturers. He was responsible for suggesting the shape the cars should take and, if I remember well, whether the body should be open or closed. There were a lot of discussions about the engine, and this was where I came in.'

Frère's subsequent involvement in detailing the new regulations was fundamental. Memories of the OPEC oil embargo were still fresh in the minds of the general public and Frère's thinking went along the lines of a formula that would force the manufacturers to consider fuel consumption. He also had taken a long look at the formula operated by IMSA in the United States.

IMSA's founder, John Bishop, was a regular attendant at the meetings of the FISA Technical Commission, and there was a mood to integrate the two worlds of sports car racing by the end of the 1970s. IMSA's headlining GTX (Grand Touring Experimental) formula had been a success (in sponsor and spectacle terms) since the inception of the series in 1971. As has been mentioned, Bishop's nagging concern was that the success was almost entirely in the hands of one manufacturer – Porsche. He wanted more variety.

Bishop brought a promoter's view of racing to the table, rather than any idea based on what was needed to please the manufacturers or the environmental lobbies.

The IMSA formula was based around a complex series of vehicle weight and engine capacity ratios, with the engines themselves being segregated by their production or race origins, and whether they were normally aspirated or supercharged in some way.

These equivalency formulas suited the needs of the varied machinery that came to the line in the United States and favoured particularly the freely available American production-based engines. The IMSA formula accepted that manufacturer interest in sports car racing there was low and that success depended on the participation of well-funded private entrants. The

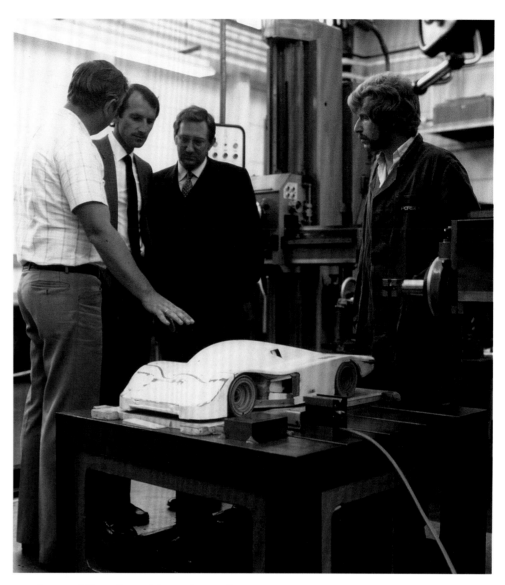

result was full grids and lots of actual racing – exactly the kind of entertainment that the fans wanted.

Quite clearly, there was a significant disconnect in the show IMSA wanted to put on for race fans and the technology-promoting formula being suggested by FISA.

Paul Frère continues: 'It was always understood within the Technical Commission that a race must be attractive enough to draw large crowds, but in those times, the sponsors were not a major issue and neither was television.' Which, unlike IMSA, underlines the fact that neither was present.

'We were not prepared to accept handicaps, to compensate for inferior engine specifications. I was

From his appointment as the new chief executive officer at Porsche, Peter Schutz (to the technician's right) was fully behind the development of the new Group C car. Here he talks to Norbert Singer (left) and Manfred Jantke.

particularly virulent about it – my point of view was that victory should only reward those who had recourse to superior engineering, not to those who used the handicap to win with obsolete material.

'I detested the so-called "equivalency formulae" as were, at the time, implemented by IMSA,' says Frère. 'They were trying to give equal chances to overhead-camshaft and pushrod engines, two-valve engines and four-valve engines and so on. And at the time, turbochargers made things more difficult.

'The technical committee's majority had decided that to all intents and purposes, the capacity of a turbocharged engine should be multiplied by 1.4. It was pure guesswork and as the factor was, as foreseeable, too low, it was later upped to 1.7. But as the minimum weight of the cars was linked to their nominal engine capacity, this led to absurdly heavy turbocharged cars.'

FISA wanted the manufacturers to be attracted to sports prototype racing and needed a formula that challenged the engineering departments within these corporations.

'The only fair and logical measure of a car's overall efficiency is its fuel consumption,' continues Frère. 'Give them a certain quantity of petrol for the race distance and allow the manufacturers complete freedom for the engine that swallows it.

'I was determined to get such a formula accepted. It would put all engines, whatever their size and whether they were turbocharged or not, on equal terms. It would also set manufacturers a technological target that would hasten progress in a direction that was equally important for their production cars: the best fuel economy for a given performance.

'It would also allow manufacturers to base their racing engine on production engines because very high revolutions are detrimental to fuel economy – the friction losses increase as the square of the crankshaft speed.

'I had a lot of discussions with the manufacturers' responsible engineers, sent bags of letters and also managed to convince Schild that this was the right thing to do. But we still had to convince the rest of the committee before discussing it officially with the manufacturers.

'Only Porsche was prepared to accept anything, provided it was fair and that the regulations would remain stable for a reasonable duration.'

Norbert Singer, of Porsche's motorsport department, represented the Stuttgart company in the discussions. Singer had joined Porsche in 1970 and was well-versed in the art of extracting the most from technical regulations for the benefit of his company. His credentials at that point included his work on the aerodynamics of the 917, the development of the remarkable 911 Turbo-Carrera prototype and the rule-stretching 935s – including the famous 'Moby Dick'.

Despite his incredible results with the 935s, Singer accepted that the Group 5 cars were not the way forward.

'It was clear by the end of the 1970s that production car prototypes, as demonstrated by the 935, were not really the future.' So as a result, Singer's first reaction to FISA's proposal of a fuel-consumption formula was one of interest rather than rejection. Once the principle for the new formula had registered with the manufacturers, a heated discussion followed about how the restriction could be applied.

'One thing was discussed for a long time,' continues Frère. 'Whether to limit the fuel consumption for the race, or to limit the real-time fuel flow by a flow meter. That had been suggested by Keith Duckworth [the head of Cosworth]. But we couldn't find a suitable device and it would have been necessary to have one designed, built and very thoroughly tested for accuracy and reliability. There was no time for that – and one still doesn't exist today.'

Singer remembers the exchange of views. 'They had some ideas about regulating the fuel with a meter. It was a very complicated idea. But it turned out it didn't work because an engine will always need a lot of fuel for a very short time (when it is accelerating) and with the regulator, the engine wouldn't run. On the other hand, it wasn't straightforward to limit the air intake with a restrictor either. We didn't know what happened when you did that to a turbocharged engine. The turbocharger might not work.'

With fuel flow regulation eliminated, that left a simple restriction on the fuel amount available for each race. As a result of the discussions and after coming to this conclusion, the Technical Commission proposed a set of draft regulations in 1980.

Through the first half of 1981, the fuel consumption requirement discussion raged on. Frère says that by Le Mans, in June, the limit had been set (and as a point of fact, Frère says the actual consumption of the winning Porsche 936 was not taken into consideration in the deduction).

'Finally the principle was accepted by all, but we had only won the first skirmish (rather than the battle) because the amount of fuel to be allocated for the race duration – 1,000km in most championship races – still had to be settled.

'As a basis, I used the consumption of the Cosworth DFV engine, yielding around 430bhp in endurance trim, that had won or finished high-up at Le Mans. They were using less than 30 litres per 100km [9.5 miles to the imperial gallon or 11.4 miles to the US gallon].

'In view of this, I thought that a limit of anything between 30 and 35 litres/100km would be a fair limit. But several manufacturers flatly refused any limit under 60 litres/100km, insisting that they would not race if a lower consumption was imposed!

'I can't remember the numbers,' says Singer. 'But yes, you looked in the files and said well, 30-litres doesn't make any sense. We had engines that needed a little more – whatever that might be, but on the other hand, there wasn't an idea of how much power there should be either. He took the Cosworth and said well, the power is about 450bhp and that should be our goal. There was a lot of discussion and finally we gave them a total quantity and said that's what we would accept.'

'Finally,' underlines Frère of the very protracted negotiation, 'we had to accept that view. The manufacturers also had to accept that the fuel allocation would be reduced by 10 per cent at the beginning of the third season [1984].'

For 1,000km races (and, at this stage, six-hour time events), each car would receive no more than 600 litres. The cars were not allowed to make more than five refuelling stops during the course of the race. This aligns closely with the agreed fuel consumption rate of 60 litres/100km. For the Le Mans 24 Hours, another time event, there would be an allowance of 2,600 litres with a maximum of 25 refuelling stops.

As we shall see, there were some mistakes made in the execution of the new regulations, not the least was that the distance covered during a dry time event could significantly exceed 1,000km. They did have agreement in principle however, and Frère takes some satisfaction about the way his theories for the fuel consumption formula turned out.

'As forecast, it enabled the manufacturers to base their successful racing engines on production units. Porsche, Mercedes-Benz, Lancia and Jaguar proved it.' Nonetheless, this seasoned sportsman is pragmatic about its criticisms.

'The formula turned out to be popular with manufacturers, but it was not with the public. It happened [in the races] that sometimes a leading car would get out of fuel within sight of the finishing line or might be forced to slow down. It was not popular with the drivers, who hated to have to do this and watch a fuel gauge. And it was not popular with race organisers because it required very vigilant observers to prevent cheating.'

Unfortunately, the new FISA proposals did not find favour with John Bishop either. During 1980, when he understood what was going to happen in Europe, he (understandably) decided to opt out. He set about refining the IMSA formula based on the proven weight and engine capacity formulas. However, he did align, largely, the chassis regulations.

For 1982, IMSA implemented a new class structure based around Grand Touring Prototypes (GTP), to replace the previous top GTX formula. GTP was

Prime movers in the new Weissach motorsport department were, from left: 956 project manager Norbert Singer, Porsche research and development head Helmuth Bott, motorsport head Peter Falk, and turbo engine specialist Valentin Schaeffer.
(Peter Falk collection)

generally similar to what would emerge as Group C, except for the fundamental differences in engine definition and fuel usage. In Europe, with the new formula pretty well defined for the coming 1982 season, it was left to the manufacturers to consider the type of car that would be required.

1981 had been a year of substantial change at Porsche. On 1 January, Peter Schutz had taken office as chief executive officer. Schutz was born in Germany and had been raised in the United States. His career before Porsche was in marketing and he was a strong champion of the saying: 'win on Sunday, sell on Monday', when it came to the value of motor racing.

Schutz knew well the needs of Porsche's principal export market, the United States, and he turned his attentions immediately to a product range which in earlier years had lost its way. In parallel, he set about rejuvenating the company's international image.

Among his first actions, he changed the development focus away from the water-cooled 924 and 928 models and back to the ever-popular 911 range. And when the subject of motorsport was discussed, he wanted to know what Porsche was doing at that year's Le Mans 24-Hour race.

'Originally,' says Peter Falk, who at the time was a Weissach project manager, 'we were going to go to Le Mans in 1981 with three 944 Turbo cars. We had done it in 1980 with the 924 because Dr Fuhrmann (the chief executive officer before Schutz) wanted to go to Le Mans with production cars to improve public relations. But when Mr Schutz came at the start of 1981, he asked Mr Bott (head of the engineering department) and me, what cars we were going to take.

'We told him about the 944s and he asked: "Can we win with those cars?" and we said "no". He couldn't understand how we could go to Le Mans when we couldn't win! Then he asked if we had a car that could win Le Mans. Mr Bott and I said there were the museum cars and that maybe we could take those.'

The museum cars to which Falk refers were the ageing 936 prototypes that had first seen the light of day in 1976. The car had won Le Mans in 1976 and 1977 and had received a major make-over for 1978. That year, the 936s had been overcome by a Renault team determined to make up for the defeats of the previous two years. An unsatisfactory double retirement was witnessed in 1979, but that outing did at least confirm the cars were still highly competitive. Fuhrmann's insistence on running the production-based 924 Carrera GTs in 1980 had consigned the two potential race winners to the Porsche museum in Zuffenhausen.

On Schutz's orders, in the spring of 1981, the pair of 936s were dusted down and taken to Weissach for very thorough upgrade. The scene was set for another major Porsche assault on the famous 24 Hours. In the event, Jacky Ickx and Derek Bell had an almost faultless run to victory, but Schutz's interest in the Le Mans programme went further than just the efforts to restore the status quo in his first year.

The new CEO also accepted the vintage of the old car. He was warming to the idea that Porsche should build a brand-new prototype for FISA's much-talked about new fuel-consumption formula in 1982. So, even though the regulations were far from complete by the middle of 1981, Norbert Singer began developing studies and costings for a new car.

When the formal proposal was placed in front of him, Peter Schutz had little hesitation in approving the new project. As well as being a strong supporter of the new prototype, at the same time, Schutz wanted the whole motorsport operation to operate in the best possible environment within Porsche itself, and that meant delegating more autonomy for its managers. In a far-reaching re-structure of the engineering department, he separated the motorsport activities from the mainstream product and production engineering.

The organisation of motorsport within Porsche had grown from the business's earliest days, when the original competitions manager, Huschke von Hanstein, looked after both the sport and public relations activities. By the 1970s though, and in the increasingly commercial motorsport environment, that integrated organisation looked outdated.

Manfred Jantke came into Porsche in 1972, being given the traditional joint responsibilities for motorsport and public relations. He took over from Rico Steinemann, who in turn had succeeded von Hanstein in 1968.

Jantke, formerly editor of the top German magazine *Auto, Motor und Sport*, reported directly to the chief executive officer (then Dr Fuhrmann) and worked directly with Peter Schutz from 1981. It had been Jantke who was the first to suggest a reorganisation was needed.

'When I took over from Rico Steinemann [in 1972], my job was the traditional one at Porsche that combined the motorsport activities with PR. It went back to the old days of Graf von Trips and von Frankenberg, when racing was a gentleman's sport. But by the time I joined, racing had become completely professional and it was just the wrong combination.

'I did a study and I suggested to Dr Fuhrmann that we should have separate motor racing and PR. He said it sounded reasonable, but that we had better leave things as they were.

'We worked well together and he didn't want to change. But when Schutz came, I updated my study and presented it again, and he said: "You are absolutely right. That is what we must do". So we separated motorsport and PR.

'I continued with PR and the motorsport was moved out to Weissach (from its previous base in Werk 1 in Zuffenhausen). It was the whole thing – team management, contracts, sales of racing cars and all this. Mr Falk was put in charge of all that and I ran the public relations.'

It was timely recognition for Peter Falk, the quiet-spoken engineer who had joined Porsche in 1959 as a chassis development engineer. He had become involved in the competition activities from 1964. He and Herbert Linge had driven a near-standard 2-litre 911 to fifth overall in the Monte Carlo Rally.

Working for the inspirational Helmuth Bott, Falk became one of Ferdinand Piëch's elite core of engineers, and was instrumental in the success of cars such as the 908 and 917. He developed a strong reputation as test driver of the racing cars until he had a narrow escape testing a long-tail 908 spyder at Hockenheim in 1969.

From that point, he became a focus for Porsche's remarkable test and development activity, first conceiving and then evolving the punishing destruction or bump test that would do so much to build Porsche's reputation as a maker of solidly built production and racing cars. Through the 1970s he became more broadly involved with the chassis development of the production cars, but he never became detached from the competition activities.

'We didn't have a dedicated race department before 1982,' he recalls. 'But at the end of 1981, Mr Schutz said we should have a real racing department. Before that it was a small part of the development department and not autonomous. Mr Bott agreed and that was when I became race director.'

The new department moved out to a collection of wooden huts on the southern edge of the large proving grounds at Weissach, underlining the fact that they could no longer be involved directly in production car development.

By coincidence, the spring of 1982 would witness the short, but ferocious war between the British and the Argentinians over the Falkland Islands in the South Atlantic. It wasn't long before the new motorsport department at Weissach was also tagged 'The Falklands'.

'I think we had about 10 or 15 people in the workshop for the chassis,' Falk says, 'and 10 or 15 working on the engine with perhaps three or five on the engineering design side. We were very small in the beginning!'

But this team was hand-picked. 'They were all involved in racing before. There was Norbert Singer of course [who would head the design and development of the new chassis]. Klaus Bischof and Walter Näher [race engineers] a little bit later. For the engine side we had Valentin Schæffer, Werner Entz and Julius Weber. They were all racing people for a long time before this, but previously they were all sitting in different departments in the main building.'

Each of these engineers and technicians were experts in their own field – engines, transmissions, chassis, suspensions, aerodynamics, electronics, race preparation and so on.

'It was a very nice time,' continues Falk. 'Mr Bott said to me at the end of 1981 that I could choose whomever I wanted and whatever I needed to do the job. That was great!'

More importantly, Falk was given little restriction on his budget. 'Well, not too much! The budget was mainly Mr Bott's thing,' he laughs at the memory. 'I didn't have to do the calculations and say that now we had to slow down a little bit here or there. Nothing at all. He would come to me and said we have spent 20 millions (Deutschmarks) or 25 millions and you have to slow down a bit, but that was all. It was very easy for me!'

Falk wanted for nothing at this stage. He had complete autonomy, a sympathetic boss who kept the company's bean counters off his back and a team of hand-picked engineers at his disposal.

Is it any wonder that they would subsequently make motor racing history?

DEFINING 2 AIR

THE TYPE 956 PROJECT began officially on 1 August 1981, despite the fact that even by this time FISA had not confirmed parts of the new regulations.

By any measure this was a very late starting point for a brand-new car that would require extensive testing ahead of a season due to commence the following March. However, Singer and his engineers had completed much ground work and had been studying possible options and alternatives through that summer.

Several manufacturers had begun their design programmes much earlier, hoping they could

In 1981, the use of aluminium sheet for a racing car monocoque was new territory for Porsche.

anticipate the missing parts of the rules. This was to prove a risky policy and when the final details were published in the latter part of 1981, two manufacturers found their cars did not comply. BMW withdrew completely after this fiasco, while Lola was forced to redesign its T600 which became the T610, to comply.

As a concession to the late publication of the full regulations, FISA cancelled the first two rounds of the 1982 championship (at Mugello and Brands Hatch) to give the teams more time to build and test their new cars.

Norbert Singer's initial approach to the new project was to proceed carefully, using the first months for comprehensive research into the two areas about which they knew least – the design and build process for an aluminium monocoque and the workings of underbody aerodynamics.

While Singer led the aerodynamics work, chassis design engineer Horst Reitter began an information-gathering study on aluminium structures.

The use of aluminium monocoques was commonplace in racing by 1981, but for Porsche, it was effectively a new technology. The only previous close encounter with monocoque construction had been fully ten years earlier during the Can-Am programme.

In 1972, in the early days of their co-operation with the Roger Penske team on the Can-Am programme, a McLaren M10 had found its way to Weissach. The McLaren had been extensively studied and compared with Porsche's tried and tested aluminium space-frame designs. At the time, the engineers were unable to identify sufficient performance advantage and they placed their trust in what they knew best. The results achieved with the 917/30 and the later 936 sports car suggest this was a very sound decision, but ten years on from that experience there had been significant advances in the thinking and materials used for monocoque chassis design, particularly in Formula One.

The quest for ever-stiffer structures, accentuated by the huge increase in forces introduced by ground effects, had resulted in the widespread use of aluminium-honeycomb (an aluminium sandwich with excellent rigidity and energy absorption properties). Some constructors were also experimenting with high-strength aramid materials such as Kevlar and carbon-fibre to achieve a super-rigid structure.

There was also increasing concern that the chassis structure should contribute more towards the protection of the driver in the event of an accident. The perception was that a wholly integrated monocoque could offer better crash-protection than a tube-frame. At this early stage in the implementation of regulated safety measures in racing car design (in this specific area), the FISA regulations advised, rather than defined, the direction in which chassis designers should go.

'The regulations were quite open on a lot of things,' says Singer. 'It had to be a closed car and it was also possible to use ground effects, whatever that meant. We had no idea at that point.

'We started to think about an aluminium monocoque, rather than a space-frame, but Mr Bott was not in favour of this. He said a space-frame was much lighter and with it we could have nearly the same stiffness. He couldn't see the need to change.

'When we got the first draft of the regulations – and there were several drafts – there were various safety proposals. When I talked with Mr Bott, I said we had to do the monocoque for safety reasons. What we had then was only a draft, but from what we could see, we had to do it.

'We couldn't meet the safety requirements with a space-frame – aluminium or magnesium.' Singer was also mindful of the fact that accommodating the large underbody venturis (to generate the ground effect) would not be an easy task with a space-frame design. This was particularly so at the rear, where the suction effectiveness depends on there being as little obstruction to the airflow as possible.

Another compelling reason to switch construction methods was based on Porsche's own experience of the tube-frame cars in the rain. With little more than a sheet of plastic for the flat underbody on cars such as the 936, the cockpit was soon awash when it rained, and the car would pull more water from the underneath into the cockpit than came in from the top.

'When Mr Bott agreed that the spaceframe was no longer suitable, we started to think about how to do a monocoque,' says Singer. 'We started to collect information. We went to Dornier. I knew some people on the aerodynamics side there and we spoke to them about making aircraft things in aluminium.'

In keeping with Porsche tradition, it never occurred to the engineers to contract out the work to a specialist. Singer would say that this was the correct 'Porsche-minded' thing to do, to use in-house ingenuity, do the job a little bit better and tease out a small performance advantage.

In parallel with all the strength calculations and design, they built a test structure to evaluate the performance of sheet aluminium and find a suitable fastening and bonding system. Following the debate about whether they should adopt a sheet aluminium chassis over a tube-frame construction, it was inevitable that the Porsche monocoque would be a relatively conservative design. The new chassis did not use honeycomb or carbon, but this was a decision

The Group C regulations advised, rather than compelled, directions for a chassis' passive safety design. This photograph of 001 in construction shows the aluminium roll-over cage.

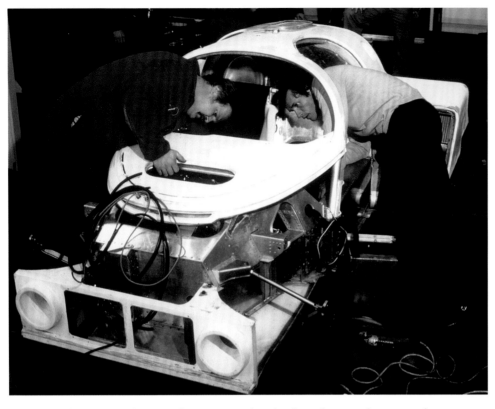

Jacky Ickx takes a close look at 001 during its construction. Unlike earlier sports car designs, the Group C regulations required the fuel tank to be positioned between the cockpit and the engine.

that went a lot further than a shortage of time or a reluctance to take large steps.

In F1 the technical demands on a chassis are quite different to an endurance sports car. F1 cars are built to win races that are around 200 miles long, not the 24 hours that would be expected of the new sports car. The differences came down to a main concern about durability. In 1981, there was still significant debate about the strength of carbon-fibre over time – its fatigue resistance. It didn't matter so much in an F1 car, but on an endurance racing car that was a question that needed answering.

Aluminium-honeycomb was also assessed, but not used. Singer explains: 'It was considered at a certain stage, but when we had built our test chassis, we were surprised with its stiffness. We knew what we had with that would be just fine.'

The first analysis results suggested that the new monocoque would have more than double the stiffness of the old tube-frame construction. Responding to later comments that the sheet-metal monocoque's stiffness was still not all it might have been, he says philosophically: 'It depends where you are coming from.

'We got some ideas and information and we talked to other people. Honeycomb might have resulted in a lower-weight monocoque, but this wasn't so important for us.

'At the beginning of Group C, the minimum weight was 800kg (1,764lb), which when you compare it with Formula One, is a lot. But on the sports car you have an enclosed body, the headlights, windscreen and windscreen wipers, all this kind of equipment. In the end we were a little over 800–810kg I think – which was just fine.

'The minimum weight changed after two years, when we had to go to the steel roll-over cage. They raised the weight to 850kg (1,874lb) and later to 900kg (1,985lb), and with that extra minimum weight, we could start thinking about putting in more stiffness. With a ground effects car you need stiffer springs and then you need a stiffer chassis, and so it goes on. The development never stopped.'

The chassis discussion would continue to simmer through the life of the 956 and the later 962, with certain Porsche customers becoming convinced the route to a winning advantage lay with a lighter, stiffer, chassis. But in late 1981, convention was the most expedient route for Singer and his team.

'Right from the start we decided to build a test monocoque first, that would not be a racing car. We built it so we could understand the stiffness and see how we could improve it. We did a lot of testing in-house by getting special pieces together, gluing and riveting, riveting and gluing, heat-treating and not heat-treating. It was a very big job and we did very intensive testing and research work on that. And after three months or so, we were ready to start on the first monocoque.'

The final design emerged as an extremely compact structure that was no wider the car's cockpit and used an aluminium-alloy roll-over cage with a simple tubular structure to support the engine, transmission and rear suspension.

Far from just refusing to let go of the beloved tube-frame chassis, this was simply the most expedient way to maintain access to the turbo engine's complex pipework and ancillaries.

'We knew what engine we would use. It could not be used as a stressed member, so we had to have some kind of frame. I think some cars did it with aluminium-sheet pontoons, but we thought about it –

and we saw the stiffness and weight – and we decided to do it with a frame.'

It was, no doubt, a decision that pleased Mr Bott?

'Partly!' he laughs, 'but you need access to the engine. When you build a monocoque and fit the engine, you can't get to any of the spark plugs or the turbos. It was very tricky.'

The regulations suggested the design should incorporate crash protection against a frontal impact and around the cockpit in the event of a roll-over, but this was before mandatory crushable structures were required, particularly on the sides of the car. As a result, the open side-bays became housings for items like the battery and the various radiators.

'People were only thinking about safety at that stage,' says Singer. 'So nobody did anything. It didn't say you had to have a crash structure – that only came later. You had to have a certain volume of crash structure. But at the beginning it was just an idea to get safety in. The way the regulation was written, it was not really defined that you had to meet any specific requirement.

'Of course this was where Mr Bott came back and said to us: "Ah! Can you show me you need a monocoque?" and we had to admit it had changed a little bit! But he was happy with what we said, because by that time we had learned how to make the chassis and we had understood the other advantages like stiffness. We had also found that the precision of the anchor points for the suspension was much better. He agreed that we had an advantage but that it wasn't just for safety, it was for all the other reasons.'

The Group C regulations demanded the fuel tank be positioned within 650mm (25.6in) of the longitudinal axis of the car and entirely within the wheelbase. The only suitable place was between the cockpit and the engine. That layout results in a long car, even if the driver is placed well forward.

When the draftsmen had finished, the 956 came out with a wheelbase of 2,650mm (104in). It was much longer than the traditional 2,300mm (90.5in) dimension of the first Porsche racers and even exceeded the long-legged 917/30's 2,500mm (98.4in).

'The 917/30 was the first Porsche to have a wheelbase longer than 2 metres 30, because on that car we had tried variable wheelbases.

'We learned that with a longer wheelbase, the car became more flexible because it was longer. You had

to stiffen it up, get some extra weight in, but even with these disadvantages, you had a better handling car. So the door was open for different wheelbases.

'The [Group C] package actually gave us the wheelbase – you have a certain cockpit size, a fuel tank, an engine and a gearbox. We ended up with 2 metres 60-something.'

The extended wheelbase also demonstrated graphically how pure mechanical considerations were being overwhelmed by aerodynamic influences.

In the old days the 2,300mm wheelbase would have been considered critical for a fast turn-in and nimble handling. Now it didn't matter so much, given there was more than enough aerodynamic downforce available to control the car's behaviour.

The suspension was completely new, with new uprights all round and a very compact rocker/pushrod geometry at the rear. The pushrod arrangement allowed the rising-rate titanium coil springs and Bilstein dampers to be mounted on the top of the gearbox and well clear of the underbody airstream.

The front suspension was a relatively conventional, unequal-length wishbone layout with outboard, rising-rate titanium coil springs over the gas dampers.

From August 1981, Norbert Singer took a regular monthly slot in the University of Stuttgart's one-fifth scale wind tunnel.

The outboard-mounted brakes were the next iteration of a development that had been in progress from the mid-1960s. It was a typically Porsche-minded programme, that had been run entirely in-house for more than a decade.

'At the beginning [of the 956 programme] we ran the double-caliper system, which the 936 didn't have. We did the casting, machining and we had also developed a kind of dyno here, where we could simulate a Le Mans lap. We developed a special steel disc for Le Mans.'

The need for two calipers on each disc was explained by the restricted tyre sizes permitted in Group C.

'You were fixed to the tyre diameter. It was 16 inches and we didn't have very good 16-inch tyres at the start. We had had some problems when we tried them on the 936 [which normally used 15in tyres].'

Through the latter part of 1981, the detail design for the new car took shape on the drawing boards at Weissach. In the experimental department, the chassis engineers built the test chassis and evaluated its stiffness and other properties. From 17 August, Singer and his small team of development engineers booked a regular monthly slot in the one-fifth scale wind tunnel at the Forschungsinstitut für Kraftsfahrwesen und Fahrzeug-motoren, the FKFZ – the Institute for Driver and Motor Vehicle Research – in the University of Stuttgart.

This tunnel was a classic in itself, being made entirely from wood and largely eclipsed by more modern installations elsewhere, but it was familiar ground to Singer. The tunnel did not have a moving ground surface, although its variables and accuracy were well understood.

The first test model was constructed with a general arrangement that used the team's extensive aerodynamics experience, while incorporating the packaging determined by the regulations. Unlike earlier developments however, the 956 tests had to consider a whole new scenario.

'Of course, we did a lot of tests on the upper side, but at the beginning, we spent much time working on how to get the ground-effects under the car.

'This was in the days when F1 cars were running with side skirts, but we were not allowed skirts. In between our tests we would always put skirts on the model, to see if we could see at what stage the ground-effects would start. But it never worked!

An early model representation of the upper bodyshell, dated October 1981. The radiator inlets are located in the top sides of the mid-section, but the NACA inlets would evolve into much larger ducts as the development continued.

'We soon learned that just copying an F1 car on a two-seater car just wouldn't work. So then we started to find our own way and each time we put a skirt in, it got worse!' At first this was puzzling the engineers, but when they began to consider the problem from basics, they began to make progress. 'From that point,' Singer says, 'We knew it had to work somehow.'

It came down to accepting the differences between the pencil-thin floor of an F1 car and the necessarily wide floor of the sports car. As well as the extra width caused by the two-seat cabin, the mandatory 1m by 0.8m (39in x 31in) flat floor section (defined for Group C) meant that the two long side-ducts, as used in the single-seaters, were not feasible. Singer says the flat section was actually quite useful.

'The airflow is different to what you would expect normally. You think you would get an airstream under the car which goes in through the front, along the ducts and exits through the rear – and that's ground-effect. No way! You need the air that comes in under the car from the sides. When you put the skirts in, you lose that – and you lose the ground-effect. That gives you some direction for the shape of the ducts you need under the car. We had to learn that and it took us quite a long time and it gave us an entirely different attitude to working on the car.'

'It's hard to say, but maybe 50 per cent of the air going into the ducts came from the front of the car and 50 per cent came in from the sides – perhaps 60 per cent.

The model evolved with two large underbody ducts, which began just behind the flat section (which itself began just behind the rear edge of the front wheels) with the duct inlets pointing out towards the sides of the car. These ducts developed internal height towards the rear of the car and finished either side of the gearbox, with only the aerodynamically clean rear suspension arms and special, small-diameter steel driveshafts breaking the airflow.

To improve the efficiency of the ducts, the entire engine and transmission assembly was lifted up towards the rear of the car by five degrees. For the dry-sumped engine and gearbox this canted installation required no special modifications. The power train was already more than capable of coping with the oil surge experienced during acceleration and braking.

While the exits for the two rear ducts were visible from the back of the car, another cavity was also formed in the underbody in line with the front axle and ahead of the flat cabin section. Air entered this section from the front of the car and was exhausted through the wheelarches and under the flat cabin section, to the rear ducts.

While the over-worked scale model received continuous underbody changes, work also progressed on the airflow over the body.

Right from the start there was an understanding that the car would not only need low-downforce (minimum drag) bodywork for the long Le Mans lap, but also a high-downforce configuration for most other circuits.

'We knew we had to have a high-downforce car, to do the races at places like the Nürburgring. And of course, there was Le Mans. Le Mans was always a very special thing for Porsche and at Le Mans without the chicanes you needed a car without the downforce and without the drag. In the past we did the long-tail cars like the 917 and the 908. But the new thing here was to be able to convert the same car to each configuration.

'In the old days we had special cars made. It was a Le Mans long-tail car and that's it. Now we wanted the possibility to convert the high-downforce car that you raced at Silverstone and then, within a few hours, convert it to a long-tail car for Le Mans. That was the plan and we went for that.'

Singer established that copying Formula One ground-effect design did not work on the wide underbody of a sports car. This 1981 view of the underbody shows thinking had progressed to a small cavity just behind the front wheel axis and two large ducts drawing air from both the front of the car and each side.

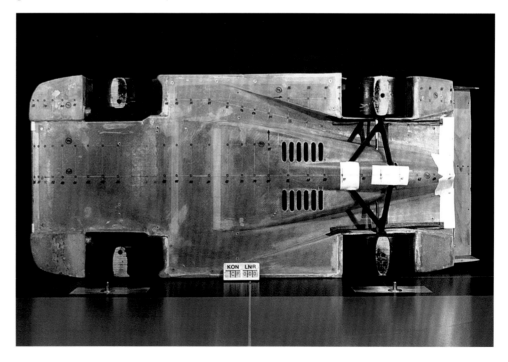

Another factor that influenced the layout of each body shape was the regulations. Both the long-tails and the short-tails had to be the same overall length.

The result was two bodyshell options that should correctly be called high-downforce and low-downforce bodies rather than short-tails and long-tails. The low-downforce tail is set lower and the rear-wing chord (the dimension between the leading and trailing edge) is narrower. At the front, the low-drag nose was given less of a sculpted concave centre-section than the high-downforce nose.

If the development of the new car presented Singer's team with a huge step into the unknown, then the engine and transmission they wanted to use would be a known quantity.

Group C applied no restriction on engine capacity and the only concern was achieving a reliable 600–650bhp on race boost with a fuel consumption that did not exceed an average of 60-litres per 100km (4.71mpg) over the course of a race.

At Le Mans in 1981, the team had run a new engine in the 936 that handed them such performance on a plate.

The two wins with the 936 in 1976 and 1977 had been achieved with the old air-cooled, 2.1-litre turbocharged engine, but it was recognised that this engine design was at the limit of its development (and the 1977 win was achieved with the car running on five cylinders).

As the first results emerged from the wind tunnel testing, so technicians began work on developing a body pattern for the new car.

In 1978, Porsche's race engine head, Hans Mezger, had run the first variant of a family of engines with a new four-valve, water-cooled cylinder head design. For Le Mans, the 3.2-litre engine had been fitted to both 935/78 'Moby Dick' and the 936. Besides problems with the transmission, the engine revealed weaknesses in both its fuel system and cylinder heads and the race had been lost to Renault. Unfortunately, no budget was made available to resolve these issues in time for the 1979 entry.

That year, the two 936s were both stopped by fuel system problems, and by this time Porsche's CEO, Dr Ernst Fuhrmann, had directed the motorsport effort into IndyCars. He also wanted a GT-based entry into Le Mans for the following year.

Mezger switched his flat-six development focus to another version of his new engine 'family' – the 2.65-litre version for Indianapolis. While the car and engine were developed to race-ready status, the project came to a standstill amid the feuding between the United States Auto Club (the organisers of the Indy 500) and the Championship Auto Racing Teams (the entrants' organisation). Sadly, the Ted Field/Interscope Porsche P6B never raced, but its development was not entirely wasted.

When Peter Schutz gave the green light to a new 936 Le Mans programme for the 1981 race, the team was also able to take advantage of a relaxation that year in the regulation governing the turbo equivalency factor for the engine. This factor was a very loose method of aligning a turbo engine's output with a normally aspirated engine, based on its capacity.

'The Le Mans people changed the regulations for 1981,' Singer explains. 'In 1981 there were fewer restrictions on the turbo engine. Previously, there had been an equivalency factor of 1.4 and this gave us the 2.1-litre capacity for the earlier turbo engine [to equate with the maximum 3-litre capacity limit for Group 6 normally aspirated engines].

'The Le Mans people decided to lift that limit. Following 1978 and 1979, when we had engine problems – there was some trouble with the cooling between the valves – we needed to do some more engine development. But that didn't make sense to us. So when the regulations changed, it opened the door to using the 2.65-litre Indy engine.'

The crucial difference was that the water-cooled, four-valve cylinder heads on this engine were considered to be less stressed and that, after adjustment of things like

Virtually every part of the new car was constructed in Weissach. Here work continues on the form of the upper body.

The Interscope-Porsche P6B IndyCar provided the basis for the Group C engine. The single-turbo 2.65-litre Indianapolis engine came from the same (935/71) family as the 3.2-litre flat-six in the 'Moby Dick'. Incidentally, this car was designed by Roman Slobodynskyj – who would contribute much to the successful Busby-Miller 962s at the end of the 1980s.

Although the cylinder heads were water-cooled, the barrels were still air-cooled. The vertical cooling fan is visible at the front of the engine. The exhausts for each bank of cylinders emerged from the body just ahead of the rear wheels, but there was no repeat of the early 917's deafening noise.

The rear of the engine was carried on a large casting mounted in the extension between the clutch housing and transmission. The carrier was known as the 'ox-bow' because of its appearance.

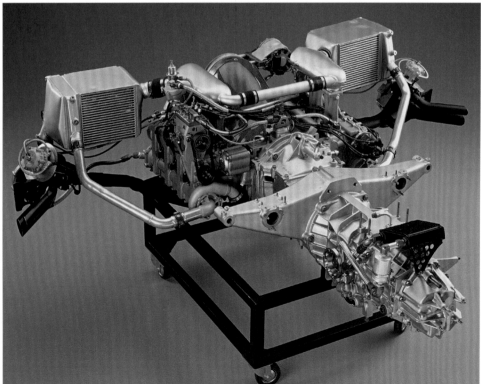

the compression ratio and mixture (the Indy engine ran on methanol whereas the endurance engine would run on petrol), it was very suitable for Le Mans.

'We developed this engine further, with changes to the heads and so on,' says Singer. 'We put that engine in the 936 and it turned out pretty well.' One of the 936s captured a relatively straightforward victory, although the other team car had a fraught race.

Importantly, the win demonstrated that the new engine was more than capable of returning a fuel consumption rate within the limits being discussed for the following year's Group C. This first version of the Group C engine used a carefully tuned combination of the proven Kugelfischer mechanical fuel injection and Bosch mechanically timed ignition to meet the needs of the new regulations.

The final piece in the matrix of elements that would make up Porsche's new Group C car was the transmission. The 936's five-speed gearbox had proved to be a weak link prior to 1981, causing problems for the factory cars in 1978 and for Reinhold Joest in 1980.

For the 1981 race, the older, but much stronger Can-Am 917/30 four-speed gearbox had been used without problem, but the versatile old campaigner wasn't going to be the best solution for the 956. The usable revolution range of the 2.65-litre engine was only around 3,000rpm, so a five-speed gearbox was considered an essential requirement, particularly for when the car was raced at the shorter circuits.

A new all-synchromesh gear cluster had been developed for the 944GTP programme. This had sufficient torque capacity for the 2.65-litre engine and fitted into a new casing would prove to be an ideal solution for the 956. That the transmission was all-synchromesh, rather than the more typical dog-ring type used by manufacturers such as Hewland, only underlined the continuing concern the engineers had for gearbox durability at Le Mans.

The 956 would also continue the custom on Le Mans Porsches of using a solid-aluminium spool to prevent differential movement of the rear wheels.

Several details about the engine and transmission installation are of interest. It may come as a surprise to learn that even though the cylinder heads were water-cooled, the Nikasil-coated aluminium barrels were still air-cooled.

A vertical cooling fan drew air from a small NACA scoop let into the cockpit roof, but the engineers were faced with the problem of how to exhaust this cooling air out of an engine bay that was completely boxed-in. The only obvious solution was to cut some slots in the underbody. This induced a measurable reduction in the effectiveness of the suction-producing ducts. This didn't matter so much at the beginning, when the Weissach 956s were the only state-of-the-art Group C cars, but later it would represent an opportunity to improve the car's downforce.

The other intriguing aspect of the installation was that the exhausts came out of the body just ahead of the rear wheels. On the first 917 such a layout had been used because there wasn't room for the extended pipework needed with the long-tail body.

The drivers had been deafened by the proximity of the open exhausts in those early cars, and there had been problems with the pipes overheating the nearby fuel system components. The 956 had presented the engineers with a similar accommodation problem.

'At the start we tried taking the pipes out the back of the car,' says Singer, 'but it wasn't so easy to get through the suspension and along the gearbox to the back. At the tail there were the underbody ducts

coming up. You had to get the exhausts into the ducts, but that didn't work because it spoiled the airflow. So we had no room. So we had the idea to take them out through the sides.

'There were cries of "Oh the 917! That doesn't work! Forget that!" But we thought about it and considered that this time we had the turbos in there also, so it might be different. We did it and in the end it worked perfectly. We saved weight and we had no problem with space.'

But was it noisy?

'Oh it's pretty noisy! You used to get a funny noise. You could only hear three cylinders and it sounded terrible. I remember later, when we fitted the single-turbo engine to race in America, we had it altogether in one pipe at the end of the car and it sounded wonderful!'

The first prototype, 956 001, was built up in the early months of 1982. At the end of March, and still in unpainted glass-fibre finish, the car was taken to the full-size wind tunnel at Volkswagen's Wolfsburg base. There the theoretical tests were benchmarked against the results of the full-size car.

'The surprise was that we came close to our model figures,' says Singer. 'I didn't really expect that. There's always a difference. A little later, I made a graph to illustrate where we were for Mr Bott and Mr Falk. It was to show them what we had created aerodynamically. It was a graph where I put the downforce versus the drag. I put on the 936, the 935s, the 917s and even the 917 Can-Am car, and [on

This cockpit view of 001 shows the simplicity of the early instrumentation including the round knob to adjust the turbo boost.

the 956] the downforce was nearly twice as high as the Can-Am car with its big wings and so on.

'I don't think Mr Bott believed it. He said he wanted to have a comparison in lap times, at Weissach. It would be a 917/30 with well, it wasn't the 1,000bhp, but about 8–900bhp, and it would be against the 956 with about 600bhp. He said: "You are always saying you have a lot of downforce. Now I want to see." I said that I have the numbers. It has a lot of downforce! But he wanted me to prove it.' Singer chuckles at the memory.

'We did that test. Derek Bell did it in Weissach. We got the 917/30 from the museum. I got some new tyres from Goodyear – they were 19 inches wide! The 956 only had 16in-wide tyres. So the 956 had less power, smaller tyres, but lots more downforce, and in the end I think Derek was about a second faster than in the 917. To be fair though, he could only do about 15 laps in the 917 because he had a problem with the engine. But he started with the 917 and went to the 956 – and he was faster. So we said to Mr Bott: "There it is. That is all we can do".'

After the first Wolfsburg wind tunnel test and a thorough inspection, 001 had been given its first run around the Weissach proving ground on a cold, dry day. It fell to customer racing manager and 1977 Le Mans winner Jürgen Barth to give the car its first laps. Peter Falk recalls the moment.

'In the early years it was something I or the master mechanic in our workshop used to do. To him it was important that if he built the car, he should drive it first. He was a good driver, but later on, the cars became so fast that I said to Mr Barth: "You do it. You are the racing driver".'

'This was a custom that had started with the customer cars in the 1970s,' echoes Barth. 'These were all the RSRs and 935s. I always tested them before they were delivered and it carried on with the new factory cars.

'It was quite late in the evening,' he says of his first 956 drive. 'It had taken them all day to make the car ready. I remember being quite excited because this was a brand new car.

'My first impression of the 956 was that it was a fantastic car. In less than two laps you could really start to push it and find out what it could do. It was the first car with ground effects, so it was very interesting to drive. On the first run, we had set the car up to understeer (push), so it wasn't dangerous at all.'

Jürgen Barth gives 001 its first drive on 27 March 1982. Afterwards, he reported the car as 'fantastic'. As can be seen, at this stage the car still had NACA-style entry ducts to the radiators.

'The first time was 27 March 1982,' continues Peter Falk. 'It was really successful because in one or two hours we didn't have any problems. The car looked very nice on the road – it was very, very stable.

'I said to Mr Singer, I remember it very well: "I congratulate you on this car. It looks very good. I have seen the first runs of many Porsche cars in the past and this one looks the best".'

The new car had passed its first test with flying colours. But in parallel with the development of the new car, there was much activity on the commercial front.

Manfred Jantke, in his new role as public relations director, had been talking to a number of potential commercial partners for the new racing programme.

Just after he had joined Porsche in 1972, Jantke had negotiated the contract with Count Gregori Rossi's Martini organisation and from then on, the personable ex-journalist showed a strong flair for the commercial side of race team management.

Martini and Porsche had enjoyed seven happy years together, including two Le Mans wins with the 936 and a back-to-back World Manufacturers' Championships in 1976 and 1977 with the 935.

'When Peter Schutz came to Porsche (in January 1981),' says Jantke, 'the first thing he said was: "What are we doing with racing?" Mr Bott replied that he was racing the production cars and that we had been doing all those things with the 924 and then with the 944.'

But everybody involved with that programme, including Jantke, knew that the four-cylinder cars stood no chance of overall victory. The team understood the reasons for trying to promote the production cars, but it wasn't like competing with a prototype for overall victory.

'This was a downswing in Porsche's glorious sports car history,' he says with the frustrated passion of one who clearly invested much personal effort at the time. 'It was the worst thing. If you go racing, you should always race to win overall. Anything else is bullshit! And that was the point at which he [Schutz] gave us the instruction to make a winner.'

Sponsorship was an essential part of the new programme. 'These were times when the auto business and especially the sports car business were going through some very rough times. We had faced the energy crisis, other fuel shortages and the business wasn't too good. The racing budget was always too small.'

The cooling air exits were also opened out and NACA ducts were added to the top of the rear body to help cool the rear brakes.

Unfortunately, Martini was now involved elsewhere. When Porsche pulled out of front-line competition after the 1978 Le Mans race, Martini wanted to stay involved.

'Count Rossi was very much a car enthusiast and they were zesty people with style and class. When we told them we didn't plan to run factory cars in 1979, they were very disappointed and they went to Lancia.'

The sponsorship arrangements that Porsche made with Essex Petroleum (1979) and Jules Toiletries (1981) were one-off deals for the Le Mans programmes in those years. There had been no intention or opportunity to consider longer-term relationships, but it was obvious that the new Group C programme was here to stay and that Jantke could negotiate a proper arrangement.

'The connection with Rothmans came through Jochen Mass. Jochen had raced a Rothmans-sponsored F1 car and they were unhappy there because they were unsuccessful, but he knew the people. He told me that Rothmans-Carreras were based in South Africa and that they had a European base in London. Jochen made the first contact and told me I could speak to somebody there. It happened very quickly.

'The initial talks were with some executives, but once we agreed that we should do something, we worked with a guy called Sean Roberts and his people.' Roberts headed Rothmans public relations activities at the time.

The contract with Porsche wasn't planned by Rothmans, but it clearly had enough benefits for the cigarette company to merit special consideration. Their existing arrangement with March in F1 (with Mass as the driver) had been very unsatisfactory although the link with the factory Opel rally team had been very popular. The attraction of an association with the top sports car racing team and visibility at a global level was irresistible. So with senior management approval, the deal was put together by Roberts and Jantke at remarkable speed.

'We started with a two-year contract and that arrangement continued and continued,' recalls Jantke. It was structured in terms of what the new team would be called, how the cars would look, and I remember that uniforms were a big thing.'

Sean Roberts was undoubtedly the right person in the right place for both Rothmans and Porsche. He had clear views on how the team should be presented and clothed.

'The blue and white livery came out of rallying,' he says. 'Originally, we had all-white overalls, but the rally folk would wipe their oily hands on their trousers! So we changed to a dark blue bottom and white at the top.' That design was carried over to the cars, along with a requirement for clear brand identification.

Roberts hints that the first year's contract with Porsche was worth more, but not much more, than £1 million. He also says Rothmans spent as much again on promoting their link with Porsche and sports car racing to the world at large.

'They said that we should qualify on the front row for all our races,' remembers Jantke. 'Qualifying was very important. They used to film the start of the race, so they said whatever happens, they wanted us to start from the front row and take the lead for the first two laps. They had a helicopter waiting that took the film straight to London. They developed the film and then they sent copies to every TV station in the world, for free – Africa – everywhere! There were many stations that would take anything they could get for free. Rothmans were very, very good in promotion and public relations.'

While the new car was at Wolfsburg, time was spent cleaning up the underbody ducts. Here, duck tape and card are used to evaluate an improved airflow through the rear suspension.

The all-important race filming was looked after by Brian Kreisky's production company and most of the subsequent Group C coverage (including the in-car photography) is down to his enthusiastic efforts.

Roberts would initiate a TV pool arrangement where all the teams contributed to a fund that paid for the races to be televised. In 1982, satellite TV was an emerging technology and Roberts found an enthusiastic outlet for his 'free' coverage with these stations.

Paul Davies, Roberts's assistant in those days, adds: 'My own efforts involved providing information to both the specialist motorsport and the more general press worldwide. Middle East journalists were flown into the races to see what happened. Often they were sent back with a complete story ghosted by yours truly! We used to distribute previews and results by telex to Rothmans offices around the globe. These offices in turn used the information for promotion in their own regions.'

The Rothmans publicity machine would, in time, attract a lot of additional support, particularly for the smaller teams. Davies says: 'With the formation of OSCAR [the organisation set up to manage the series on behalf of the smaller teams], it made it possible for them to travel to the more distant – from Europe – races.'

The relationship between Porsche and Rothmans quickly developed a very high level of trust, a fact endorsed by Peter Falk.

'Rothmans were absolutely perfect and very nice to work with. Everything went through Mr Sean Roberts and he was often in Weissach and came to all the races. We agreed with them which races we should do and made our schedules together, and they asked the drivers to do appearances for them. At the end of the year we built them a show car, which wasn't a problem by then.'

'We never had to look at the contract,' Jantke continues. 'We told them about driver choices, everything. It was a real partnership.

'Later, there was one year [1984] when Porsche boycotted Le Mans for some reason. This was such a big race for the sponsor, but we told them and they agreed. They agreed that we would not race at Le Mans and they didn't even ask for one pound back.'

The subsequent success of the Rothmans-Porsche relationship comes down to the energy and enthusiasm that not only Jantke and Roberts showed, but also the honesty and trust that grew between both parties.

The blue and white Rothmans livery was first seen on the Rothmans-Opel rally cars. It would become a very familiar sight in international sports car racing during the coming years. This is actually the one-fifth scale wind tunnel model that Norbert Singer had used to develop the 956's profile – it needed extensive restoration to look like this!

ECONOMY RUN

The Porsche motorsport team ready to go to Silverstone in May 1982. Falk, Schaeffer and Singer oversee the team of six mechanics. (Peter Falk collection)

O NE OF THE MOST IMPORTANT elements of any racing team is the drivers. Because Porsche was the strongest manufacturer in endurance racing in 1982, it might seem odd that the race team did not choose to have reigning F1 world champions driving their cars.

However, far from selecting the single-minded hotshots of the moment from grand prix or IndyCar racing, Porsche often looked for different qualities in its endurance racing drivers. These qualities remain

the benchmark for any serious long-distance racing effort to this day.

Any driver who experienced working with the Porsche racing team in the 1970s and 1980s will always begin the discussion with tales of the fantastic family atmosphere within the team. This spirit was no coincidence of chemistry, for its success can be squarely laid with Helmuth Bott, Porsche's head of engineering of the time.

Before he had joined Porsche in the 1950s, Bott had

been a mathematics school teacher. He certainly had a passion for Porsche and moreover, he had a natural leadership ability. But perhaps those early tutoring years had taught him how to create exactly the right environment for his staff to excel.

At Porsche in the 1970s, he had surrounded himself with a core of like-minded experts – engineers who stood above the rest in their chosen disciplines – but importantly, were team players signed up for a common goal. Far from seeking individual glory, what satisfied each of these loyal lieutenants most of all was to see Porsche do well.

Each could claim both achievement and experience in their established careers. They seemed to have the same calm determination to succeed – determination that did not burn uncontrolled like a petrol fire, but delivered results with the control of a blow-torch's flame. And when it came to the drivers, Bott's philosophy for a winning team was no different.

Porsche had always practised a policy of employing only experienced drivers, largely on the basis that the cars themselves were already superior to the opposition and that it was unnecessary for the driver to take risks to get results.

Unusually for this time, they chose drivers who could be ambassadors for Porsche, not self-centred and single-minded, but those who would put Porsche first. Of course, to drive at Porsche in the first place, a driver had to have a strong track record of both success and versatility, but how he handled himself off the track was also noted.

It wasn't enough to be able to claim pole position and then retire after an hour's racing with a missed gear and a blown engine. Every driver had to have a well-developed sense of mechanical sympathy and importantly, not have a reputation for crashing.

In short, Porsche wanted drivers who understood that in endurance racing, the chequered flag only goes to those who are around at the finish, but it didn't end there. Whatever the calibre of driver, once they had been selected, they all received coaching in how to drive Porsche racing cars. Manfred Jantke recalls that nobody was excused from these tutorials.

'All the drivers had serious instruction on endurance racing by the Botts and Falks and so on. Very serious. They told them how to race endurance, how to avoid risks, how to save the gearbox.

'We talked a lot with them, especially before every

Professor Helmuth Bott cultivated a unique team environment among his engineers and drivers, and was the foundation of Porsche's racing success.

Le Mans race. We would sit together and talk about exactly how we wanted to win the race.' Not drive the race, you might note, but win the race.

'The main message was that the distance was long enough to be able to give a few tenths of a second away. They were told not to take risks when passing and to save the gearbox for the later part of the race.

'At that time there was this problem, if you didn't declutch properly and shifted roughly, sooner or later third gear would stretch or you would lose it altogether. So we told them to shift slowly, saying "twenty-one, twenty-two", just like that – slow.

'They had lessons on how to repair the car themselves if they broke down on the track. And after

Norbert Singer (left) talks to Jochen Mass and Peter Falk some time in 1982. (Peter Falk collection)

Norbert Singer with Derek Bell at Silverstone in May 1982. After being involved in the development testing at Paul Ricard, Bell was none too impressed with the first Group C race.

The distinctive Rothmans colour scheme on the 956 was the product of Scottish designer 'Ginger' Ostle, who worked within Tony Lapine's Porsche design studio. Rothmans later asked Porsche to run the central stripe straight back to the tail.

be as hot as the young ones, but they would have the self-discipline.

'They said the young guys might get an extra second, but they crash too often. They crashed the cars and we didn't have the budgets, so we could not afford, young, hot drivers – and it worked.

'Since we had the dominant cars, we could afford to run drivers who dropped half or a full second a lap, but step-by-step, we brought some young drivers in.

'I signed the contract with Jacky [Ickx] in 1976. He was the toughest guy to deal with! In Formula One, he had been runner-up in the World Championship for Ferrari, but it was all behind him and he was already focusing on endurance racing. He had won Le Mans in 1969 with the GT40 and with Derek [Bell] had won again in 1975 in the Mirage.

'We signed him for more money than Porsche usually spent, but he was worth it. And I must say he was the most impressive driver I worked with during my whole time with Porsche.

'Jacky was a highly intelligent, charismatic person who was enormously dedicated to his racing and he had management qualities. He would take care of his entire environment in racing. So from the first practice to the end, he collected all the details he needed to win a race. He took risks and he went to limits you wouldn't believe. He could move mountains! But the nice thing was that he was quiet and wasn't big-mouthed. He could really push it if necessary, so we

all that [classroom instruction] they weren't young-sters any more, they were endurance racers.'

Jantke negotiated the driver contracts at Porsche during the 1970s and early 1980s, so shared the responsibility for driver selection. He was well aware of the qualities that were needed for someone to be considered as a factory driver.

'When I joined Porsche [in 1972] the policy was very much to rely on the older, more experienced-drivers. There were all the old guys like Herbert Müller and Gijs van Lennep. It was not easy to open the door for new drivers. The team's managers, like Mr Bott and Mr Falk knew the older guys would not

all had enormous respect for him and the way he handled his races.'

By 1982, Ickx's credentials to lead the Porsche team were impeccable. He drove for Porsche from 1976, winning Le Mans that year (with Gijs van Lennep) and in 1977 (with Hurley Haywood and Jürgen Barth), both times in the 936. He delivered an heroic performance that year, and again in 1978, chasing home the winning Renaults after much lost time. He retired from the race in 1979, but was runner-up in 1980 (with Reinhold Joest) after another gritty drive and many laps at the head of the field. In 1981, he partnered Derek Bell to yet another win in the 936.

Ickx would lead the newly revitalised Porsche team in 1982 and for the long-distance races he would continue the partnership he had forged with Derek Bell.

'Ickx and Bell were a dream!' Jantke remembers. 'Maybe Derek didn't have the ultimate speed, but he was a very good driver and the ultimate racing professional. He was a team player and he was a fantastic representative for our company and for the car.

'Derek could handle people and not only important people. If kids came up to him, he was so nice. He was the perfect ambassador for Porsche racing, which we loved. He was fast enough and he didn't make mistakes. He was one of the very, very good drivers and when we started Group C, we badly wanted Bell. No doubt about it.'

Peter Falk endorses this view. 'It wasn't so much his driving, because he wasn't so fast or even good with fuel consumption. But he was absolutely consistent. He had no accidents with us. We knew that if Derek was driving the car, we could go and have a meal or get a drink somewhere else! He will do his ten laps and then he will come in, no problem. That was his real value.'

Derek recalls his recruitment into the new team: 'I remember walking into Professor Bott's office in October 1981 and he said, "Derek, we would like to offer you a new contract for next year". I said thank you. They were the most incredible words to hear from the head of Porsche engineering, and he continued: "We've never run a monocoque before, we've never run a ground-effects car before and nobody has ever put a horizontally opposed engine in a ground-effects car before." He paused at that moment, "but we've never been wrong before!"

'He was such a fantastic guy. He spent his whole life

building incredible racing cars. Mind you, he didn't think drivers should be paid much and wouldn't allow us to be paid more than he earned because he thought that was wrong!'

The other lead driver in the new team would be Jacky Ickx's partner from the 935 days, Jochen Mass. 'Jochen was the only German grand prix driver at that time,' says Jantke. 'He was racing uncompetitive cars and he was very unhappy. We talked about this in Porsche and we felt we should have at least one German driver.

'So we asked Jochen. He was ready to step out of F1 and do sports car racing. He was a very easy-going, happy man who did not prepare for the races too much. He always came at the last minute, but he was a very able driver. He would jump in the car and do a great job.

'When he was out of the car, he wouldn't give racing a thought. He was easy to negotiate on money. You made him an offer and he said: "OK, if you think that is right!" He was exactly the opposite of Jacky. We

The 956 with its rear bodywork removed shows how compact the engine and gearbox were packaged in order to accommodate the deep underbody ducts. The vertical strut at the rear is the lifting jack.

got along very well, but it was always Jacky that was dominant, and like Derek, he assisted Jacky very well because he was quick and didn't make mistakes.

'I remember one time when he came into the sports department in Zuffenhausen the day before the Nürburgring race. He said: "Has anybody seen my racing bag?" My secretary said that we had put the stinking thing in the archive, so we couldn't smell it! We brought it out and it still had his wet overalls in it from the last race. He had taken them off in the back of the transporter and forgotten about them. He only thought to look for them the day before the next race! That was Jochen.'

Ickx was the first one to drive the new car, coming to Weissach soon after Jürgen Barth had given 001 its first exploratory laps of the proving ground's 'Can-Am' course on 27 March 1982. The still-unpainted car was then taken to the Circuit Paul Ricard at Le Castellet, near Bandol in the south of France.

For this first circuit test, Jochen Mass joined Ickx to give the new car a thorough workout. The pro-gramme was fairly conventional for Porsche, who had been bringing their Le Mans contenders to Ricard for many years.

'Of course, we had done some lap time calculations,' says Norbert Singer, 'and we believed that with the amount of downforce we knew we had and with that power and those tyres, we ought to be able to do so-and-so times. We knew what the 936 would do and we expected the 956 to be a lot better.'

At first the two drivers struggled to match the times of the 936. 'But they kept saying the new car was much better than the old one. I remember it well. There was a very fast Esses after the start/finish line. After a while, Ickx came in and said: "These Esses could be flat", that was at 280kph [175mph] or so in those days.

'He said: "But I'm not going to be the first person to do it! When Jochen does it, that is fine and I will do it immediately after him. I don't want to be the first one. I'm not brave enough!"

'This was very nice. We had the numbers in the wind tunnel, but you really don't know what you have on the road, and at the beginning we hadn't seen a big step. We thought it had to be faster. So when Jacky said it could be flat, we knew the lap times could fall by two seconds. And they did. They had to adapt

The startling Lancia LC1 was a very different kind of prototype to the Porsche 956, as can be seen from this view. This is Piercarlo Ghinzhani in the 700kg car. The 1.4-litre, four-cylinder motor developed a screaming 420bhp – and the result was record-breaking laps and enough durability in 1982 to win at Monza, the Nürburbring and Mugello. (LAT)

themselves to the increased downforce and at first you didn't see it on the stopwatch.

'They got faster and faster and it was clear the ground effects were working on the circuit. Years later, I remember we were doing a test there and we had a problem during the afternoon – it was the engine or gearbox. By the time we had fixed it, it was getting dark. We said: "OK, let's do a short check and then we can start tomorrow from the beginning."

'Jochen Mass did the check and by then it was completely dark. He did three, four, five laps and I think for the last two laps he went completely flat through the Esses. When he came in, I said to him: "Are you completely crazy? In the night! You can't see anything!"

'But by then it was easy, running flat and nobody questioned it. He said, "It's no problem. There's a mark on the road and when I see it, I turn in and that's it!".'

The first runs at Ricard were followed by an intensive period of durability testing at Weissach. This was another area of racing car development that set Porsche apart from its opposition and in which the

Reinhold Joest ran this 936 coupé in the World Manufacturers' Championship in 1982, with backing from Belga Cigarettes. To accommodate the new requirement for a central fuel tank, the wheelbase was extended by 110mm (4.33in) to 2,510mm (98.8in). The flat-bottomed car was no match for the 956, but achieved consistent results.

Vern Schuppan shared this 936/81 with Jochen Mass (driving here) at Le Mans in 1981. In complete contrast to the sister car of Ickx and Bell, number 12 had a troubled race.

Hurley Haywood first attracted Porsche's attention in 1973 when he and Brumos principal Peter Gregg won the Daytona 24 Hours in a Carrera RSR.

company had made huge progress since the Piëch 'fast but fragile' era of the 908s and 917s.

In those days the cars would usually have blistering pace, but then retire from leading positions – sometimes because of simple failures.

In his role as manager of the experimental department from 1970, Peter Falk had developed the very severe 'Destruction' or 'Bump' test for the production cars and in turn, this had been adapted for the racing cars. Additionally, by 1980 the racing cars could run a simulation of the Le Mans lap on what was called a test bench or chassis dyno.

A car could be driven almost exactly as it would in a 24-hour race, for a full 24 hours or more, to ensure the reliability of all the major system components and assemblies.

The long-suffering prototype 956 001 would be subjected to both these durability tests in April and May 1982. The tests were driven by factory technicians Roland Kussmaul, Klaus Bischoff, Falk himself and several other willing volunteers from the factory. Even Jacky Ickx became involved, wanting to see the extent of the testing.

The Bump test was performed after the first run at Paul Ricard. 'It was very severe.' Singer says. 'It wasn't

100 per cent the same as the test the road cars get, because there were some tests on our back straight [at Weissach] that were not really suitable for a race car. I think we did more or less 80 per cent of the test for the road car. In those days, the road car did 10,000km and we did only 1,000km. But it was pretty rough.'

The test yielded much valuable information. A host of detail modifications were incorporated into the first three race chassis that were being built in parallel for Le Mans. But there was no rest for 001. After a check-up it was sent back to Paul Ricard with Ickx and Mass. This time, Derek Bell was invited to join them.

Derek had been involved in the exhaustive testing of the earlier 924 and 944 four-cylinder GTs. But unlike Mass, who had found the little cars disappointing, Derek was enthused by the way Singer and the other engineers had gone about developing their potential. He couldn't wait to become involved with the new 956.

'It was one of the most interesting development programmes I've ever done, he says. 'The 956 didn't have any ugly characteristics at all. At first it always seemed that the stiffer we could make it the more stable it was, because the air flowed under the car more smoothly.

'It was basically an understeering car. That was due to the way the rear wheels clicked in, we had a solid differential at all times. We always seemed to need a stiffer roll bar on the front.'

A limited-slip differential was briefly compared with the locked differential, with the team deciding to keep the traditional fully-locked set-up.

'Jochen tried one,' says Bell of the limited slip differential. 'When he came back he wasn't happy. I think it was probably unfair to use Paul Ricard as a yardstick. I would have liked to have tried it somewhere else. I still believe that was the way to go.' But for Le Mans, tradition prevailed, and as with every Le Mans Porsche for the previous ten years, the solid spool remained.

Derek also remembers driving the car with the low-downforce Le Mans bodywork for the first time. 'The long-tail was like having a trailer on the back. You'd come up to corners and the tail would step out and you'd always be trying to balance it. There was no understeer then, you'd always be trying to keep the tail from coming all the way round in a corner. It had very little downforce.'

Peter Falk also recalls from the Ricard tests that the drivers' well-being became a hot topic of discussion, the more they pushed the car.

'From the first test in Paul Ricard they were complaining about their sore necks!' he smiles. 'But the other thing was that they couldn't find the limits of the car in the fast corners, and Paul Ricard has some very fast corners!

'The corner at the end of the straight and the Esses after the pits were very fast. They knew what other cars could do without ground effects, but they couldn't get used to going much faster than that at the beginning. It took us a while to learn how to set the cars up for this, but [at least] Mr Singer had already calculated from the beginning that very hard springs were necessary.'

The team chose to enter the long-suffering 001 for the Silverstone Six Hours on 16 May, the second round of the World Endurance Championship. They had accepted early on in the programme that they would not be ready in time for the championship opener at Monza on 18 April and indeed, it wasn't the plan at that stage to do anything other than a campaign based around Le Mans.

The British race gave the teams an opportunity to run their cars at similar speeds to Le Mans, understand fuel consumption and work on strategies for the big race. For the media and general public, there was another surprise in store from the new Porsches.

When 001 was rolled out of the transporter at Silverstone, it was painted in a dazzling new Rothmans red, white, blue and gold colour scheme.

This was the first time the new colours had been seen in public. The car looked sensational – the scheme being a triumph for Rothmans themselves and the Porsche design studio. Under the leadership of Anatole Lapine, a Scottish designer named Arnold 'Ginger' Ostle had devised the dramatic swirls in Rothmans' corporate hues.

'We had a very, very good guy do this,' says Jantke. 'Ginger Ostle did the Martini scheme on the 936 and the Safari Carreras in 1978 – where the Martini colours were used in the style of a giraffe.

'I remember Rothmans got deeply involved in the new scheme. The first design looped around the back of the cockpit [as seen on the launch photos and at Silverstone], but later they asked us to take the stripes straight back to the tail.'

Silverstone was the first time the competition (and the paying spectators) were able to see all that year's competition side by side – and there were some big surprises.

Lancia-Martini had ignored the start of Group C and exploited the fact that they could run a Group 6 car for this final transitional year. They had built a new car that could run outside the very restrictive Group C fuel-consumption regulations. But the downside of that was that they were ineligible for the World Championship of Manufacturers. Their attention was focused on the new Drivers World Endurance Championship.

In the lightweight Dallara-designed LC1 (it was about 140kg lighter than the 956), they were able to run a highly tuned 1.4-litre turbo engine without fear of using too much fuel. Highly rated team manager Cesare Fiorio hired top Italian F1 drivers Riccardo Patrese, Michele Alboreto, Piercarlo Ghinzani and Teo Fabi for his team. This 'hotshot' strategy (and they were all Italians!) was in stark contrast to the Porsche team's driver philosophy.

The other manufacturer in Group C that Porsche were anxious to quantify was Ford. The C100 had made its debut late in the 1981 season at Brands Hatch. At that race, it had been fast enough to take pole position, but didn't have the reliability to finish

As the drivers tuned themselves into the capabilities of ground effects-assisted manoeuvring, so the spring rates progressively rose in a bid to keep the car as flat as possible during cornering. Visible here are the progressive rate rear springs operated by push-rods from the hubs.

the race. At the first race of the 1982 season, the car had run again at Monza and, despite the best efforts of top drivers Manfred Winkelhock and Klaus Ludwig, had grossly under-performed.

Ford had brought in experienced German touring car racers Zakspeed to take over the team's management and had Tony Southgate – a highly respected adversary of Porsche – design a new aluminium-honeycomb chassis. This was built by John Thompson and powered by the 3.9-litre Ford-Cosworth DFL, the same engine as used by Jean Rondeau to win the 1980 Le Mans 24 Hours.

The remaining Group C competition came from Rondeau and Lola, with Sauber and John Horsmann's Mirage team still developing new Group C cars. All used the Ford DFL.

The best Porsche-based competition came from Reinhold Joest. Joest himself had hung up his helmet after Le Mans in 1981 and was now embarking on a new career as a team owner. His 936C was a coupé version of the venerable spyder and despite its lack of ground effects would prove to be a strong competitor for the long endurance races.

Rothmans-Porsche team manager Peter Falk began

By the time Le Mans came round in mid-June 1982, the 956s were fully prepared for what was expected to be a fierce battle with Lancia and Rondeau.

Silverstone qualifying with the 956 in race trim and went carefully through a series of checks to confirm fuel usage. Car 001 was fitted with the high-downforce bodykit and, to the assembled spectators, its initial performance was slightly underwhelming.

Running with low, 1.1 bar turbo boost, the 2.65-litre engine was good for around 600bhp. In this form, it was easy for the best of the other competitors to get the impression that Porsche's new challenger wasn't all that highly rated.

Towards the end of qualifying, Lancia held the best time, but given the contractual commitment to their new sponsor, there was never any doubt about from where Jacky Ickx and Derek Bell would start the Silverstone race.

With minutes to go, the boost was turned up and Ickx swept to pole position with a time that was a second and a half faster than Patrese's best effort in the Lancia.

The race wouldn't be quite so straightforward. The Rothmans 956 led the pack away, but after leading through the early stages, Ickx and Bell had to back right off. The others didn't miss their opportunity and streamed past.

'The Silverstone race was a Six Hours, not a 1,000km,' explains Peter Falk. 'In six hours we did more than 1,000km. I think at the end it was something like 1,140km, but they only gave us 600-litres of fuel, the same as for a 1,000km race, so we had to slow down.

'The race started very fast. It was dry and there were no pace car periods and no problems with the car – nothing that resulted in a long pit-stop. We knew that by the halfway point that if we went on at that speed we would be in trouble with fuel. So we had to back-off the throttle.'

Derek Bell partnered Ickx that day and was totally unimpressed by events, especially after the stunning qualifying run.

'Peter Falk came up to me after practice and said we weren't going to win the race. I didn't know what he was talking about. I'll never forget it. Jacky had done a 1min 17sec in practice, but in the race we were doing 1min 22 or 23sec. I remember being so outspoken, because I'm that sort of person.

'I didn't think it was fair on the paying public. They would have seen that Ickx and Bell did a 1:17 and the Lancia did a 1:18 or something, and that that would make a very exciting race. And then what happened? The Lancia disappeared up the road because they didn't have the same fuel restrictions and we were cruising around in fifth gear. It was a joke!'

The 956 trailed the Lancia home three laps adrift. At least it did win the Group C class, although that was of little consolation for either the crowd or the drivers. However, the six-hour run did provide more valuable data in preparation for Le Mans.

Silverstone also demonstrated that the rest of the field were not really in the same race. The Reinhold Joest 936C finished third, but like the 956, was reduced to covering the Silverstone lap mostly in fifth gear to get the most out of its fuel allowance.

The feared attack from Ford didn't materialise either and that team was handicapped by corporate Blue Oval doubts about the future of their sports car effort. As with all the DFL-equipped teams at Silverstone, the car was not on the pace of Porsche (in practice anyway), or Lancia. The new Southgate C100 was slowed by a leaking radiator and struggled home to an unimpressive eighth place.

After the event, FISA accepted the discrepancy between 1,000km and six-hour races. There were no

The 956 was caught out by the new fuel regulations on its debut at the 1982 Silverstone Six Hours. The Group C teams were given a fuel allocation for a 1,000km race, and in the event, the winning Lancia covered 1,132km. Jacky Ickx (here) and Derek Bell finished second overall, running much of the final part of the race in fifth gear to save fuel. (LAT)

more six-hour time events on the 1982 calendar and the following year, all qualifying Group C races were 1,000km distance events.

Porsche returned to Weissach to continue the preparation of three brand new cars for Le Mans, just four weeks later. After its Silverstone run, there was now more time to subject 001 to the gruelling chassis test bench.

This unique test called for attributes well outside the job descriptions of all those involved, not the least of which were personal durability and courage.

'We could put the whole car on the test bench,' says Falk. 'We had a special Le Mans programme. That meant more or less full throttle for 30 hours. That's good for the engine – or bad for the engine – and very difficult for the gearbox and driveshafts, and for us drivers! We drove for 30 hours and it was not so easy.

'Looking back I would say it was also very dangerous. It consisted of a little wind tunnel and the car on a rotating drum. We fastened the car and had many hoses for cooling the radiators. Then we sat in the car shifting, accelerating, braking against the resistance of the drum. We would go first, second, third, fourth, fifth. We had a little map of Le Mans and we had a stopwatch. It wasn't quite the right layout, but nearly. After a few laps we knew how to do it.

Running endurance tests in this way proved to be more practical than attempting a 24-hour test at Paul Ricard.

'We tried that often, but something always stopped it! When we saw that the test bench was OK, we didn't try to do it on the road. You can destroy a car immediately on the road, whereas on the test bench only the engine blows up, and we don't destroy the car.

'The dangerous thing was that the car was fastened to the ground, with the wheels running and the left and right side doors were fixed because of the big hoses that were there to cool the radiators. If there had been a fire, the driver couldn't get out very easily, because the hoses blocked the doors! It was very hot in the car and sometimes a lot of exhaust gas got inside, so we wore gas masks!

'We had a wire connection to the outside, so it was no problem. They could tell us if something happened or if the temperature went too high. But the main thing was that we always went full throttle – for 30 hours. It was very, very hard . . . but it was a success.'

Car 001's short, but hard-worked life was coming to an end. Before Le Mans it would be worked mercilessly around Weissach, testing new components and modifications, but for Le Mans, it would serve only as a spare car.

Peter Falk says there were many details that needed attention in those very busy weeks before Le Mans.

'I think we had about 30 or 40 points to change or improve on. It wasn't important things, but details. The main thing was the bodywork. The body had come loose or the doors came up a little bit.'

Singer agrees. 'There were a lot of tests during that period. We had started at the end of March and we raced in May at Silverstone. We tested in Weissach a lot and at Ricard. We went twice to Ricard before Le Mans. It was very, very busy, but it was good development work because the car wasn't perfect straight away. We reinforced supports, the gear change, the radiators, everywhere.'

In an interview for the British magazine *The Motor* before Le Mans in June 1982, Derek Bell talked of the intensive testing he had recently completed at Paul Ricard, saying that the 956 would be good for 235mph (378kph) on the 3.5-mile Hunaudiéres Straight at Le Mans. That was around 10mph (16kph) slower than he had experienced in the 917 long-tail in 1971. The reduction, he believed, was because the older car had a flat bottom. Of course, the overall lap time of the 956, ignoring course differences (like the new Porsche Curves installed in 1972), would have been much faster because of the vastly improved cornering downforce.

As the weeks before Le Mans passed and the drivers became more adept at working the ground effects to their maximum advantage, the spring rates also continued to increase.

'I think this is usual,' Singer says. 'We started at Ricard and found a set-up that worked with that specific Dunlop tyre. Then at Silverstone we changed it and at Weissach we changed it again. That was what we would have expected.

'At that stage there was also some concern about the speed of the Lancias, particularly whether they would find enough durability to last 24 hours at Le Mans.

'Their first reaction was that we had no chance against a Group 6 car,' says Falk. 'They were lighter, they had no fuel consumption regulations, they had a very good engine and very good drivers. But we resigned ourselves to the fact that maybe 1982 would be a learning year.'

Besides the development issues, the other task that pre-occupied Falk, Jantke and no doubt, was discussed at length with Helmuth Bott, was driver selection. With three cars, the team would have to expand for Le Mans.

The leading car would be driven by Jacky Ickx and Derek Bell, that was obvious. Jochen Mass would be in the second car and they chose to continue the association he had formed in 1981 with Australian Vern Schuppan.

'Vern was a good friend from the old days,' says Manfred Jantke. The Australian driver had competed at Le Mans for the first time in 1973 with John Wyer's Gulf Research team. That first appearance had finished upside down in the sand at Têtre Rouge, but since then he had established an enviable string of finishes in every subsequent event. What also impressed the Porsche men was that he combined an obvious mechanical sympathy with a dogged determination to succeed, with virtually no personal resources.

'He was an extremely reliable driver and a very modest person,' Jantke says. 'What all our drivers had in common was modesty. This was Schuppan.'

Vern had run his own McLaren at Indianapolis in 1981 and had been able to afford just one Cosworth engine. He qualified the car on the first weekend and used the same engine for the race. He finished third.

'It was just after that I received a call from Manfred Jantke,' he remembers. 'He asked me to take over Rick Mears's position in the team, because Rick had been hurt at Indy.

'So I drove the 936 with Jochen Mass. We had a lot of trouble. He went out and right away the car was misfiring and it turned out to be a broken spark plug. We had started the race with it like that. So immediately we were down in last place. We got back up to second or third and then the car failed on me right out on the circuit. Something was wrong with the fuel injection. By some miracle I got the tail off and got the engine running. But we'd lost an hour out there and we had to dismantle the injection. We did finish, but it was down in twelfth place.

'That really got me the drive for the following year. Helmuth Bott came along and he said: "You have created a stone in the throats of all the mechanics!" He said then that he wanted me to drive for them at Le Mans again.'

The third 956 broke with tradition. The tests had revealed that the ground-effect cars were more tiring to drive and so car number three would run with three drivers. Jürgen Barth would share with Americans Hurley Haywood and Al Holbert.

'Ickx and Bell were a dream!' says Peter Falk of the two leading drivers in the 1982 Rothmans-Porsche attack.
(Rothmans International)

Barth, son of Porsche factory driver Edgar Barth, had joined Porsche as an apprentice in 1963. The quiet-spoken Barth junior had inherited his father's determination and driving skills, beginning his competition career in rallying in 1968 and racing shortly after. He drove for the first time at Le Mans in 1971.

In the early 1970s, he developed a strong reputation for finishing races with the Carrera RSR, particularly with Georg Loos and Reinhold Joest. He consolidated that reputation from 1973 after driving a 917 Spyder in the European Interserie Championship.

His big break into prototype racing came in 1976, when he drove the new 936 with Joest. They retired, but in 1977, he partnered Hurley Haywood and Jacky Ickx to victory.

That result remains one of the most memorable by the factory Porsche team. After an early set-back had left the car at the tail of the field, a spectacular effort by all involved, motivated by a dazzling performance from Jacky Ickx, seized victory with a car running on only five cylinders. By this time Barth was also very well known within the motorsport industry through his contribution in Porsche's customer sport business. Through the late 1970s and early '80s, he would appear regularly in factory or the best customer cars, and invariably, his presence in a car would result in a podium position. It was he, who with Manfred Schurti, drove the 924 Carrera GT to a remarkable sixth place in 1980 and followed that with seventh in the GTP version of the car in 1981.

Barth was an obvious selection for the factory team at Le Mans in 1982. He was proven and reliable, had been deeply involved in the 956's testing, and had a particular knack of getting a crippled car to the finish.

Hurley Haywood first caught Porsche's attention in 1973. Recently returned from military service in Vietnam, the young Haywood had formed a strong racing relationship with Peter Gregg, owner of the Jacksonville, Florida Brumos Porsche dealership.

The spotlight fell on Hurley when he and Gregg won both the 1973 Daytona 24 Hours and Sebring 12 Hours in quick succession. Hurley followed this with a strong season in the Brumos 917/10 in that year's Can-Am. By coincidence, this was the year when Manfred Jantke was tasked by Porsche's then-

CEO Ernst Fuhrmann to try to persuade the Sports Car Club of America to let the 917 stay in Can-Am racing.

Jantke went to the last race at Riverside, where Mark Donohue simply crushed the opposition, but Hurley finished second. The discussions with the SCCA were a disaster and Porsche was ruled out, but the young driver from Jacksonville, Florida had firmly registered with the factory's talent spotter.

Haywood was invited into the factory team for Le Mans in 1977 and found himself in the winning 936 with Jacky Ickx and Jürgen Barth. From that first drive, he experienced the total involvement that came with driving for the factory.

'I remember the first time I drove,' he recalls. 'Professor Porsche was there. He said to me in a very earnest voice: "We must, shift, very, slow: 1 – 2 – 3 – 4 – 5, like that, very slow." And he continued: "We are giving you the very best car and it is now your responsibility to bring it home to victory."

'Back then, driving for Porsche was an honour, because driving a factory Porsche, especially in those long-distance races, was practically a guarantee you were going to get the win.'

By 1982, his was a very mature head on still-young shoulders. When it came to choosing drivers for the third 956 in 1982, Haywood was an obvious choice.

'Haywood was always a factor,' says Jantke. 'Especially in the Group C times. Peter Schutz was an American and America was our booming market. I think we sold a large percentage of our production to the States and the marketing guys said we must have an American, and it was always going to be Hurley. I wouldn't say he was the fastest, but he was always very lucky. We used to say you need Haywood in the car to win. Whenever he was in the car, we finished high.

'Hurley carried the car at a decent speed. He was very soft on the car and he was also a nice person. At Porsche we were very much interested in people who were team players and who liked each other. We would never have somebody who was arrogant or didn't fit.

'You know, for decades, Porsche didn't look at passports – it wasn't important where a driver came from. It was down to whether he was a good driver and a good person. That's all we asked for. We wanted a good team spirit and we succeeded. Hurley was one and Al Holbert was another.'

Al Holbert won the IMSA Camel GTP title two years in a row in 1976 and 1977 driving this Chevrolet Monza. (Geoffrey Hewitt)

Al Holbert, pictured in 1979 at the Watkins Glen Can-Am. (Geoffrey Hewitt)

Al Holbert from Warrington, Pennsylvania, had Porsche connections that went back a long way. He would partner Barth and Haywood in the third 956 at Le Mans. His father, Bob, used to race Spyders during the early years of professional sports car racing in the United States and was well known to the senior Porsche staff.

Al's degree in mechanical engineering from Lehigh University led him to a job at Penske Racing where, in the early 1970s, he worked closely with Mark Donohue. The Penske experience undoubtedly honed the young Holbert's reputation as being almost obsessive when it came to detail. One driver would later comment that he got upset even if his name was not quite in the right place on a car.

After Donohue's fatal accident in 1975, Holbert found inspiration in his friend's achievements as he forged his own career in Trans-Am and IMSA sports cars. He won the IMSA Camel GT title two years in a row in 1976 and 1977 driving a tube-frame Chevrolet Monza.

'Mr Bott really loved Al Holbert because he was such a good character,' says Jantke. 'It went further than him being an engineer. He was such an honest person, a wonderful man and a good driver. He would also develop into a good manager because he ran his own team at the top level.'

So how did Holbert compare to the team's leading drivers? Peter Falk remembers him as being as fast as Derek Bell. 'Not too fast, but he was reliable. It was quite a thing with Al Holbert that he was an engineer. It is not easy to work with a driver who is an engineer!

'A driver says that car is doing this or that, but an engineer says I would change this or that, and Mr Singer would say: "No! I know that!" It wasn't so easy sometimes, but normally he agreed with Singer.'

It might be concluded that Porsche was seeking to develop a close engineering relationship with Holbert that mirrored the one they had had previously with Mark Donohue from 1971 to 1973, but Jantke is quick to respond.

'It is easy to answer this: not at all,' he says emphatically. 'Al Holbert did not have a big ego, he just did a good job. In Can-Am the Penske group, including Mark Donohue, were racing very much for themselves and their own reputations. Mark Donohue was a brilliant technician, maybe the best engineer/driver combination Porsche had met, but how can I say it? In a way he was a bit selfish.

'At the end of the successful Can-Am times there was a book published which was the biggest disappointment for the Weissach people. If you read this book, you get the impression that he (Donohue) had developed the car because he was such a good technician. The Weissach people were left asking: "What did we do on the car, didn't we develop these things?" No. Al was the opposite. He wouldn't take as much credit as he should have done. Al Holbert was a friend and Donohue was a partner, like Roger Penske. They were great partners, extremely able, high-quality people and highly successful. And of course not every good partner can be your friend. But Al was.

AS EASY AS A-B-C

IN THE WEEKS RUNNING UP to the race, the drivers were expected to prepare thoroughly for the upcoming 24-hour marathon. Each received a package of potions and dietary advice that had been prepared by the team's physical well-being adviser Dr Huber and his assistant Dr Schmidt.

'I remember I was staying in America,' says Vern Schuppan, 'at a doctor friend's house, when this kit of vials and all sorts of things arrived.'

The down-to-earth Australian was clearly not impressed by the package of homeopathic supplements. 'I showed them to this doctor and he joked that I should flush them down the loo! He said he wouldn't take that stuff. But we were supposed to be taking it for about a month before the race.

I didn't know what I was going to do. There was Royal Jelly and then in the race they gave us this electrolyte drink. That made me absolutely sick – it was really horrible.'

Peter Falk recalls the supplements. 'We always had two doctors at Le Mans – and later at the overseas races in Japan and Malaysia. They told the drivers what they should eat and drink.'

Rothmans were responsible for the catering at the races, but the drivers were always to be seen sucking on pasta, other high-efficiency foods and particularly drinking fluids. 'It isn't so much the food, but the drinking, adds Falk. 'During the race it is very important.'

'Eventually I just started gagging on it,' says Schuppan, grimacing at the memory. 'It was really nasty. It didn't do me much good at all. If it had been Gatorade or something it would have been OK. But they were very much into the old diet.'

The weekend before the team was due to set off for Le Mans, Derek Bell stopped by at Weissach to give two of the three brand-new cars – 956 002 and 956 003 – a shakedown run to check everything was working. It proved to be a perfect example of how Porsche went about their racing.

'I turned up and ran the first car around the test track. I did five laps and came in and there was an oil leak from the back. One of the rear wheel bearings was coming out of the upright. They told me to take it down to the race workshop and they went to work on it.

'While I was waiting they said I could take the next car out and precisely the same thing happened with that. When I got back to the workshop, there were all the engineers huddled in the corner working on the

Porsche put great faith in having special diet guidance for its drivers. At Le Mans Dr Huber (left) and Dr Schmidt were on hand to ensure the well-being of the drivers during the race and to attend to any team maladies as they occurred.

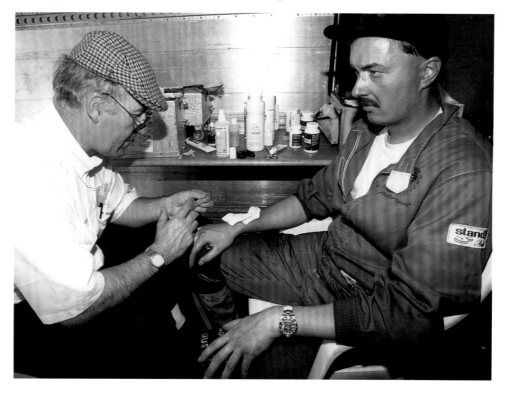

problem. They were all in different-coloured coats and they were all scratching their heads discussing what to do, but there was no panic. It was all very sombre and yet, well, at midnight that evening the truck was due to leave for Le Mans!

'After a while they all turned around and went their own ways and they told me to come back in two hours. In that time they drove to the factory, made up some new parts and drove back out to Weissach and fitted them! We tested them later and that was the problem solved. They loaded the cars into the truck and they were all ready to go!

'Now that to me was Porsche. Incredible, no fluster. In all my years with Porsche I never saw a mechanic run. Never leaping from a counter, never dropping spanners, nothing. When I compare that with the Horsmann (Mirage) era, the journalists would gather round because they knew it was going to be hilarious. They knew he was going to end up throwing the mechanic out and doing the job himself!'

It wasn't only new cars that Porsche introduced at Le Mans in 1982. That year was the first year the team garage was not based in the village of Teloché, some five miles south of the circuit.

Peter Falk was responsible for all the logistics of the team when in France and remembers that it became impractical to drive the racing cars on the roads after each practice session and the race. 'The ground clearance became so low [with the 956] and it became impossible to go in and out of the paddock with the big trucks at night. It was too full.'

But this old tradition didn't completely die at that point. Throughout the Group C times, the mechanics and engineers were accommodated in Teloché, in private houses, as they had been since the 1950s. 'It was cheaper and it was the tradition.

'The size of the team for Le Mans was around 50. For each car we needed two mechanics for the chassis, two for the engine and two for the fuel – six per car. Then in addition we needed mechanics for the electrics, the plastics and for the tyres – and some to just bring the fuel and tyres to the pits. We needed other people for the timekeeping – on the big chair – and one for the telephone to the Mulsanne pits.'

In those days, when radio contact still owed more to luck than Marconi, all the teams stationed signallers just after the Mulsanne Corner, so that they could indicate a driver to come into the pits. It was a

'In all my years with Porsche, I never saw a mechanic run,' says Derek Bell. 'Incredible!' The small motorsport team at Weissach formed a very closely knit operation that fed off its own enthusiasm. This photo is simply titled: 'Peter's Mannschaft'.

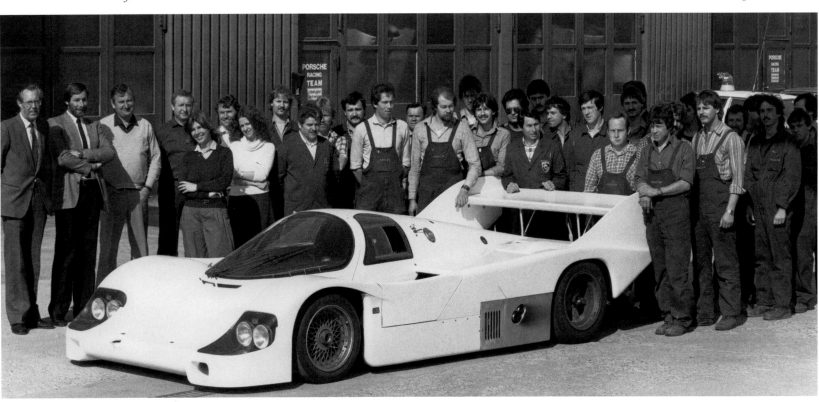

safer place to hang out lap times than on the start/finish straight.

By 1982, Porsche had a standard routine for running the cars during Le Mans week, which had been honed to perfection over decades of competition. Even 20 years later, Peter Falk easily remembers the preparation required.

'We had two spare engines per car. We could do the engine change in the garage, but not rebuild it. After the Wednesday practice we would change the first engine. If that new engine was good during the Thursday practice, then it would stay in the car. If we had a problem with the second engine on Thursday we would change it again for the third.'

Considering the slow publication of the regulations for Group C at the end of the previous year, Le Mans in 1982 promised much. There were no less than 29 Group C cars entered.

Lancia was there of course with two Group 6 cars, the 1.4-litre turbocharged spyders fresh from overall wins at both Silverstone and the following race at the Nürburgring. From a technical standpoint though, questions remained about the durability of the Italian horsepower on the fast, 8.467-mile (13.623km) course.

Reinhold Joest's brand-new Group C 936 offered possibly the most sustained threat to the factory Porsche team, not least because he had gained so much knowledge of running the Porsche flat-six at Le Mans.

His car, with a wheelbase extended by 110mm (4.3in) for improved stability, was running a 2.5-litre turbocharged engine and used the reliable Can-Am-specification four-speed gearbox. The all air-cooled engine was slower revving than the factory air- and water-cooled 2.65-litre units and particularly in the hands of Strasbourg's Bob Wollek (teamed with the Martin bothers), was more than capable of turning up a surprise.

Wollek had matured into a rapid sports car driver by this time and his reliability behind the wheel made him a natural for Joest's new team.

'Wollek had driven with Kremer before and he was good,' says Joest. 'He was strong and he was gentle with the car. He was also very good at setting up the car and knew what he was doing when he was in the car.'

Kremer's new CK5 was another 936 coupé adaption, although this car was only finished just before the race. It was powered by a 2.8-litre air-cooled engine.

Jochen Mass and Vern Schuppan were delayed early in the 1982 Le Mans 24 Hours by a fuel metering problem, but recovered quickly and ran through the rest of the race in a comfortable second position.

All the 956s were fitted with the low downforce tails for Le Mans. The fastest car was timed at 221mph (356kph) on the long Hunaudières Straight

The first 956s were actually very hard work to drive because the steering was so heavy – but few drivers complained because it was far and away the best car in the Group C field.

These two tube-frame Porsches were backed by a remarkable selection of high-technology 935s. The best of these was the Bob Akin IMSA car – the Hudson Wire machine being a full prototype Chuck Gaa-built monocoque save for its unmistakable 911 glass-house. John Fitzpatrick ran a Joest-built 'Moby Dick' replica, using a spaceframe chassis. Fitzpatrick followed Joest practice and ran a proven 2.6-litre air-cooled engine for the race.

By this time, the 3.9-litre Ford-Cosworth DFL was also a well-proven motor for Le Mans. Jacky Ickx and Derek Bell had won the race in 1975 with a 3.0-litre DFV and in 1980 Jean Rondeau won using the larger capacity DFL. Rondeau was back in 1982 with three cars each driven by top drivers (Pescarolo/Ragnotti, Jaussaud/Rondeau and Spice/Migault/Lapeyre).

Rondeau and Pescarolo had won the Monza 1,000km earlier that year, but like the Joest car, the Rondeau was an adaption of an earlier Group 6 machine. All the French cars were said to have been completed only just in time for the race.

The two Zakspeed-run Ford C100s should have been the class of the many Ford-Cosworth competitors, but the team had little experience of endurance racing. Similar stories surrounded the Jeff Hazell-run Lolas and the two ground-effect March 83Gs, powered by the proven 5.7-litre Chevrolet V8.

Lola, Rondeau and Yves Courage's Cougars all used the Ford engine in either 3.9-litre, 3.3-litre (DFL) forms or as the basic 3.0-litre DFV. There were few consumption problems among the Cosworth teams. Paul Frère had based his original fuel usage estimates for Group C on this engine's performance at Le Mans. Their problem though, would be containing the damage caused by engine vibration.

Domingos Piedade managed Peter Sauber's emerging sports car team. The Swiss C6 chassis had been strengthened by chassis specialist John Thompson in an attempt to overcome the Ford DFL's persistent vibration problem. One car was driven by young German hotshot Hans-Joachim Stuck, Jean Schlesser and the experienced Dieter Quester, while the other would be driven by Walter Brun, Sigi Müller and Stuck.

Two Nimrods, using Lola-built chassis and the 5.3-litre Aston Martin V8, plus four Chevy-powered Marches gave Le Mans some deeper music to the shrill Cosworths and whispering Porsches.

The Rothmans-Porsche drivers knew which cars they were getting, about a week before the event. But when Jacky Ickx used the first practice session on Wednesday evening to blow everyone else away, there was much back-handed discussion about him running a special qualifying engine. This wasn't true.

There may have been a few horsepower difference between car number one and numbers two and three, but the reality of the fast times was down to the adjustable boost control. For the fast time, the boost was turned up to 1.2 bar for 620bhp (race boost was 1.1 bar or around 590bhp). The fast time was down to the extra horsepower and Ickx's familiarity with both the car and Le Mans. He didn't even have to resort to qualifying tyres to claim provisional pole position – a time of 3min 28.4sec. This was one second faster than his best the previous year in the 936 (which had been on special qualifying tyres). Ickx's 956 (956 002) was clocked through the speed trap at a maximum speed of 221mph (356kph).

If Ickx, Bell, Mass and Barth were familiar with the new cars as a result of the extensive Paul Ricard testing, then Vern Schuppan, Hurley Haywood and Al Holbert only had their first taste of the 956 during practice on the Wednesday evening.

All of these very experienced drivers were, by then, Porsche team regulars used to the exquisite performance of the 936. But nevertheless, the first experience of the 956 was not what they expected.

'It was my first real experience with a closed car,' says Vern Schuppan. 'It was like the 936, because obviously they had the same motor. But you just felt you had something much better than anyone else out there. And it wasn't just driving the car, it was the whole way the Porsche guys operated. When it came to your turn to drive, you'd get in and drive some laps. I just remember being incredibly quick.

'But those first cars were very, very heavy on the steering. They had tremendous grip and with the heavy steering, there were times on the faster corners when you just couldn't believe the tyre would stay on the rim.'

He was also in for a big surprise during the first qualifying session.

'I blew a tyre on the Mulsanne Straight just after the hump and the car was at top speed at that point. There was this explosion from the rear. I didn't know what had happened, but the car went all over the road and tore the rear bodywork off, but luckily it didn't hurt the suspension.'

Leading the Porsche team at Le Mans in 1982 were Jacky Ickx and Derek Bell. Here, they are talking to Norbert Singer (left) and Porsche Engineering head Helmuth Bott.

Car 003 was repaired hurriedly and Jochen Mass made the rebuilt car fly with a time that was less than a second behind Ickx.

Haywood, Holbert and Barth ran into problems with dirt in the braking system of 956 004. The two Americans were using the restricted running to get used to the brand-new experience of driving the ground-effect car, while Barth was frustrated from setting a representative time. The problem was only solved when the team changed the entire braking system.

Hurley remembers it wasn't the best way to get acquainted with a new car.

'It was very hard to drive,' he recalls. It wasn't what I would call a piece of shit, but it was difficult. The steering effort was enormous. I remember thinking that I couldn't drive the car. They worked very diligently later to reduce that steering effort, but those first runs were very, very hard.

'It was a combination of the ground effects and the length of the wishbones. It was the geometry at the front. We would go into a corner and we would pin the front. It would bind up the steering rack, so it was difficult to turn the wheel.'

Reinhold Joest's 936C led the opposition during qualifying with Bob Wollek a second slower than Jochen Mass, and the two Lancias close behind.

The other prototypes seemed to struggle and few seemed to have the level of professional preparation that is so essential to a competitive Le Mans attack.

Many failed to find high-speed stability on the long straight, and even when they had found that control, they were more than 10mph (16kph) adrift of the 956s and slower still around the rest of the course.

At the team's pre-race conference on the Friday, Falk outlined his proposed race strategy. Everyone was concerned about fuel consumption after Silverstone and the possibility that they wouldn't be able to drive at full race speed. For the 24 Hours, the fuel allowance came to just 2600 litres (572gal), or 650 litres (143gal) every six hours. That was only 50 litres (11gal) more per six hours than they had had at Silverstone. But Falk was bullish.

'I said to the drivers before the race that we would drive as if we did not have any fuel consumption concerns. I believed that if we had some trouble with the car, it would stay in the pits for minutes or maybe a quarter of an hour. If we had a pace car, it would be the same thing. If we had rain, then we would have to go slowly, and we get some spare fuel.'

Two factors would improve the 956's fuel consumption at Le Mans. The first was the new low-drag bodywork that had been developed by Norbert Singer alongside the high-downforce set-up seen at Silverstone, and second, there had been a small improvement in the engine's fuel consumption. The Bosch engineers had been working hard on optimising the fuel delivery from the mechanical fuel injection. The system included an additional electronic control valve that reduced the fuel flow as the volumetric efficiency reduced with higher engine revolutions.

For the first time, the drivers would also have a read-out in the cockpit showing fuel flow in litres per hour, which helped them stay within the fuel consumption rate agreed with the team.

If the race was incident-free and it stayed dry throughout, then they would just have to hope the opposition would break.

Given the investment by Porsche, the huge amount of preparation and the fact that the engine had been found to be too thirsty, the outcome of the race was nonetheless far from obvious. Peter Falk went to great lengths to stress to the assembled media at Le Mans that 1982 was Porsche's learning year. The Silverstone experience had demonstrated that even with the most advanced car in the world, if you didn't have enough

The start of the 1982 Le Mans 24 Hours looks more like a southern European rally than a motor race! (LAT)

fuel, then overall victory was at risk. Despite all the preparation and durability testing, it appeared Porsche's fate still lay outside their own control.

Falk's gamble paid off. His reading of his own team's preparedness and the lack of it on the part of his opponents proved to be faultless.

There were no team orders about who should win. Hurley Haywood recalls the instructions. 'It was a free for all. Porsche never had team orders, but it was made very clear that we were the professionals, that we shouldn't crash into each other. But we could race for the win.'

The opposition just fell away and by half-distance the three 956s were racing among themselves. The Ickx/Bell car suffered a high-speed misfire as the night air became cooler, and this dropped them behind the other two team cars. As dawn broke, so the air warmed and the misfire cleared.

Norbert Singer says this was probably due to the mixture being set too lean – an attempt to save more fuel – and that had caused the engine to misfire during the cold hours of the night. Fortunately, no significant damage had been caused and Ickx and Bell worked hard to make up time, benefiting along the way from the others' misfortunes.

Vern Schuppan remembers putting the Ickx/Bell car under pressure. 'We were very strong there and we did lead the race.' But niggling problems delayed the second car. They lost a lap while a rev-limiter was changed to cure a high speed misfire and then during the night the fuel-metering unit required some work.

After leading for a time during the night, the third car had suffered more serious problems. The driver's door blew off and then a rear wheel bearing failed. As a result the Haywood/Barth/Holbert car lost nearly an hour in the pits and slipped to ninth place.

These dramas left Ickx and Bell back with a five-lap lead at daybreak, with Schuppan and Mass chasing behind. When Ickx picked up a puncture, the lead over the chasing Mass/Schuppan car shortened to three laps.

'The Ickx/Bell car ran almost faultlessly,' remembers Vern. 'Under normal circumstances, the little problems we had wouldn't have been enough to stop us from winning it. The time we lost was the difference between where they finished and where we finished. It was a tremendously satisfying race for me. It was a two-driver race, just Jochen and myself

Streaming down to the Esses on the first lap, two Rothmans-Porsches lead the Joest 936C, the two Lancias and one of the Zakspeed Ford C100s.

driving. And it was hot. I know at the end I was tremendously dehydrated.'

Third place had been held by the Joest 936C until two hours from the end, when the engine broke. That allowed the third 956 to slip into its formation-finish slot behind the other two (albeit 16 laps adrift). This was after the drivers had launched an heroic recovery from their earlier problems. Haywood, Barth and Holbert finished 11 laps ahead of the John Fitzpatrick 935.

Of the 55 cars cars that started only 20 finished the race and no fewer than 10 of those were Porsches. The

three 956s finished in the order of their starting number: 1-2-3. They had made it look easy. It was the most dominant display by any manufacturer in the race's history and wouldn't be equalled for fully 20 years, and then by Audi.

The pre-race concerns about fuel consumption came to nothing as competitor after competitor ran into problems that kept them in the pits rather than on the racetrack.

On Ickx's first double stint, he turned up the boost and drove hard to please Rothmans and to put on a good show after a typically careful start. Running 1.1 bar boost, he managed 12 and 13 laps between his stops, but from this point it was left to (a frustrated!) Derek to set up a pattern of running around 15 laps between stops, running with yet lower boost and a lower rev. limit to recover the consumption average. Their mid-race lap times were around 30 seconds slower than in qualifying.

'And I tell you what,' adds Derek, 'it's a damn sight more difficult to put it [the fuel] back than to use it!'

The Ickx/Bell partnership recorded a third joint victory and Ickx a record sixth. It confirmed the value of this unique partnership in the winning car, but Derek still finds it difficult to explain why he and Ickx formed such a strong team.

'For the life of me I don't know,' he says. 'There was something about he and I driving together. We never overstressed the car and both believed the other guy would bring it home. And we both had great mechanical sympathy.'

Before the race, Ickx had discussed with his partner whether they should have a third driver in their team. Testing had shown the car was more tiring to drive than the older 936, due to the much stiffer suspension (itself due to the ground effects), the 956's heavy steering and the high temperatures in the cockpit.

'The ground effects on these cars was fairly limited,' Jacky recalls. 'If you compared them to what we had in Formula One at that time.

'The basic difference was that the long-distance car had bodywork and big wings and a huge nose

section, but for me, it wasn't exceptional. The problem was that these cars had no power steering or power brakes. They were very physically demanding to drive.

'They were closed cars and they needed a lot of strength to drive them when the track was demanding. But it did depend on the circuit.'

In later years, when the ground effects were optimised still further, three-driver teams would be an essential requirement. For 1982 (and 1983) however, Jacky accepted his regular co-driver's opinion that the two of them could do the job.

'He said Le Mans was getting much harder to do,' continues Derek. 'Jacky was clever like that, because it just hadn't occurred to me.

'I had accepted that Jacky and I would drive as a pair and the others would always drive with three because, I supposed, that was what they wanted. I never thought of the physical side. I remember saying to him that I couldn't think of anyone they could put with us. I was totally conceited! It was like I didn't know anyone else I would trust, and he accepted that.'

'It was completely demanding,' adds Jacky. 'But it was endurance racing, so you had to compromise and you had to make the engineering side last to the end. So you had to spend your capacity and effort through [the whole] 24 hours, and keeping something back to meet a specific situation and some power for the right moment. Today, it is a grand prix for 24 hours, so you need three drivers.'

There was more to the pairing than simply sufficient stamina however.

'It was because we had the same sort of skill,' he adds. 'The same sort of philosophy and mentality. We only ever drove with a two-driver team in Le Mans, never three. The fact we knew each other so well and didn't have to have a long conversation to know what to do. We knew the goal was to win. It wasn't necessary to be on pole. We matched so well together. I trusted him totally and he trusted me totally.'

The 1982 win at Le Mans is still rated by many of the Porsche team to be their greatest victory. It wasn't so much the convincing way they defeated their

With Le Mans behind them, Porsche turned their attention to developing the Motronic engine management during the remaining races of 1982. It was not a popular decision with the team's drivers, but Jacky Ickx rose above it all and claimed the World Endurance Championship for Drivers. (LAT)

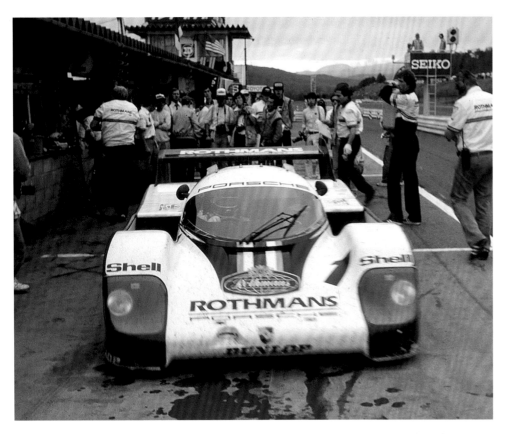

Jacky Ickx (in the car) seized a fine victory over Lancia at the Mount Fuji circuit in Japan, in October 1982. (LAT)

race opposition (which, of course, was the objective), but more, it was a very satisfying conclusion to a massive development effort that had begun 12 months previously.

Le Mans had been the main target in 1982, but as the Silverstone race had demonstrated, the new car could be fast enough at the shorter races – fuel quantity permitting.

'Le Mans was the main goal of the Porsche team at the time,' recalls Jacky Ickx. 'At Le Mans the only consideration was that the straight was 5km (3 miles) long. You had to find a compromise there for speed and downforce and that was the only place where you needed that. Everywhere else you had the short (high) tail with maximum downforce.'

The Silverstone race had been run with the high downforce bodywork and this had proven particularly effective. The rear wing even recalled the massive device that had been used on the back of the Can-Am 917/30 ten years earlier.

'I think it was clear from the beginning,' says Peter Falk of the decision to continue racing the 956 after Le Mans. 'Maybe if we had lost Le Mans, the decision

would have been different, but after the victory, it was no problem.'

Porsche had their eyes on the FIA World Endurance Championship for Manufacturers.

Before Le Mans, there had been three qualifying rounds. At Monza, Rondeau had won Group C; at Silverstone, the lone Ickx/Bell 956 had won, with Rondeau third in the class, and at the 'Ring (which the 956s did not attend) the highest-placed Group C car was again a Rondeau (second overall).

At Le Mans, the best Rondeau had managed to finish sixth in class. The combination of two wins and three more placings had put them ahead going into the final, decisive, round – the Spa-Francorchamps 1,000km in early September. Porsche weren't about to let them win that easily.

After the Le Mans win, it was a relatively easy decision to continue racing with the 956 in that year's World Endurance Championship. Jochen Mass demonstrated the speed of the 956 (using the old prototype) at a non-qualifying race at the Norisring at the end of June, but the interval after Le Mans and before the next championship race at Spa (in early September), was used to make further improvements to the cars.

During this time, Singer's team, ever-concerned about the fuel consumption issue, began to evaluate a completely new 'engine management' system developed by Bosch.

Digital Motor Electronics or DME had appeared on the 1979 BMW 7-series and a year later had found its way on to the limited-edition 924 Carrera GT road car. Its application in racing however, was brand new.

Since the announcement of FISA's intention to reduce the fuel allowance in Group C from the start of 1984, the Bosch engineers, led by Dr Udo Zucker, had been studying a race version of their new electronic system.

Robert Bosch had bought Schäfer Einspritztechnik GmbH, the makers of the Kugelfischer fuel metering pump, in 1974. The closer integration must have significantly helped the development of the later ground-breaking and all-electronic systems.

Bosch were not alone in this field, particularly in racing. Later, they would face up to the system being developed by Weber-Marelli for Lancia, but Motronic would be perhaps the greatest – and most influential – technical development of the Porsche Group C effort. It would thrust Porsche into the electronics age, using an on-board computer to control both fuel delivery and the electronic ignition.

The Porsche strategy at Spa was one which combined a new motivation to win the championship but, typically, one which continued the relentless development of the cars. Consequently, one 956 would run the proven mechanical injection set-up and the other would trial the experimental Motronic.

The race would be no push-over as Rondeau were very serious about keeping Porsche at bay and winning the championship themselves. Cosworth had incorporated a new crankshaft damper for the vibration-prone DFL engine and the Keith Greene-managed team entered with three cars. Both Lancia LC1 prototypes were present, but as they were running under the old Group 6 rules they were competing only for the Drivers' Championship (which didn't interest Porsche at this point).

Jacky Ickx was teamed with his rapid partner from the Martini 935 days – Jochen Mass – and this pair drove the proven mechanical injection car. Derek Bell led the attack in the second, Motronic car, and was teamed with Vern Schuppan.

To this day, Derek remembers the decisions made regarding his new partner and the new technology, with some considerable passion.

'I threw a wobbly about that!' he recalls. 'Jacky (Ickx) was a very clever driver, who always made sure he was in the right car. He would always make sure he had all the right extras and you'd think, that's unbelievable! Jacky's got it and I haven't! He always cultivated the right environment around him and made it work. But good for him. That's one of the reasons I wanted to drive with him.

'He might have thought I wasn't as quick as Jochen. That might have been the point, but I wasn't that much slower than him.

'But they said, "put Bell with Schuppan" and they seemed to want to test the Motronic on our car! Why our car? Because Jacky didn't want it!

'I said it was very unfair that I should have to drive the second car and I remember saying Vern is an unlucky driver. He had never been that successful and things always seemed to go wrong. I'm not blaming Vern, but I was never that lucky [either].'

In the race both Porsches were mindful of the fuel allowances. A wet start allowed them to build a reserve of fuel and further into the race Ickx and Mass were able to wind up the boost and by the end, led everyone.

However, from the first pit-stop, it was clear that Bell and Schuppan were being delayed by a misfire. The car was also difficult to drive as the throttle lag appeared to be made worse by the new Motronic system. They finished third, three laps behind a Lancia and ahead of the best Rondeau, which was fourth in class.

Rondeau believed that with their fourth place at Spa they had done enough to win the championship, but they had not counted the points that had been earned by a Group B 911 Porsche Turbo back in May at the Nürburgring. This unlikely addition to the Porsche points total gave the championship to the German manufacturer.

The remaining three races of the 1982 season counted only for the World Endurance Championship of Drivers. This championship wasn't so important for Porsche (not a viewpoint shared by the drivers!) and as a result, the team missed the next round at Mugello in Italy.

They did make the journey to Japan in early October for the Fuji Six Hours. This was more in recognition of the growing importance of the Japanese

Sadly, the partnering of Derek Bell with Vern Schuppan (seen in the car here at Mount Fuji) did not work out during 1982. (LAT)

market to Porsche than as part of any specific attempt to defeat Lancia's drivers.

The race witnessed a continuation of the frustration with the new Motronic system. But despite these teething troubles, Spa and subsequent further development had shown that the new electronics signalled the end of the 956's fuel consumption problems. However, at this stage, its driveability was still poor.

So while Ickx and Mass seized a fine victory over Lancia in Japan, the second Porsche failed to finish. After a strong start, Derek Bell brought the car in with a split oil line, which lost them five laps. Schuppan took over but later, a right-rear tyre failed on the very rough surface and the suspension was damaged. What was it that Derek had said about Ickx controlling his environment?

If the Japanese race came as a bonus to the programme, then going to Brands Hatch a few weeks later for the final round of the drivers' championship was a concession to vanity. Jacky Ickx was now in a position to win and he persuaded Porsche to let him and Bell drive a single car there.

They won and Ricardo Patrese of Lancia was denied the drivers' championship that had been the whole reasoning behind the Italian manufacturers Group 6-based campaign. The lone 956 benefited from a complicated race that was affected by a stoppage and changeable conditions. Jacky Ickx returned a champion's performance in conditions that recalled Pedro Rodriguez's great drive at Brands in the 917K in 1970.

The 1982 season had turned out to be more successful than anyone at Porsche could have dreamed: Le Mans, the Manufacturers' Championship and unexpectedly, the Drivers' Championship.

The racing for that year wasn't over yet. The team sent two cars to the non-championship Kyalami Nine Hours in South Africa. In Rothmans-Carreras homeland, this long event was no small undertaking. The strongest opposition came from the Joest 936s – the Group C coupé (fitted with a four-valve engine after Le Mans), the earlier Group 6 spyder – and the John Fitzpatrick Joest-built 935 that had finished fourth at Le Mans.

Once again the race revealed the simmering dissent over the indifferent performance of the still-improving Motronic engine management.

'You know, Mr Bell? He was really not – well – he was really very upset!' Peter Falk says delicately and remembering his English driver's wrath. 'It was misfiring and it had a poor transition out of the corners.

'If you went slow or fast on the throttle, you would get nothing. It took us over a year to get it right.'

Derek's recollection of the first Motronic systems is slightly more colourful than Peter Falk's engineer viewpoint.

'I remember Jacky and Jochen going out,' says Bell, 'and this was like the final race of the year. They were two seconds a lap quicker!

'Our engine wouldn't pull all the way round. You had to get on the throttle before you'd finished braking to get it all to work. And when it came to the night practice, you couldn't even see the corners! How could you possibly put the power on when you couldn't see where you were going? Through those very fast corners at Kyalami, you know, they were bloody quick, I also remember thinking "this is crazy!"

'I recall coming in after night practice and I was so verbal. I wasn't screaming, but I was saying: "Peter, I just can't handle this". He spoke to someone and when he came back, he said he would put it on Jacky's car. Or maybe Jacky said to put it on his car. I never heard his side of the story. I thought at the time that was bloody good!

'So I remember the night before the race, I had dinner and went down to the track to see how the boys were getting on. It was about 9.30 at night, and I get in there and there's a lot of dust and fire trucks around.

'I asked what was happening and they told me that Jacky's car had caught fire! I asked what they meant and they said that they had just swapped the numbers on the car he was driving with mine. They had fired up the Motronic car on the trestles and as it was squirting neat fuel, the turbos backfired and it all went up. So Jacky ended up with the same car as me. He had the spare with ordinary injection. I couldn't believe it!

'It was the one time when Jacky might have been caught out, and yet he still went home smelling of roses!

'Anyway, there was no bad feeling afterwards. I did my whingeing Pom thing, but I never heard anybody ever really complain about that.'

After nine hours of racing, Ickx and Mass won by a single lap from Bell and Schuppan.

ALTERNATIVE MEDICINE

THE LAST RACE OF 1982 at Kyalami had brought to a head the amount of work that was still required on the new Bosch Motronic engine management system.

Many criticised the fact that in virtually every Group C race in 1982, one or more of the best cars – the Rothmans-Porsches – were to be seen cruising to conserve fuel. The artificial constraint had put a damper on the races where Porsche and Lancia might have gone head to head. So, from many viewpoints, including the paying spectators, the first year of Group C was not too impressive.

With the Motronic system the first signs were seen that the vision of Paul Frère and his colleagues at FISA was justified. The only serious manufacturer in the formula was being forced into research and development to improve the fuel consumption of a racing internal combustion engine – such a development was then unheard of in modern motor racing. The knock-on effect was that digital motor electronics integration was accelerated into sports car racing far earlier than it might otherwise have been.

'We couldn't do much with the mechanical fuel injection,' remembers Peter Falk. 'We had to change to the electronic system. We had known about Motronic since before Silverstone, but it took time to adapt it to our engine. They already had a production version of the electronic injection (on the 924 Carrera GT road car) and during 1982, Bosch began experiments on the 956.

'In this case it didn't go from the race cars to the production cars, but the other way! It was much better than the mechanical system because the metering was much more accurate.'

'We were sure it would have a fuel advantage,' adds Norbert Singer. 'but at that early stage you had to get it running, then go for the consumption.' It was not surprising that the luckless Bell and Schuppan had so much grief in the later stages of the season.

The system that found its way onto the first 956 was known as Version 1.2. It was fairly basic and allowed the driver to adjust the fuel mixture and ignition advance manually. That might sound like a recipe for disaster, but Singer says it was controlled within limits.

'Of course, he had some mapping options and he could change between normal and lean mapping. That was the difference. But he couldn't ruin the engine. It was the same for the ignition. It wasn't fully adjustable, but it was possible for the driver to play a little bit without ruining the engine.'

The final item in the Motronic jigsaw puzzle was integrating the effects of the cockpit adjustable boost.

'The development of this [Motronic] became a kind of race within a race,' says Singer. 'It helped us bring the development of the system forward much faster. You could put a given mapping into the engine and if it was necessary, certain parameters could be changed by the engine guy to a specific revolutions or boost scale. He might say to himself: "I need a little bit more or a little bit less or whatever out of that corner," and he could do it, but the limits of what the driver could adjust were given by the mapping.

'We could replace the chip at the track. The engine engineer had a computer where he could programme the chip. He took this chip out and put it in the car. It wasn't until the 1.7 [the later Motronic version that appeared in 1988] that we could just plug in and do it on the car.'

The algorithms, or mathematical formulas, that held it all together were established on the dyno in Weissach.

Stefan Bellof was the new driver in the Rothmans-Porsche team for 1983. The young German driver would probe the full limits of the early 956 – and more.

The development of the Bosch Motronic engine management for the 956 became, in Norbert Singer's words, a race within a race. This is the 956 ready for the start of the 1983 season, photographed at Weissach.

'There were a lot of parameters that were sensitive on the system. For instance, temperature was very important.'

The development of Motronic would accelerate quickly in race conditions. Today, the work would have been performed out of sight by a test team, but in 1982, development in race conditions was typical, and particularly so for Porsche.

It wasn't only the cars that went through a learning experience in 1982. The Kyalami race also highlighted a confidence crisis between Derek Bell and Vern Schuppan.

After poor runs at Spa and Fuji, both drivers were becoming frustrated with their apparently incident-prone partnership.

Vern takes up the story. 'I was driving with Derek that year and it was one of those seasons where we just kept getting silly problems with the car. It appeared I wasn't as quick as him. It was only when we went to Kyalami that I found out that I had been running a lot less boost than Derek.

'It was my first full year with Porsche and they would say that I must use 1.2 bar boost. Being the new boy, I stuck to that rigidly. But in Kyalami, Derek

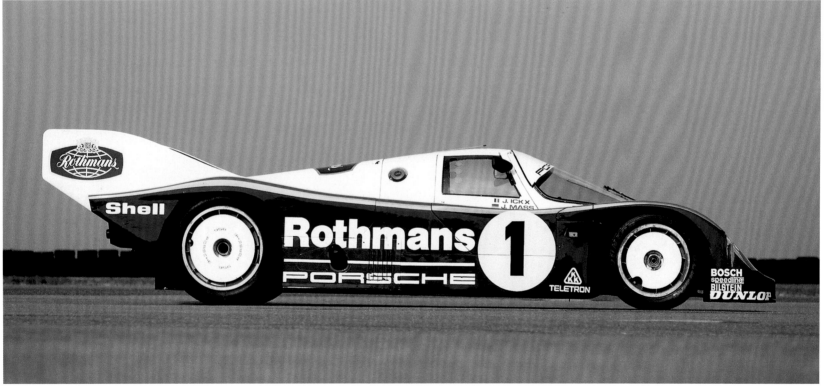

was testing one car and Ickx the other. Then he came in to go to the loo or something and Norbert Singer asked me to take this journalist around in the car. He was a cameraman. So I jumped in and I was quicker than I had been by myself! When I came in Norbert said: "We must send somebody with you all the time!" But Derek had been using 1.4, and he hadn't put it back. You could turn the [cockpit adjustable boost] wheel half a turn and get 50hp more. I'm pretty sure it had happened before and it caused some problems in other teams as well. That upset me a lot because it made me look bad.'

Derek had continued to be unhappy about not driving with Ickx all the time and the string of retirements with Vern only served to reinforce his own opinion that the partnership wasn't working. Derek began to feel that there was almost a jinx on them.

'It always seemed to go wrong,' he remembers. 'Whenever we were doing well, the gearbox would go wrong or something. I'm not blaming Vern.'

The result was that Schuppan found himself in the wrong place at the wrong time without necessarily having put a foot wrong.

'We changed Schuppan and Bell for 1983,' says Peter Falk. 'Because we thought Schuppan was slower than the other ones. We said it to him at the end of 1982: "Vern, sorry." We showed him the lap times. We told him he was a little bit too slow and that we needed another driver. We promised to take him as a driver for our third car in Le Mans and there were other possibilities.'

So Vern Schuppan lost his seat in the second Rothmans car for the 1983 Manufacturers' Championship. By possibly accepting that the playing field had not been quite level, Porsche would continue to take care of the Australian driver in 1983. Nonetheless, it meant there was a spare seat in the Rothmans team.

'We chose Stefan Bellof,' continues Falk. 'He was a German driver. This was reason number one. We had four non-German drivers and we needed a German driver, and we knew he was extremely fast. We knew that that was not necessarily a good thing for the long-distance races, especially for Le Mans, but together with Bell, that was a good combination.

'Bell was a guy who didn't crash the car. He was not so fast, but he was consistent and we had no problem with him, but in practice Bellof was

incredible and if we needed to go fast in the race, we called for him again.'

'I had seen Stefan Bellof race in Formula Two at the Nürburgring,' remembers Manfred Jantke. 'He was in a Maurer car in the rain and you could see from the outside, his performance was exceptional. I was so impressed that at the end of the race, I went to his garage and not knowing him, I introduced myself and said how great his drive was. I said that if he had some time at the end of the season, he should come and visit us at Weissach. And he did.

'I must say that nobody [at Porsche] was enthused to have a young, hot driver. But then he came and Stefan was such a positive individual – a great person. He laughed a lot and at the end of the meeting, they all liked him, and that was because he was such a nice guy and so open. So they agreed to take a young guy and he got the contract for 1983.'

In fact, in Formula One terms, Bellof wasn't that young. He was 25 when he first drove a 956, and one year after first driving for Porsche, he would make his Formula One debut for Tyrrell.

The other major activity over the winter of 1982/83 was to build a small series of customer 956s. This

The 1983 956 with the high-downforce body kit. A central stripe was taken straight back to the tail on the 1983 cars (rather than curving around the rear of the cockpit), on the instructions of Rothmans.

decision was not taken without some considerable discussion in Porsche.

'I had talked about this subject in earlier times with Professor Fuhrmann,' says Jantke. 'Was it right or wrong to sell customer cars or should we race just works cars?

'There were internal politics involved as well. We couldn't decide on Porsche's position. You could always find Porsches on the racetrack of course (even if there were no factory cars). Even later, when we decided to quit Group C, the private cars were there, but of course, they were beaten.

'We considered the fact that [when we weren't racing] we were no longer in a position to decide our fate. But the tradition was so strong [to build customer cars], and we needed the money!'

Peter Falk agrees that tradition won the day in this discussion.

'It was always a tradition to build customer cars, so I think it came from both sides that we should build them.'

There was no element of selection in the process. 'We did not say to anyone, you cannot have a car, no.' In fact, there is some evidence that initial order uptake was below Porsche's expectations.

Over the winter, customer racing co-ordinator Jürgen Barth accepted orders for the 956 from Reinhold Joest/Dieter Schornstein (two), John Fitzpatrick (two),

The 956's underbody aerodynamics proved to be remarkably effective right out of the box. The sculpted underbody would be continuously developed by Porsche – and by several of its more serious customers.

Alain de Cadenet, Jürgen Lässig/Axel Plankenhorn, Richard Lloyd, Yoshiho Matsuda, Nova Racing, Preston Henn and Brun Racing.

These chassis were given numbers which began with the number 1, as opposed to factory chassis which began with 0.

'It is just to tell the chassis apart,' says Singer. 'At the end of that season we knew we were selling [replicas of] the factory cars, and outside they would become mixed up. So we started with 101 for the customer car and 001 for a factory car.'

The list price for the 956 was a very reasonable Dem630,000, collected from the factory. This was equivalent to around £150,000 or US$247,000

Over the winter 11 customer cars were built to the 1982 factory specification, with 2.65-litre engines (with water-cooled cylinder heads) and mechanical fuel injection. When the cars were delivered to their customers during the first quarter of 1983, it seemed like a very good deal indeed.

For Reinhold Joest, the purchase of two 956s was a carefully planned expansion of the recently retired driver's activities.

'I saw the potential to make a business out of racing [with Group C],' he says. 'We had had very big sponsorship from Belga Cigarettes in 1982 and we built our own car – the 936C. You couldn't buy the 956 at that stage, so we did our own car for one season. Then we started planning the next season with two cars. I placed the first order for 956s with Porsche.'

He bought one car and Dieter Schornstein another, with Joest maintaining and preparing the second car. 'To buy two cars was a very big expenditure. There was the driver cost and when you buy a car you need two of everything – bodywork, engine, gearbox and lots of things.' But Joest continued his skill for attracting sponsors who were prepared to fund a proper racing budget. His number one car would be supported by cigarette manufacturer Marlboro, while Schornstein's car would be turned out in the yellow, white and black colours of the New Man fashion house.

Importantly, the Absteinach-based team was now managed by ex-Sauber team manager Domingos Piedade, who brought another string to Joest's bow in the war of strategy with the factory cars.

When Alain de Cadenet had to cancel his plans to run a 956, the Kremer brothers lost no time in picking up the vacant order.

Vern Schuppan shared this Nova Engineering-run 956 with local driver Naohiro Fujita in the inaugural Japanese Sportscar Championship in 1983. Despite the low-downforce bodywork, the Porsche was the class of the championship. (LAT)

The Rothmans team cars were comprehensively beaten by Reinhold Joest at Monza in 1983. Here, Jacky Ickx prepares to go out after Jochen Mass (just visible on the left) has done his best.

The Kremers had been long-time Porsche customers, since the late 1960s. In the 1970s, their 935s benefited from significant development.

After Weissach withdrew in 1978, it was the Kremer 935s that became the cars to beat in endurance racing's Group 5 category. The K3 in particular had become the accepted customer racing sports car on both sides of the Atlantic.

Of the other customers, all had impressive track records in long-distance sports car racing. John Fitzpatrick had established a very strong record in endurance racing and IMSA with the 935K3. His team would be strengthened by another well-known endurance racing team manager Keith Greene, who had run the successful Rondeau squad.

Richard Lloyd had just completed two strong seasons in endurance racing with a 924 Carrera GTR. His success had been enough to convince his principal sponsor, Canon, to buy a 956 for the new season.

Preston Henn's 935s had been an influential feature in IMSA even before he bought the 956. Henn, founder of the huge Thunderbird Drive-In and Swap Shop leisure complex in Fort Lauderdale, had become a consistent points scorer in a Kremer 935 in

the early 1980s. He switched to an Andial-built 935 in late 1982 and immediately found himself among the winners. In February 1983, he had won the Daytona 24 Hours in the car, driving with Bob Wollek, Claude Ballot-Lena and US racing legend A. J. Foyt. He wanted to drive in Europe (and had driven at Le Mans in 1982 in a Ferrari BB) and in early 1983 set up a European base for his new 956 in London with Dave Charlsey.

Matsuda was Japan's foremost Porsche collector while Nova Engineering was a new name to the racers at Weissach. The Japanese team was unknown to the men at Porsche and they feared it could be a cover by the Japanese manufacturers, just to get their hands on the 956. But Nova had no links to any manufacturer and it soon became clear to the Europeans that they were as thoroughly professional about their racing as Joest or Kremer. They got their 956 and strong links developed quickly.

'The president of Nova, Ryouiche Inose, and I visited the motorsport office in Weissach,' recalls Nova team manager Moto Moriwaki. 'It seemed to us that by this time they knew who we were. They did ask some questions about the Japanese manufacturers, but on this trip we bought the 956.'

Vern Schuppan was to benefit from Nova's interest in Porsche. Moriwaki hired the Australian as his number one driver, sharing the car in the very competitive All Japan Sports Car Championship with the experienced Naohiro Fujita.

By this time, Nova Engineering was a well-established team with about 20 staff and a business that included importing, design and construction work for manufacturing industry and of course, the racing team. For Vern Schuppan, it renewed an earlier relationship, as he had driven a GRD for Nova in the mid-1970s.

Despite the sceptism at the start, Nova was a big break for Porsche. The importance of the Japanese market to Porsche had been underlined by the factory team's presence at Fuji the previous year, and having the top Japanese team buy one of their cars was a perfect way of increasing visibility through the whole season.

Schuppan would turn what appeared to be a lateral posting to his own great advantage in the coming years. In 1983, his 956, complete with far-from-ideal Le Mans bodywork would face the factory might of Mazda, Toyota and Nissan.

Walter Brun adopted the policy of: 'if you can't beat them, join them' when it came to the 956. He began 1983 trying to make his Cosworth-powered Sehcars competitive against the new cars from Weissach, but after Le Mans he gave up. He would run his new Porsche for the first time at Spa in August.

The new customer 956s came ready to race, which surprised those who were not used to buying racing cars from Porsche.

'Group C was the happening formula at the time,' remembers Richard Lloyd. 'and we could see the potential of the 956. Canon were very enthusiastic and provided all the budget. We bought an old truck from the VDS team and went to Stuttgart to pick up the car.

'We turned up at the factory and we went into an underground car park. They switched the lights on and there were eight brand-new 956s in plain white.

They were all slightly dusty, so I think they had been there a while. They showed me my car, 956 106 and gave me the key. I remember asking for a Porsche key fob, but they wouldn't give me one! So we put the car on our truck and came home!'

Each car came with a complete owner's manual and parts list.

'They got a nice booklet,' says Norbert Singer. 'It described how to service the car – to adjust the camber, toe-in, engine, gearbox and gear charts. It was all that sort of thing. And when we sold the cars we also sold the support for the cars as well.'

Porsche would send a customer racing support truck to every race, meaning that owners didn't need to carry an (expensive) inventory of spare parts. However, as more than one ex-956 team owner has since pointed out, the replacement parts were not cheap!

Preston Henn ran his new 956 at the 1983 Silverstone 1,000km. His partner was the experienced Guy Edwards. Porsche's Jürgen Barth (left) looks on as his customer makes a pit-stop. The 1981 Endurance Drivers' Champion, Bob Garretson (with yellow collar behind the car), urges on the mechanics. (LAT)

'It was an amazing service,' continues Lloyd. 'But it was very expensive. We were never stuck for a part at any race. The bill didn't used to arrive until two or three weeks after and then you would start to ask whether we really used all that stuff!'

Weissach decided the cars were to be delivered in Le Mans configuration, which seemed to be a fairly unsubtle way of generating extra spare parts business.

If the cars were to be used anywhere else, sooner or later the customer teams would have to buy a high downforce tail. At least Reinhold Joest spotted this before his cars were delivered and corrected his order.

Six new 1983-model cars were also built for Rothmans team use. These 956-83s included many additional detail modifications, the most welcome being new front suspension with 2° of castor rather than the original 1.5° – to make the steering slightly lighter. The 1984 956B would have 4° and that it was still a concern in 1985 is obvious with the IMSA 962 having fully 9°. But there was no doubt that with this and other improvements to the hub design, the cars became progressively less exhausting to drive.

What the customer cars did not have in 1983 was the new Motronic engine management that was being developed on the Rothmans cars. For some customers (but as we shall see, not all), this was a point of contention, especially when they thought they had

just bought a 956 to the previous year's specification, but from Porsche's viewpoint this made sense.

Motronic was still unproven in race conditions at the beginning of 1983 and anyway, the Weissach team still wanted to have some kind of 'unfair advantage' over their customers!

'The customers had the same kind of cars as we did,' says Peter Falk, 'and if we had some parts that were a little bit better than the customers, they came to us and said: "Why don't we get these!" But it was agreed with them that they would get all the new parts, only three months later.

'We needed those three months just to get the parts from our suppliers. We said to the customers: "You can see we have these new parts – like the injection," but we had to make them and then prove they worked. We couldn't give the new parts to them [immediately] because, what if they had a problem with them in a race? They would come back and ask why. We had to prove anything new at our own risk and we said that they had to agree to that.'

Often that wasn't enough of an explanation for the fiercely competitive customers, but the new cars would prove to be a lifesaver for the fledgling Group C championship. Very quickly it became obvious that if a professional race team wanted a competitive car, then there really wasn't any other choice than the Porsche.

Ford had cancelled their Group C programme at the end of 1982 and terminated the development of the 3.9-litre Cosworth DFL. At the same time, Lancia team leader Cesare Fiorio was faced with either leaving sports car racing with his lightweight Group 6 spyders or building a brand-new Group C car and sourcing an engine that would comply with the fuel consumption regulations. His cars had been very quick throughout 1982 but had lost an early season advantage over the factory 956s. His gamble had failed. But against all expectations, Fiorio – one of racing's great team managers – maintained the team's support from drinks manufacturer Martini, and found the budget to develop an entirely new Group C car for 1983.

The new ground-effect coupé, called the LC2, was again sourced from Gian Paolo Dallara and was powered by a purpose-designed Ferrari 2.6-litre twin turbo V8. On paper at least, the new car looked as though it might offer a serious challenge to the 956.

Reinhold Joest ran Dieter Schornstein's 956 twice in the WEC during 1983 in the colours of the New Man clothing business. The car failed to finish at the Spa 1,000km in the hands of Bob Wollek, Volkert Merl and Hans Heyer.

With the new customer Porsches and the new Lancias to take on the Rothmans cars, there were good reasons why everyone was optimistic for Group C's prospects in its second season.

The first race was at Monza in April and, based on the form at the close of the previous season (and the newness of the Lancias), most were expecting the Rothmans cars to be comfortably on top. But there were some surprises in store.

The speed of the new Lancia LC2 was staggering. Driven by grand prix drivers Piercarlo Ghinzani and Teo Fabi, the new coupé looked superb. The new Ferrari engine appeared to have far more reserves than the previous year's highly stressed, blown four-cylinder. Around the Royal Park, and despite a voracious appetite for its Pirelli tyres, the quickest Lancia took pole position by nearly a second over the fastest 956 – and that 956 was not a Rothmans-Porsche – it was a Marlboro-Porsche!

Bob Wollek and rising Belgian star Thierry Boutsen hurled Reinhold Joest's brand-new Marlboro-liveried 956 around like it was a formula car, and Wollek's speed was clearly no stroke of luck.

Several of the new 956 teams had run their cars a few weeks previously at the first round of the Deutsch Rennsport Meisterschaft (the DRM – the German sports car championship) and gained valuable experience ahead of the world championship opener. Wollek had won that sprint in the Joest 956 from John Fitzpatrick in his new JDavid-sponsored version.

With a thoroughness that would become typical, Joest had been working on the competitiveness of his new cars since well before he received his new cars.

'I had special ideas for that number one car,' says Joest. 'I needed that car to be delivered with the short-tail and the high-downforce bodywork and the second one with the long-tail [the low-downforce bodywork]. Customers couldn't buy the high-downforce body at that time, but that's what I ordered.'

Unbeknown to his rivals, Joest was already experimenting with the power-to-fuel consumption balance of the mechanically injected engine.

'The second step was that when we got the engine, we rebuilt it completely. We put in better pistons, a higher compression ratio and so on. The engine was stronger and the whole point of it all was to improve the fuel consumption.'

John Fitzpatrick's 956 made an immediate impact on Group C in 1983 if only for the unusual product of one of the sponsors: Skoal Bandit was a chewing tobacco.

Peter Falk's race summary of the 1983 Silverstone 1,000km, showing Bellof's spectacular lap times compared with all the other competitors.

'We had learned a lot by then, you know.' As he says this, Reinhold Joest cannot conceal a winning grin. 'That was how we were able to win our first races. It was a really good first step.'

In practice for Monza, Wollek and Boutsen had no answer for the speed of Piercarlo Ghinzani's Lancia.

RENNEN: *1000 KM SILVERSTONE* ☒ WM-Lauf
DATUM: *8.5.83* Nicht-WM-Lauf

Streckenlänge: *4.712* (km) Wetter: *NASS / TROCKEN*
Einsatzfahrzeug: *956.005* Fahrer: *ICKX / MASS* Start-Nr.: *1*
956.007 *BELL / BELLOF* *2*
....
....
Ersatzfahrzeug: *956.004* ...

Ergebnisse Rennen: 1. *BELL / BELLOF ... 956 ... 212* Fahrzeit: *5:02.42,93*
2. *WOLLEK / JOHANSSON .956. 212* ....
3. *LLOYD / LAMMERS / BOUTSEN 956. 205* ....
4. *LÄSSIG / PLANKENHORN / GROHS 956 201* ....
5. *JONES / SCHUPPAN ... 956 ... 189* ....
6. *CLEARE / DRON ... KREMER CK5 186* ....

Trainingszeiten: 1. *BELLOF ... 1.13,15*
2. *WOLLEK / JOHANNS. 1.15,10*
3. *ICKX / MASS ... 1.15,30*
4. *ALBORETO / PATRESE 1.16,03 (LANCIA)*
5. *GHINZANI / FABI 1.17,43 (")*
6. *FITZPATRICK / HOBBS 1.17,72 (956)*

Schnellste Runde
Rennen: *ALBORETO / PATRESE 1.18,39 (LANCIA)*

Probleme: ....

Ausfallursachen: ① *UNFALL MASS RUNDE 114* km bis Ausfall: ....

RENNVERLAUF:

Fahrzeugdaten
Motor: *2.6 LITER MISCHKÜHLUNG* ....
Getriebe: *SYNCHRONGETRIEBE* ....
Übersetzung: 1.: ...... 2.: ...... 3.: ...... 4.: ...... 5.: ......
KT ...... Differential ....

Fahrwerk:
Federn: vorn .... hinten ....
Dämpfer: vorn .... hinten ....
Stabilisator: vorn .... hinten ....
Felgen: vorn .... hinten ....
Reifen: vorn .... hinten ....
Misch.: vorn .... hinten ....

Bremsen
Bremszange .... Kolben Ø .... Belag ....
Bremsscheibe .... Bremskraftverteilung ....

Sonstiges: ....
....

The Marlboro car lined up alongside the Lancia, with a surprised Jacky Ickx and Jochen Mass in the leading Rothmans car, trailing in third place.

In the race the new Lancia quickly showed it lacked durability and it confirmed its hunger for Pirelli tyres. The inconsistent performance set the pattern for the Italian cars throughout the season – quick in practice, but completely shaded by the 956's reliability in the race. It was a pity.

If the Italian cars were disappointing in the race, then Joest's new 956 was a revelation. Bob Wollek seemed to be able to control the pace as he wished. He was able to lead the Rothmans cars and still get an extra lap between his fuel stops. It should be noted that the factory cars were using the supposedly more fuel-efficient Motronic engine management systems.

The Ickx/Mass Rothmans car just wasn't able to maintain the same speed as the Joest car, but did at least finish on the same lap after 1,000km. Three laps behind them and just to rub salt in the wounds of the Rothmans team, was the second Joest-run car driven by Rolf Stommelen, Hans Heyer and Clemens Schickentanz.

The Bell/Holbert factory car fell right back, supposedly running to a safe fuel regime, but it lost a lot of time when a rear wheel bearing seized.

'We had a very special wheel bearing at the rear,' notes Norbert Singer, 'and I think we only had a problem once and that was because of poor brake cooling.'

Ironically for Bell, the run did nothing to improve his run of poor finishes in the 956. They finished an unmemorable seventh.

This wasn't quite what the Weissach team had expected when they sold the new cars to customers, but for Group C and the spectators, the encouraging aspect was that at Monza, of the five customer 956s running, five finished. Together with the pair of factory cars, these 956s finished in the first seven places!

Unfortunately, the highly successful opening performance by the customers at Monza drew a strong response from the Weissach team, and one month later, at Silverstone, the old order was re-established.

Two new 956s joined the Monza debutants – Preston Henn entered his car with Guy Edwards, while the Kremers put Alan Jones in their car with Vern Schuppan.

Despite being a part-timer among all the hardened professionals, Preston Henn had no apprehension about driving the ground-effect 956 for the first time in a world championship race. 'Oh, it was very, very good. It was easy and forgiving,' he remembers.

'That was my first race in the car. I got there and Al Holbert – the nicest guy in the world and he'd driven with me a few times before – I remember he was worried about me. He said in a really nice sort of way: "Preston, are you up to this?" He didn't want me to hurt myself. We had Bob Snodgrass [of Brumos Porsche in Fort Lauderdale] and some other people there as well. And I can tell you, I amazed myself how easy it was to drive, compared to the 935. Don't get me wrong, I wasn't driving really competitively like the top drivers. But for a gentleman driver like me, it was easy.'

Weissach had further developed their own engines for Silverstone in a bid to counter Joest's speed in Italy. Importantly, the 2.65-litre engine used a compression ratio increased to 7.5:1 from 7.2:1. The engineers had spent a lot of time on the dyno playing with the Motronic's algorithms to get to a higher balance of maximum power for a given fuel consumption – suspected to be the reason for Reinhold Joest's speed at Monza. There were also new nose sections on the works cars at Silverstone.

The early 956s with the high-downforce tail had a tendency towards understeer, which had been difficult to balance with the early nose (and in fact was controlled by trimming the tail-section). Norbert Singer had continued his exhaustive research in the Stuttgart University wind tunnel to improve the situation.

The new noses were characterised by a deeper concave section between the wheels. This was combined with a front, horizontal edge that dipped closer towards the road at the front. However, as well as the improved car, Porsche's real ace-up-the-sleeve at Silverstone was new driver signing Stefan Bellof.

'I remember Silverstone in 1983 very well,' smiles Manfred Jantke. 'We were running for pole position and we couldn't make it. There was the Marlboro car

Reinhold Joest's new 956 won the first World Endurance Championship race of 1983 at Monza. It was no stroke of luck that Bob Wollek (here) and Thierry Boutsen were able to get more miles to the gallon than the works cars. (LAT)

driven by Stefan Johansson [and Bob Wollek] and the Lancia [of Patrese and Alboreto]. 'There must have been about 12 or 14 minutes left in qualifying. Of course Jacky had been privileged to qualify the car and up to that point Stefan had had to wait. Then Mr Falk said it was time to try the young guy.

'He got into the car and I think he went around maybe three times and he got the pole!'

Peter Falk's timesheets for the meeting show that Bellof's time was 1.95 seconds faster than Wollek's in the Joest 956 and fully 2.15 seconds faster than Jacky Ickx had set in the other factory 956. This, it should

The new Group C Lancia LC2 was very quick right from its first race at Monza. Sadly, it did not have the reliability. (LAT)

be noted, was with a qualifying lap time that was not on a scale of long minutes like Spa, Le Mans or the Nürburgring. His pole-position lap time at Silverstone was just 1min 13.15sec. In Britain, he was a country-mile faster than anyone else.

The race took place in changeable conditions and Jochen Mass crashed during a shower while in the lead. Wollek and Johansson ran at the front in the Joest car but, unlike Monza, had to ease off as they ran over budget on fuel. This allowed Bell and Bellof to win, and what made the victory sweeter was that they had fuel to spare, thanks to the improvements since Monza. Lancia were blown away – they led at the start but fell out with overheating engines.

After a steady debut at Monza, the Richard Lloyd Canon 956 finished third at Silverstone, driven by Jan Lammers and Thiery Boutsen. Again 956s filled the first five places, with Kremer's CK5 in sixth. Preston Henn's debut run in the Swap Shop 956 ended with a blown engine.

The following Nürburgring race marked the end of an era, because it was the last 1,000km event on the old Nordschleife. The slightly shortened, 12.94-mile (20.8km) lap didn't include the southern loop as by this time they were building the new made-for-TV circuit.

Bellof put the outright lap record out of reach with a staggering time of 6min 11.13sec which was an average speed of over 125mph (200kph) and his time remains the benchmark for every aspiring Ringmeister to this day.

By comparison, Jochen Mass's best was 6min 16.85sec. The other hot driver of the moment was Stefan Johansson in the Joest 956 and he lined up third with a time of 6min 31.59sec. These are very big differences, even when taking into account the length of the old German course, and if nothing else, Bellof's time demonstrates his completely fearless approach to driving. The young German from Giessen, just north of Frankfurt, was making a sensational impression, and particularly so on the Porsche management.

Derek Bell found it easy to work with Bellof, but he soon had concerns about the lack of team control on his partner's speed. 'I called him my son,' he says. 'and we had a great rapport. It was great really.'

'He was so electrifyingly fast at the Nürburgring. The kid goes out there and every lap he is going five seconds quicker in the race. I'd done a stint and he'd done a stint. We were two or three minutes ahead of

Jochen and Jacky, because they had a problem. We only had to cruise to win the bloody race and every time they put the board out it was 6:29 or 6:24, you know. I went up to Professor Bott and Peter Falk and I asked them why they didn't just tell him to hold. And they just thought he was marvellous. I just said OK and then, the next lap, he didn't come round.'

Bellof had lost control of the 956 at high speed at the Pflanzgarten, one of the 'Ring's infamous flying places. The car was totally destroyed. Bellof stepped unhurt from the very crumpled monocoque (at least demonstrating the inherent strength of the structure), but Derek was seething.

'I didn't understand that. I was outspoken about it. The guy needed some guidance. I had such great respect in every other aspect for Porsche except the way they couldn't control him. They didn't try and mould him into a driver. Nobody really did.

'Maybe Ken Tyrrell did later on, I don't know. It's different when they are bringing a driver on from Formula Three, after that they just want to get the best out of him. But I don't know why Porsche had him in the first place and then [at the end of the year] let him go. They were just hypnotised by the lap times.'

The two-part race was won by Ickx and Mass in the other Rothmans car despite a six-minute stop to replace a broken rear suspension arm. As at Silverstone, Reinhold Joest's car was second and Richard Lloyd's third.

Such was the standing of the Nordschleife (and this being the last international on the course) that Lloyd enjoyed the services of current Formula One World Champion, Keke Rosburg. The Swedish star shared the Canon car alongside rising F1 driver Jonathan Palmer and regular driver Jan Lammers.

Lloyd was setting a standard (that only a few other teams could afford) that he would retain all through his Group C years. The team would only use professionals who could get the best from the car. 'I didn't want track performance compromised and I always had the satisfaction of knowing I had the best drivers I could get in the car.'

Like everyone else, Derek Bell was astonished at Stefan Bellof's speed, but the young German driver lost control of his 956 at the notorious Pflanzgarten during the 1983 Nürburgring 1,000km. Bellof was unhurt, but his team-mate was unimpressed. (LAT)

THE HOLBERT ADVANTAGE

Every detail of the team's attendance at La Sarthe was considered. This is a layout of how the team trucks would be arranged in the paddock.

AT THE END OF 1982, Vern Schuppan had thought his career was over with the Rothmans-Porsche team.

'What happened was that I didn't just get the sack,' he says. 'Helmuth Bott called me into his office and said: "Derek just feels that maybe you are not so lucky for him".

'But they had sold a car to Nova Engineering in Japan and they wanted a factory driver to drive it, somebody who had experience of the factory cars. So Porsche asked me if I was interested in that. I was, very interested. I thought it would be a terrific thing

to do. I had an absolutely fantastic season in Japan. I won the [Japanese Sportscar] championship and five races. Then Professor Bott gave me the opportunity to drive at Le Mans as well, and that was a race I really wanted to wrap up.'

His call-up to the Rothmans squad came as a very pleasant surprise and demonstrated how much he had impressed the Porsche team – and how well he had fitted into the 'family' – in his two previous appearances for them in France.

'I never had a contract. I recall another year that I hadn't heard from them about Le Mans. I phoned Peter Falk and he said: "Well, of course you are driving. You can drive at Le Mans for as long as you want to." That was how they worked and it was something I really liked.'

After so many years practice, the 'family' – under Peter Falk's paternal guidance – was running like a well-oiled machine. Norbert Singer was in overall technical control and he acted as crew chief on the (number one) Ickx/Mass car – the Nürburgring winner, 005. Klaus Bischoff looked after the number two, Bell/Bellof 956 (a brand-new car, 008) and Roland Kussmaul tended number three (chassis 003), the car to be driven by Schuppan, with Al Holbert and Hurley Haywood. This was the same car that had been driven to second place the previous year by Schuppan and Mass and had since won at Spa, Fuji and Brands Hatch. It might not have been new, but it was well-sorted.

Against the factory cars were all the European 956 customers with Preston Henn's from the USA. After their strong early season results, few felt compromised (or over-awed) by any speed advantage the Rothmans cars might show in practice.

The Andrettis, Mario and Michael, teamed with the

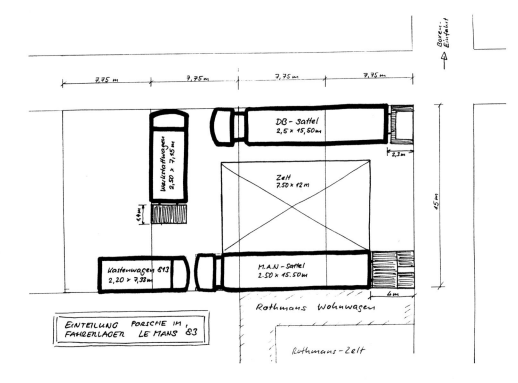

promising Phillippe Alliot in the (Kenwood) Kremer car, while Wollek and Johanssen were joined by Klaus Ludwig in the leading (Marlboro) Joest car. Joest also ran the Schornstein 956, in New Man colours, for Merl, Schickentanz and de Narvaez.

Preston Henn was ready for his first 24-hour race in Europe as a team owner. With A. J. Foyt, Claude Ballot-Lena and Bob Wollek, he had won the Daytona 24 Hours that February in an Andial 935 and he had hired Mike Colucci to run his race team. The Peter Gregg-schooled perfectionist would bring a significant strength to Henn's team. At Le Mans, he shared his 956 with Ballot-Lena and future Mercedes endurance star Jean-Louis Schlesser

John Fitzpatrick was running Guy Edwards, Rupert Keegan and himself in the Skoal Bandit 956 and Richard Lloyd's Canon 956 was driven by Lammers, Palmer and Richard himself. The latter team owner would only do a single stint in the race.

'It was a daunting experience at Le Mans,' confesses Lloyd. 'I'd been there in the 924, but in the 956! The sheer rate of closing speed [on say a 911] was phenomenal. It was my first time in a full ground-effect car at that kind of speed. It was a relaxing car to drive and it had a beautiful gearbox, but my abiding memory was dealing with the crown in the middle of the road on the Mulsanne Straight. I had to hold the steering wheel with all my effort to avoid going off the road when I crossed the crown.' Richard was fast coming to the conclusion that he would leave the driving to others.

Since reliability and fuel consumption were the key to a successful Le Mans, any one of the serious 956 entries stood a chance of causing an upset over the course of 24 hours.

Jacky Ickx and Derek Bell were trying for a hat-trick of victories and their intent was underlined by a fiercely quick pole-position lap by Ickx, using a special engine with an 8.0:1 compression ratio, larger turbos and qualifying versions of Dunlop's new Denloc tyres. Ickx's lap was an average of 155.07mph (249.51kph) and the 956 was timed at a maximum speed of 224mph (360kph) on the long straight.

In terms of outright speed, the fastest car on the track in qualifying wasn't a Rothmans Porsche; it was Volkert Merl in the New Man Joest 956.

Merl and Klaus Ludwig (in Joest's Marlboro car) had slipstreamed each other on the long straight in an attempt to seize an improved grid position. Merl emerged from the attempt with ninth on the grid (and Ludwig fifth), but with the fastest time through the speed trap of 230mph (370kph).

Mass and Bellof were beaten to the second fastest qualifying position by the Alboreto Lancia, the Martini car doing its by-now expected hot practice performance with most observers predicting a typically short appearance in the race itself. Haywood, Holbert, and Schuppan avoided the practice sprinting and got on with the job of tuning themselves and the car into the event.

There were others in this race. We could talk about Walter Brun's Sehcars, Peter Sauber's BMW-powered C7 or the three Rondeaus (one of which was co-driven by Vic Elford), but the 956s were so dominant in practice that only a fool would have bet against one of them winning.

Nevertheless, the race didn't quite go according to the Weissach master plan. On only the second lap, Ickx was barged from the rear by Jan Lammers and after a pit-stop which lost some three laps, the lead factory car fell back down the order.

Through the night the other two factory cars,

Serious discussions in the Le Mans pits for (left to right): Klaus Bischoff, Norbert Singer, Helmuth Bott and Peter Falk. (Peter Falk collection)

The winning (but only just!) Rothmans 956 of Al Holbert, Vern Schuppan and Hurley Haywood looks worse for wear after a hard night's racing. But there was a lot more anxiety to come. (LAT)

running like sewing machines, traded the lead. As the early hours unwound, Holbert, Haywood and Schuppan pulled steadily away from the rest of the field – by midnight the top ten was filled with 956s.

Mass and Bellof fell back with various problems with their 956's lights, but in the chill of the night, the engine became slow to restart. A longer stop discovered that one cylinder was down on compression. The engine had run too lean and the mechanics suspected a cracked head. The 956 struggled on, sounding more and more sickly and consuming more and more water, but like a wounded soldier, it wouldn't lie down. A holed piston finally stopped the car on Sunday afternoon.

Meanwhile, Ickx and Bell's sterling drive had brought them back on to the same lap as the Holbert, Haywood and Schuppan car. When one of the posts supporting the rear wing on the transmission broke just after dawn, it cost the number three car two laps and allowed Derek to surge into the lead. However, shortly after, when he was pulling away from the Mulsanne Corner, his engine cut and the car rolled to a stop.

Derek lifted the tail, which was no small task for one person and, with help on the radio from the mechanics, got the engine re-started. An electrical connection was broken and by the time he got the car back to the pits for a proper check-up, they had dropped six laps. Their thriller of a race wasn't over yet.

To this point the Schuppan, Haywood and Holbert race had been a near-text book strategy on how to win Le Mans – stay out of trouble and the pits, avoid the scraps and take care of the car.

When Bell pitted, number three extended its strong lead. But with around two hours to go, the Le Mans story page was about to turn again. Ickx and Bell had fought back to within two laps and were relentlessly carving away at the gap.

'It was just after I had gone through the Mulsanne kink,' remembers Vern Schuppan. 'It was like an explosion and suddenly there was this gaping hole with the wiring flapping back.' The passenger door had become detached, either because it hadn't been closed properly at the last stop or because the hinges had sheared. The first 956s had the hinges mounted off the front roll-over hoop using a single hinge pin. In later years the mounting would be substantially strengthened.

'My first thought was that I was losing the tail of the car. That has killed a few guys in the past. But then it seemed OK. We had a two-lap lead and we had led the race for 19 hours in total at that point. So I decided to keep running until they got a new door ready. I was actually black-flagged, but I stayed out for five laps and when I came in they were ready. They threw it on and it didn't fit properly [the hinges had been damaged], so they pop-riveted a strap on [to hold it closed] and I went out again.

'What I didn't know was that you had to have a working door with a catch that the driver could operate from inside the car. So while I drove round, there was this negotiation with the Clerk of the Course as to whether a leather strap could be considered a working catch. I guess they all decided what was legal and they called me back in and quickly made it workable.

'All the time, you know, with these pit-stops, the Ickx/Bell car was catching us. But what we hadn't realised was that because the new door wasn't as good a fit as the old one and the temperature on that side started going up, but it was OK when I had handed over to Holbert (to start the last stint).'

The cylinder-head coolant radiators on the 956 are located just behind each door, and their cooling air is guided into each side by critically placed channels that are sculpted into the doors. The team were discovering that if a door was not closed precisely, the airflow to the radiators was disrupted.

'So, 20 minutes or so before the end, Hurley and myself were up on the rostrum, because even though Derek had just got on to the same lap as us, it looked like we had it in the bag.'

Hurley recalls the tension of the next 15 minutes vividly.

'I just remember Vern and I were on our way up to the podium. They had come to get us. There were two or three inches where that door hadn't fitted properly and that upset the air-flow to the coolers.

'Suddenly it came over the loudspeakers that Al Holbert had slowed down and there was smoke bellowing out the back of the car. We didn't even know if he was going to make it back.'

In a 1983 interview Al Holbert said that before he made a final stop for fuel, about a half hour before the

end, the water temperature in the left-hand bank of cylinders was high but that he could control it.

Crew chief Kussmaul advised Holbert that he needed to go faster to hold off Ickx and Bell. Holbert increased the pace, but the temperature went off the gauge as the engine began to cook itself. He could smell oil and water in the cockpit as he started his last lap and at that point the left-bank gauge had dropped to zero – there was no water left in the system.

'We thought bloody hell!' adds Vern. 'We're slowing down and Derek is out there going flat-out, reeling us in!'

Of that final lap, Holbert said: 'I figured I had to chance it and maintain the same pace as I had been doing, since either we were going to finish first or not at all.

'Fortunately, it held together, but I can tell you I was really sweating it.' Holbert also had to take great care not to arrive at the finish line before 4 o'clock as he would have had to do another lap. 'And that simply wasn't on the cards for us.'

'It was pretty dramatic there,' continues Hurley, the master of under-statement. 'But Al was the perfect

The Andrettis drove a Kremer 956 to third place at Le Mans in 1983, and but for another race lap may have won. Here, Michael and Mario are at Weissach to discuss future projects with, from left to right: Helmuth Bott, Michael, Mario, CEO Peter Schutz and Peter Falk. (Peter Falk collection)

Jochen Mass climbs out of his 956 while Jacky Ickx waits to take over. The pit-stop is at the Nürburgring 1,000km in 1984, this car finishing in a delayed seventh place.

Peter Falk discusses the 956 with F1 World Champion Keke Rosberg at the Nürburgring 1,000km. The last international race on the old Nordschleife attracted a superb entry of sentimentalists all wanting one last go on the demanding course. (Peter Falk collection)

guy, because he was an engineer and he had the mindset to get the car [over the line] – it was just beginning to seize up in top gear as he began to slow down.

'He managed to get it into first gear and pop the clutch, so that it broke the engine loose and he just kind of puttered very, very slowly back to the finish. And all the time the sister car was chasing us down. Literally, I think we won that race by around 50 or 60 seconds.'

In fact, the number one car had its own problems. The punishing drive back to the head of the field had left the brake discs with serious cracks. When Ickx had handed the car to Derek for the last stint, he had said the brakes were 'gone', but Derek elected to go for it rather than waste time changing the discs. The final result would have been a very different story if their brakes had been healthy, and that result would also have been quite different again, if the race had gone an extra lap – as Derek's fuel light had come on as he came through the Porsche Curves. With Holbert stopped just after the start/finish line and Bell out of fuel, the race would have gone to Mario and Michael Andretti, driving with Philippe Alliot in Kremer's 956. The Kremer car was some six laps behind the Rothmans cars, but at least it was healthy. It would be perhaps the closest Mario – winner of the Indy 500 and the F1 World Championship – would come to completing the dream triple crown of motorsport. But it wasn't to be. Haywood, Holbert and Schuppan were jubilant – and their car couldn't move another millimetre. The last word comes from Peter Falk. 'After the finish line he (Holbert) stopped and the engine was completely seized – absolutely. We had had it before where the engine had seized, but it always went again.'

Not this time, but in a race which had echoes of the final lap in 1969, Porsche's remarkable durability and a hugely experienced driver team had paid dividends. The Le Mans win gave Porsche the 1983 World Endurance Championship.

From Le Mans in 1983, the story of the 956 moves outwards from the factory's own efforts. With 956s taking nine of the top ten places at the 1983 race, some of the customer teams were beginning to ask themselves what could they do on their own to improve the performance of the car.

To find an edge on the factory cars, some looked to

the engine options, while others looked to the aerodynamics and chassis design.

At Spa, two and a half months after Le Mans, both Ickx/Mass and Bell/Bellof were the class of the field, but the best of the customers – and Lancia – were still not far behind.

Derek Warwick drove the Kremer car and came within a couple of seconds of the Bell/Bellof car in practice (itself a second shy of Ickx and Mass on pole). The Kremer car retired during the fast race while Ickx and Mass were able to win after Mass out-smarted their sister car on fuel consumption.

Two weeks later at Brands Hatch, the Rothmans cars were themselves both out-smarted by John Fitzpatrick's team. Rain (as usual) coloured the result, but the British team had discovered a telling unfair advantage.

Fitzpatrick's team manager, Keith Greene, had blanked off the cooling air outlets in the 956's undersides to gain a significant ground-effect advantage over the factory cars. Blanking off the slots was not recommended by Singer as it could lead to overheating, but in the chilly, wet conditions of the day, it worked. The modification would be much-copied.

After completing a brief apprenticeship at Spa, Derek Warwick partnered Fitzpatrick and the Toleman grand prix driver made the 956 fly. The JDavid-sponsored car also benefited from a high-downforce nose section while most customers still ran with the early nose section and so complained universally of too much understeer. Warwick and Fitzpatrick were also helped by superior Goodyear wet tyres and they won by a lap from Ickx and Mass.

Despite the Brands result, where the weather stayed fine, there was little the customers could do against the Rothmans cars. This was amply demonstrated at the Fuji 1,000km in Japan in early October, when both Weissach 956s finished five laps ahead of the locally based Trust/Nova 956 driven by Vern Schuppan and Nao Fujita and Matsuda's 956 driven by Thierry Boutsen and Henri Pescarolo. Local knowledge undoubtedly helped the Nova car, which was the only 956 still running with the low-downforce Le Mans tail (as it had done all season). Bell and Bellof won the race, suffering less than their partners from a deteriorating track surface.

The World Endurance Championship for Drivers in 1983 went down to the final round at Kyalami. Held

in the middle of the rainy season, the race produced another win for Derek Bell and Stefan Bellof with the Lancia of Patrese and Sandro Nannini second, but Jacky Ickx's third place was enough to ensure him the drivers' title.

Derek Bell was non-plussed by it all. If his partner

Falk's race summary for the last world championship event on the Nürburgring Nordschleife. Bellof again shows remarkable speed.

RENNEN: **1000 KM RENNEN NÜRBURGRING** (*NORDSCHLEIFE OHNE START-Z ZIEL*) ☒ WM-Lauf Nicht-WM-Lauf
DATUM: **83**

Streckenlänge: **20,6** (km) Wetter: *TROCKEN / KALT*
Einsatzfahrzeug: **956 005** Fahrer: *ICKX / MASS* Start-Nr.: **1.**
 956 007 *BELL / BELLOF* **2**

Ersatzfahrzeug: **956 006** *R.D.* **3.**

Ergebnisse Rennen:
1. *ICKX / MASS* 956 44 Fahrzeit: 5:26.34,63
2. *WOLLEK / JOHANNSON* 956 44 5:30.34,99
3. *ROSBERG / LAMMERS / PALMER* 956 43 5:25.41,78
4. *LÄSSIG / PLANKENH. / HEYER* 956 42 5:29.58,27
5. *SIGALA / LARRAURI* LANCIA 40 5:30.41,73
6. *FITZPATRICK / HOBBS* 956 39 5:30.47,20

Trainingszeiten:
1. *BELLOF* 6.11,13
2. *ICKX / MASS* 6.16,85
3. *WOLLEK / JOHANNSON* 6.31,59
4. *ROSBERG / LAMMERS / PALMER* 6.39,52
5. *PATRESE / ALBORETO* 6.41,17 (*LANCIA*)
6. *FITZPATRICK / HOBBS* 6.42,12

Schnellste Runde Rennen: *BELLOF* 6.25,91

Probleme: ① *QUERLENKERBRUCH HR UNTEN*

Ausfallursachen: .... km bis Ausfall: ....

RENNVERLAUF: ② *UNFALL SPRUNGHÜGEL PFLANZGARTEN IN RUNDE 20 (BELLOF)*

RUNDE 27: *ABBRUCH DES RENNENS NACH UNFALL BRUN (BMW-SEHCAR)*
1. *ICKX / MASS* 2:20,48,06
2. *WOLLEK / JOHANNSON* 2:26.09,56
3. *FITZPATRICK / HOBBS* 2:26.49,08

RUNDE 34 = 6 R.D. NACH RESTART: ① *QUERLENKER AN HINTERACHSE UNTEN RECHTS GEBROCHEN → GEWECHSELT (STANDZEIT 5.55 MIN)*

Fahrzeugdaten
Motor: *2.6 LITER MISCHKÜHLUNG*
Getriebe: *SYNCHRONGETRIEBE*
 Übersetzung: 1.: .... 2.: .... 3.: .... 4.: .... 5.: ....
 KT .... Differential ....
Fahrwerk:
 Federn: vorn .... hinten ....
 Dämpfer: vorn .... hinten ....
 Stabilisator: vorn .... hinten ....
 Felgen: vorn .... hinten ....
 Reifen: vorn .... hinten ....
 Misch.: vorn .... hinten ....
Bremsen
 Bremszange .... Kolben Ø .... Belag ....
 Bremsscheibe .... Bremskraftverteilung ....
Sonstiges: ....

Under the experienced team management of ex-Brabham F1 and Rondeau manager Keith Greene, John Fitzpatrick's team made rapid progress in 1983, culminating in a win at Brands Hatch.

The start of the 1983 Spa 1,000km with the two Rothmans 956s leading away the Kremer 956 of Derek Warwick and Franz Konrad, followed by the Patrese/Fabi Lancia LC2-83. The Rothmans cars would finish in number order.

hadn't crashed at the Nürburgring earlier in the season, it would have been his championship.

In 1981, John Bishop had made up his mind to not follow FISA's lead and introduce a fuel-consumption formula.

The guiding force behind the International Motor Sports Association (IMSA) would pursue a formula for sports car racing in the United States that gave the spectators what they wanted – the spectacle of racing cars racing, without any artificial restrictions once the flag had dropped. Economy remained something you flew on an aircraft when the budgets were tight.

Seen from twenty years later, the failure of FISA to embrace the American promoter's wisdom is telling. So many races in 1982 and 1983 had been ruined by the best cars having to back-off in the second half of the race.

While strong-willed characters such as Jean-Marie Balestre loudly hailed the introduction of the Group C formula as an opportunity for manufacturers to use racing to develop new technology in the heat of competition, IMSA just got on with the racing, and entertaining the paying spectators.

By 1982, the IMSA-run Camel GT Championship had become a popular series with both racers and fans alike. OK, there was not high-budget, manufacturer interest with technology-moving prototypes, but the grids were full, the cars were loud and the racing was close.

The core of its support came from often well-funded, but private teams who were really not that interested in research and development, but who (and is this a surprise!) just wanted to go racing.

If the IMSA management saw a need for fine tuning, then it was only in their desire for a varied selection of winners, which usually meant finding ways to prevent a Porsche from winning.

Credit on Porsche's side for this situation rests with Josef Hoppen, who through the 1970s, was in charge of Porsche's North American competition activities. Hoppen had been extremely successful in using IMSA both as a growing profit centre for Porsche motorsport and to promoting sales of the production cars.

By 1982, after such complete domination, particularly by the 935, John Bishop was ready to introduce a new variable to break the German domination. His solution was Grand Touring Prototypes (GTP).

The new class adopted similar chassis regulations to Group C, except that each wheel had to have the same diameter and be no wider than 16 inches. The dimensions of the underbody ground-effect ducts could be greater, but unlike Group C, the rear aerofoil had to be within the plan-form of the rear bodywork, so preventing cantilevered wings.

As before, the engine regulations defined a complex scale of rising capacity against vehicle weight. There were different scales for production-based and racing engines and equivalency factors for supercharged engines. From the beginning, Porsche's four-valve twin-turbo engine (as used in the 956) was deliberately factored out of the GTP regulations with the emphasis weighted particularly in favour of the home-grown pushrod V8s.

The first year of GTP had produced a traditional winner, but with new hope. A tube-frame 935 had shown the way, despite close competition from Lola-Chevrolet and March-BMW prototypes and later, Bob Tullius's new Jaguar V12s.

The Spa-winning 956-83 of Jacky Ickx and Jochen Mass – the latter seen here rounding La Source hairpin.

An exhausted-looking Jacky Ickx considers the lap times with Peter Falk at the Brands Hatch 1,000km. He had just completed his last driving stint in the team's (ultimately unsuccessful) chase of the Derek Warwick, John Fitzpatrick 956. Even after a year's development, the 956 was still an exhausting car to drive. (John Hearn)

In 1983, Al Holbert had begun the season with March's much-improved 83G ground-effect prototype, running a 5.8-litre Chevrolet V8. John Fitzpatrick campaigned an extreme, Joest-built 935 and won several races, but Holbert didn't give up. From Charlotte in mid-May that year, Holbert ran a new March 83G. It was powered by a Porsche engine built up by Andial of California.

Andial had been started in 1975 by three ex-Vasek Polak employees: Dieter Inzenhofer, Arnold Wagner and Alwin Springer. By 1983, Andial had earned an enviable reputation developing the 935 and in particular, turning the factory's very strong endurance racing motors into the more sprint-based and torquey units suitable for the Camel GT Championship.

Andial's broad skills were underlined when Preston Henn bought their tube-frame but sprint-prepared 935 in late 1982 and then had taken pole and won the 1983 Daytona 24 Hours. This 935 was far from being a 'Moby Dick' copy, but was the product of the California hot-rod 'school' of race car preparation. The unique tube-frame had been designed by Durino Miller and was built by Glyn Blakeslee (who had built Don Garlitt's dragsters) with Springer ensuring the car would become a winning proposition during 1982. It was a relatively straightforward job for Henn's crew chief Kevin Jeannette to prepare the Swap Shop car for endurance racing and in Kevin's words, 'it flew straight out of the box'.

The German-born Springer makes the link between the Peter Gregg years for Porsche in the USA and the new start the German company's racing activities

John Fitzpatrick shared his 956 with David Hobbs throughout most of 1983, but made the most of having the services of Toleman F1 driver Derek Warwick to win the Brands Hatch 1,000km in September. (LAT)

were making in 1983. He is quick to credit Al Holbert's role.

'Al was a very special guy and at that time he really hit it off with Mr Bott. So after Gregg died [in 1980], Porsche needed a guy over here and Al was able to build on that relationship with Bott.'

The association between Andial and Holbert had started in 1983. 'We got together with Momo – Gianpiero Moretti – and put a Porsche engine in a March prototype,' recalls Springer. 'It was a single-turbo 935. That worked out OK and so Holbert approached us.

'It developed into a kind of triangular thing with Al and the factory, that was productive for everybody. I had my own contacts there, but we weren't endorsed officially from Porsche. They tolerated us and the results spoke for themselves.'

The engine in the Holbert March quickly became the class of the IMSA field.

'I realised,' says Springer, 'that I had a guy who drove, who financed the effort and who could really give you feedback about what it was doing. He was willing to take a chance, so we were able to – shall we say – live some of our fantasies with the engine. 'We escalated the pace of our improvements and we made a very good combination.'

The March began with a 2.65-litre, single-turbo engine and by July, this had grown to a 3.0-litre. Holbert took five wins and the championship from Bob Tullius's ever-improving Jaguar.

In all this time, Weissach's attention was focused firmly on Le Mans and the World Endurance Championship. Not only that, IMSA wasn't holding the door open to the new 956 at all, but it was the SCCA who would give the car an opportunity to show what it could do in North America.

John Fitzpatrick took advantage of the long gap between Le Mans (in mid-June) and the next world championship race at Spa, in September, and brought his car to the SCCA-organised Can-Am round at Road America (Elkhart Lake).

Fitzpatrick's 956 was not as fast as the single-seat Can-Am machines of that time, but it was more durable and he won Porsche's first Can-Am race since Mark Donohue at Riverside in 1973.

Fitzpatrick's win did wonders for the Porsche Customer Sport order book. Jürgen Barth had already begun discussions with John Bishop about bringing

The pair of Rothmans Porsches finished five laps ahead of the Schuppan/Fujita 956 at Fuji in October 1983. (Rothmans International)

the 956 to IMSA and had talks with several potential customers, although Barth found rejection with the series organiser.

There was no way Bishop wanted the water-cooled Porsche engine dominating a formula that was at last showing ample signs of obtaining a healthy mix of winners. To underline his point of view on the car, as well as the engine, he also ruled out the 956 on a safety argument because, among other things, the driver's feet projected ahead of the front axle line.

The discussion didn't end there however. Barth generated widespread interest in the 956 in North America – enough in fact that it would be worth Porsche developing a special car to meet IMSA's new regulations. However, few of those potential customers believed that Porsche would actually be prepared to make the necessary changes to produce a car that could run just in IMSA.

Nevertheless, Norbert Singer took the discussions with John Bishop simply as a clarification of the rules. With CEO Peter Schutz's backing – and after Le Mans – the wily engineer went to work with his slide rule.

'We said OK,' he recounts, like a student set a new puzzle, 'Porsche will make a car so that the American customers can run in IMSA.'

He makes light of the Type 962's design task. This

Another pitlane conference – this time in Kyalami, South Africa. From the left are chassis engineer Horst Reitter, Norbert Singer, Valentin Schaeffer, mechanics Spingler and Hillburger, and Peter Falk. Derek Bell looks on and catches some rays. (Peter Falk collection)

Andial had gained a strong reputation for building competitive race cars by 1983. Preston Henn's car took pole position and won the 1983 Daytona 24 Hours. While Group C worried over every drop of fuel, IMSA had few fuel worries . . . (Geoffrey Hewitt)

would include designing-in a steel, rather than aluminium, roll-over cage, new bodywork and of course the challenge of placing the driver's feet behind the front axle-line.

'It wasn't difficult to do this, no. It was of course a change in the monocoque, but in principle, we didn't move the pedals backwards. If you did that you would have had to have moved the driver and fuel cell and so on, so we moved the wheels forward. It was not a big deal.' The new car gained an additional 120mm (4.72in) on its wheelbase compared to the 956.

The revised bodywork meant more wind tunnel work, particularly to develop the hybrid tail. The IMSA-legal rear end was a cross between the existing two tail options for Group C. The new tail sited the wing within the plan area of the car's rear bodywork. But unlike the low-mounted Le Mans tail, the wing was located at the same height as the car's cockpit roof.

Singer's wind tunnel work also considered a slightly shorter nose, which would ensure the new car also complied with the Group C regulations and the increased size of the NACA inlet just behind the cockpit – larger to accommodate the airflow required for the IMSA-specification, 2,869cc, all-air-cooled,

single-turbo engine. With this engine, the IMSA 962 still had to carry about 25kg (55lb) of ballast to meet the relevant sliding scale power-to-weight formula.

The new 962 (962 001) was ready for the 1984 Daytona 24 Hours, held over the weekend of 4/5 February. The drivers for the all-white car were Mario and Michael Andretti. As well as being the last car John Bishop wanted to see at Daytona, the appearance of the 962 also upset three of the factory's closest US customers – Bruce Leven, Bob Akin and Preston Henn.

Leven had his name down for the first 962 and he had expected to run it at Daytona. When it was announced that the factory would be running the car with the Andrettis, there was uproar.

Technically, the factory entry ran strictly to the same policy that Weissach had used in Europe, which was that they wouldn't release the car until all the bugs had been ironed out and they were confident about building a reliable product. There was some justification for this policy, but it didn't stop a bad breakdown in communications over the issue. It is said these three influential customers had to be talked back into maintaining their intention to buy the new

The new 962 differed from the 956 in having a 120mm (4.72in) longer wheelbase, and other detail changes. This is the new car during qualifying for its first race, the 1984 Daytona 24 Hours. It seized pole position by fully two seconds.
(Geoffrey Hewitt)

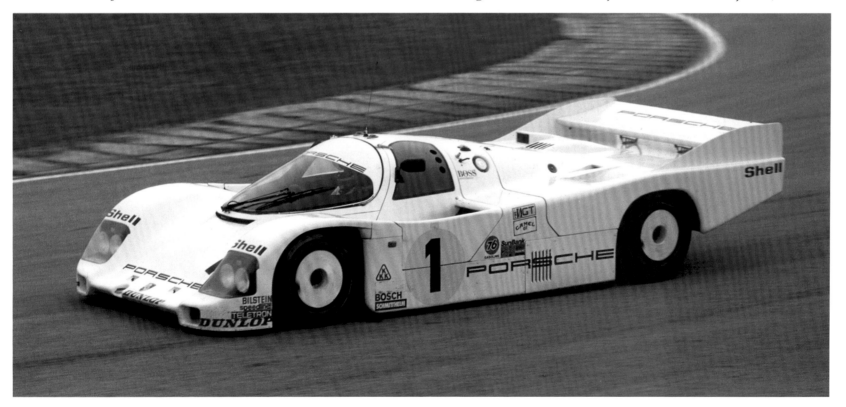

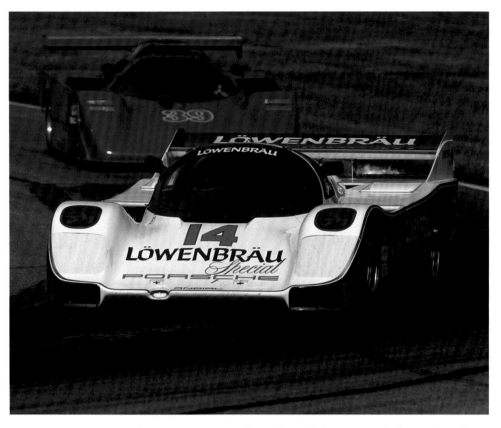

The first win for Al Holbert's new Löwenbräu team came at Mid-Ohio in June 1984. (Geoffrey Hewitt)

car. Even Al Holbert didn't get a look in; he drove Leven's 935 at Daytona that year.

The new 962 had been completed only two weeks before the event and as unloaded at Daytona, had only ran about 800km in testing. This was significantly less preparation than there had been before the debut of the 956 in 1982.

Nevertheless, Mario put the car on pole position with a lap that was nearly two seconds faster than the next qualifier. This was Sarel van der Merwe in the Kreepy Krauly-supported March-Porsche – Holbert's championship winner from the previous year. The next three followed in one-second intervals behind the March. These were the Tullius Jaguar XJR-5 driven by Tullius himself, David Hobbs and Doc Bundy; Preston Henn's tube-frame 935 – the previous year's winner built by Andial and driven by A. J. Foyt, Derek Bell and Bob Wollek, and a March 83G-Chevrolet driven by Bill Whittington, Randy Lanier and owner Marty Hinze.

By any measure, it was a class line-up and one for which John Bishop should have felt justifiably proud, if only for its variety. We can guess that the IMSA chief

allowed himself a smile when the new Porsche, which had been designed to win his championship, retired after only four hours.

The new 962 didn't have the durability. Its single-turbo installation, housed in the fully enclosed tail, overheated the gearbox on which it was mounted. Then the engine broke a camshaft. The race went to the South African team of van der Merwe, Graham Duxbury and Tony Martin in Holbert's old car from Henn's 935 and the Tullius Jaguar.

The 962 was returned to Weissach where it went into a further test programme to iron out the problems discovered in Florida. Although this car was never raced again, it would be the first of many.

A batch of customer 962s was started immediately, with the first car being delivered to Bruce Leven's Bayside Disposal team in April 1984 (962 101). In the following month cars were also delivered to Bob Akin (962 102) and Al Holbert (962 103).

Holbert was a late entry to the order books because it took some time for his new race budget to come together and when it did, he was obviously the right person to continue to lead the race development of the new cars. After the Daytona retirement, (and all the early impatience was forgotten) there were now concerns about the car's readiness and whether the 2.87-litre engine would be enough to take on the powerful Chevrolets and Jaguars in the shorter subsequent races of the championship.

Accepting this concern and Holbert's ability to sort out a new car, Leven rented his car for two races to Holbert until the latter's own 962 was available.

The new Holbert team, presenting major new sponsorship from the drinks brand Löwenbräu, made their debut at the Riverside Six Hours at the end of April. Holbert's new partner for the longer races was Derek Bell. Why Bell? There were two reasons.

The two men had first driven together, literally by accident, at Le Mans in 1980 and a mutual respect had built up since then. 'I think he saw my basic ability and mechanical sympathy,' says the British driver. Bell had also driven occasional races during 1982, driving Bob Akin's Coca Cola 935, and while he was driving for Akin, Bell had done promotional work for Camel. In turn, the contact at Camel led to an approach to Holbert from Miller. The American brewing giant had bought the US rights to Löwenbräu, the famous German beer. Miller wanted to get involved in racing to promote their new brand, and Bell had suggested Holbert.

'He had a few guys from the year before,' remembers Bell, 'but at the beginning, the car [the 962] wasn't really competitive with the March-Chevrolets.

'Like everything Porsche do, the engine was very under-stressed, because they didn't dare risk anything breaking. But when Al got hold of it, he created an amazing team around him. He was probably the best development driver I have ever worked with. He was very, very knowledgeable and he really made it work.

'He would drive the car, come in and talk to Tom Seabolt, who was the crew chief in that first year. Tom would tell the mechanics to do this, that and the other and I didn't have a clue what was happening. I had a much better rapport with the guy who took over from Tom in 1985, Kevin Durant. Kevin was a big guy, and had been a mechanic under Tom in the first year.

'I would ask him what Al had done, and he would write on his clipboard: "2 clicks on bump, one click on rebound, 2 degrees on castor, but more stiff on the roll bar, half a degree on the wing and drop the ride height half an inch" – and it would be all in one go!

'Eventually I was getting in the way, because I was stopping them doing it. But Al was so good. Eventually, I went: "Oh bollocks" and just let them get on with it! It was the same with Norbert Singer. Only they spoke in German!

'The best thing I had going there [with Holbert] was that I could tell them exactly what the car was doing. And in some ways that was the best thing. I'd come in and say it was pushing or it's pushing more, or it's faster, and they would just say, "well, it is faster".'

The 962 finished second at Riverside just five seconds behind the winning Whittington/Lanier March-Chevrolet, with Bell setting the fastest lap. They would have won but for slow pit work. Bell lost again to the same car at Laguna Seca when he was delayed by a puncture.

By May, Holbert had received his own 962, but he retired from the first race, at Charlotte, with a failed rear upright and wheel bearing. More importantly, there were now serious concerns about the competitiveness of the basic 2.87-litre engine.

The first win did not come until Mid-Ohio on 10 June, still with this smaller engine. But immediately

Bruce Leven let Al Holbert race the Bayside Disposal-bound 962 at Riverside and Laguna Seca, but drove the car himself for the first time at Mid-Ohio. The car is seen leading a typically assorted IMSA field. (Geoffrey Hewitt)

afterwards, the 3.2-litre engine from Holbert's 1983 March was fitted in a bid to get on terms with the powerful Chevys. This engine benefited from Springer's special intake manifold and intercooler layout that improved the throttle response with the big, single-turbo installation.

Springer continued the development and with the help of Weissach engine expert Valentin Schæffer, had the 3.2-litre air-cooled engine running on the new Motronic electronics by the end of the year.

Holbert and Bell won the next race, a three-hour event in early July at Watkins Glen. Back on the West Coast, the Löwenbräu car reverted to the 2.87-litre engine and graphically demonstrated its (poor) competitiveness with a third and a fourth at Portland and Sears Point respectively.

With the 3.2-litre back in, two wins followed, at Road America and Pocono. However, despite Holbert's charge in the second half of the season, the 962 didn't win the championship in 1984. The late start was too much of a disadvantage to overcome the very strong (Chevrolet) charge by Whittington and Lanier.

There was disappointment also for the other three

962 customers. Everybody had their cars, but they all struggled with the factory 2.87-litre engine's lack of competitiveness and a lack of manufacturer support.

The 1984 experience proved that IMSA GTP had become a very competitive series. Porsche couldn't just expect to turn up with a standard factory car and win. Daytona had proven that and Holbert underlined it when he spoke to *Panorama* magazine in August 1984.

'I think that racing on American tracks, with American sanctioning bodies, against American competitors is best done by Americans. There are ways of working within the rules that allow you to do certain things that make the car more competitive. That's what we'll try to do.'

In a far-reaching change of organisation on 1 September 1984, Volkswagen of America handed their Porsche responsibilities to the new Porsche Cars North America. It brought to an end Josef Hoppen's long and auspicious term as the champion of Porsche competition in North America. The head of the new Porsche Motorsport North America organisation would be Al Holbert. Now he could really put his management ideas into practice.

Bob Akin was another to receive his car in 1984, but like all the other 962 runners, found the factory 2.87-litre single turbo lacked torque compared with the Chevrolets. (Geoffrey Hewitt)

JOEST A MINUTE . . .

ONE INTERESTED SPECTATOR at the 1984 Daytona 24 Hours had been FISA President Jean-Marie Balestre. Balestre had been so impressed with the varied entry in IMSA's GTP class that he returned to Europe and announced the fuel consumption principle for Group C would be abolished from the start of 1985 and a new IMSA-harmonised formula would be adopted.

A sliding scale of engine capacities-to-vehicle weights would also be introduced. The formula's maximum weight would be raised to 850kg (1,874lb) (from 800kg/1,764lb) and from the start of the 1985 season, cars would have to be constructed so that the driver's feet were behind the front axle line.

The 15 per cent reduction in fuel allowances previously agreed for the 1984 season, which had been written into the original Group C rules back in 1982, was to be scrapped. One extra detail Balestre proposed, and which was added to make the shorter races more interesting for 1984, was that six (rather than five) pit-stops were to be allowed. It was expected this would result in faster races as the cars would now spend an extra two minutes stopped in the pits.

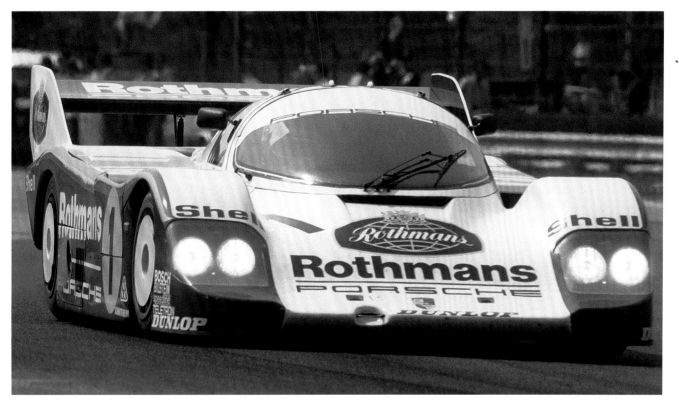

This 956, driven by Jacky Ickx and Jochen Mass, won the 1984 Monza 1,000km. All the Weissach cars, and many of the customer 956 teams, were running with the new Motronic 1.2 engine management. Monza would be remembered for its high toll on the Porsche turbo engines.

The positive aspect of these regulation changes was that by aligning Group C with IMSA, cars from each series could, once more, run together. However, Porsche had not invested so much money, time and effort working with Bosch to reduce the fuel consumption of its 956 just to see it all blown away without proper notice.

The new Motronic electronic engine management development had been troublesome to begin with, but after a concentrated development effort had come good. Further development also promised continued competitiveness in 1984, while meeting the original goal of reducing the fuel consumption by 15 per cent.

As a result, the reaction from Weissach to what appeared to be an arbitrary change to the regulations was immediate. Porsche withdrew its entry for that year's Le Mans 24 Hours and threatened legal action for a breach of the FISA's own Sporting Code (which

defined the notice period for such regulation changes). FISA was shocked into action, immediately offering a concession.

They would allow the original Group C cars to run until the end of the 1985 season, at least giving the fuel-optimised 2.65-litre Porsche and 3-litre Lancia (Ferrari) turbo engines a stay of execution. The full harmonisation would be put on hold, but from 1984, IMSA cars would still be allowed to run at Le Mans. That, at least, did broaden the show for the spectators although it was hardly the best way to begin a new season, but nonetheless, it was business as usual for the customer sport department at Weissach.

Five new Group C customer cars were built at the start of 1984 (but no new factory cars), to a revised 956B specification. These adopted the Motronic 1.2, which was also made available to the existing customer cars. Among other detail changes there was lighter bodywork and a significantly revised front

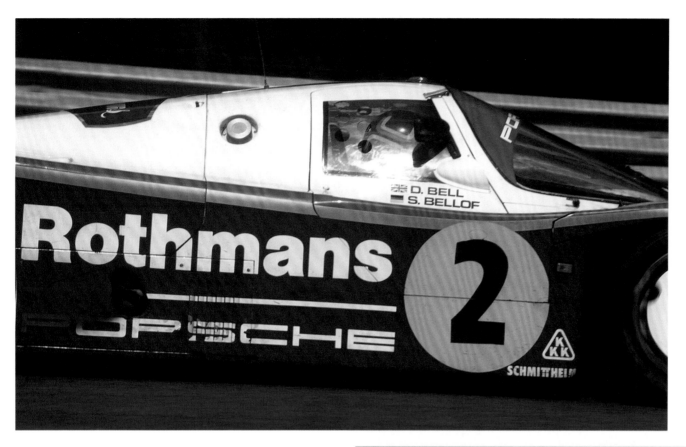

Stefan Bellof continued in 1984 as he had started the year before – showing blistering speed.

Vern Schuppan, Alan Jones and Jean-Pierre Jarier brought this Kremer 956B home to sixth place at Le Mans in 1984.

suspension geometry which included a castor angle increased from 2° to 4°. It was another step (with more to come on the 962) to reduce steering effort.

It was obvious from Monza that Bellof was beginning 1984 as he had finished the previous year – blisteringly quick. Frequently, it was left to a sometimes-unimpressed Bell to get the fuel consumption back on course after the young German's inevitable, record-breaking laps, but when Bell and Bellof won the race, they were disqualified for being 2kg (4.4lb) underweight. After a winter of sparring with FISA over the regulations, the Weissach team were in no mood for losing races. The protest was immediate, Porsche calling into question the calibration of Monza's scales. It took two months to resolve, and after the necessary checks, they were given the victory back. Ickx and Mass finished on the same lap.

Monza in 1984 will not be remembered for Bellof's speed or indeed the racing at all however, but the bills accrued by the 956 owners. The leading 956 customer teams all had the Motronic 1.2 for the first

Porsche CEO Peter Schutz and his wife Sheila.

ratio. This fact was unknown to the customers at the time and all (except Joest) who were running the Weissach-built engines, were using the standard 8.0:1 ratio, and their engines were destroying themselves. They had every reason to be aggrieved.

It is likely that the weekend's high ambient temperatures and potentially suspect fuel from the paddock petrol station gave the turbo-engines their excuse to let go. The strain on the engines was further increased by Monza's high-speed stretches and the pace forced on the 956s by the Lancias. Also of course, there was the ever-present temptation in the cockpit to wind-up the boost to get a quick lap time.

When the Rothmans team destroyed more engines at Silverstone and the Motronic runners were again affected at Le Mans, some began to wonder if the new electronics were as great as it had been led to believe. Meanwhile, Bosch and the Weissach engineers were working hard to find the right balance of mixture, timing and fuel consumption.

Ickx and Mass won Silverstone, after Patrese had captured the pole position in a Lancia, sharing the car with Bob Wollek. The surprise of the weekend once

time, and it was more than a coincidence that the race took a heavy toll on engines, including, in qualifying, even the Rothmans team units.

The factory team's own failures could have been as the result of probing the edges of their own performance envelope with an 8.5:1 compression

At Monza in 1984, Reinhold Joest's car was not as fortunate as it had been the year before. Klaus Ludwig retired the car with a blown engine after just 17 laps; bad fuel was suspected.

again came from Porsche's customers – in this case the two leading British teams.

The Richard Lloyd-entered Canon 956, driven by Jonathan Palmer and Jan Lammers, was one of the fastest 956s throughout the weekend. In the race, the red and white Canon car had forged ahead and would have won had it not fallen back to sixth place with a fractured oil line.

Others to impress had been the two John Fitzpatrick-entered cars. The Skoal Bandit cars were among the prettiest on the grid (which cannot be said of the sponsor's product – a chewing tobacco) and lead drivers David Hobbs and Thierry Boutsen surprised many to finish third.

In fourth place came Lancia – their second consecutive finish (after their third at Monza). The Italian cars seemed to have found some reliability at last and looked threatening for the coming races. After several years competing against one another, the Porsche men had the utmost respect for the apparent progress (and the potential threat) that Cesare Fiorio's team was making.

'It was one of the best relationships that I personally had with a competitor,' says Norbert Singer. 'I remember several times before the start of a race, Fiorio would come up and wish us a good race. We were not friends, but we had a good relationship. We wanted a fair race and that's all. It was ideal because he had a completely different car and a completely different engine. Of course, you could look at the car and think "Ah yes! This is a nice detail" and you might try it on your car. That's normal. But at a certain point, we shook hands and just had a good race.'

Nonetheless, despite their speed and superb driving team, in 1984 the Lancias just couldn't make that final step towards consistency. By sheer weight of numbers, the 956s prevailed.

'Maybe the team was not as perfect as he thought,' continues Singer, referring to the Lancias, 'or there was not enough time or money. It was a pity because when you looked at the car, it was nicely done.

'Bob Wollek was driving the car by then, before he came to us. He didn't tell us much about the technical details of course, but he said it was a nice car. It had lots of power, but the fuel consumption wasn't as good. So I don't know really why they weren't more competitive.'

With the factory absent from Le Mans, the race fell

Reinhold Joest out-foxed everyone else at Le Mans in 1984 by careful preparation. Here, the winning car of Henri Pescarolo and Klaus Ludwig follows the other Joest team car out of the Ford chicane. (LAT)

Reinhold Joest's victory at Le Mans in 1984 came after detailed development of the engine's mechanical fuel injection and the car's underbody.

Preston Henn began a trio of excellent endurance racing results at the 1984 Le Mans 24 Hours. The Jean Rondeau and John Paul Jnr-driven 956 would finish second in France. The Henn team also won the 1985 Daytona and Sebring classics. (LAT)

wide open for the customer teams – and for Lancia. This was the best chance Fiorio would ever have of winning the 24 Hours – if only his cars could hold together.

The Lancias went through an exhaustive test programme to improve their durability and three cars were entered. Bob Wollek captured pole position with Mauro Baldi in the sister car in second place. Ominously, the third car crashed in practice and only started 12th.

The other non-Porsche outsiders that received a lot of attention in France were the Bob Tullius-run IMSA Jaguar XJR-5s. Despite being heavier and less powerful than the Group C runners, the 6-litre V12 cars made a powerful alternative statement.

There were no less than 14 956s and two of the new 962s on the entry list. This 'class within a class' created an interesting battle to be top dog, and by this time, every team was trying to find a secret advantage over the others.

In that year's *Autosport* report Quentin Spurring quoted one team driver: 'We come to Le Mans and try out all the ideas we've had since [last year]. That's usually a waste of time and we lose the first day. We go back to the standard set-up and go from there.'

Each time the teams departed from Norbert Singer's standard low-downforce body configuration, the balance seemed to be upset.

Reinhold Joest was running a brand-new 956B, chassis 117 in the colours of clothing manufacturer New Man. Both Joest cars started immediately behind the two Lancias and were notable for not attempting to be any different from the standard factory specification (well, visually anyway).

That was because Joest had focused all his long Le Mans experience on the car's underbody and its flat-six engine. The underbody experiments would continue well after Le Mans but by this time, the engine specification was well-proven.

He had chosen the regular 2.65-litre engine and developed new camshafts, higher compression pistons and a host of other proven enhancements in the block and heads, but the real advantage would come from not using the supposedly more fuel-efficient Motronic system. This was a decision that had been taken when engines had started to self-destruct earlier in the season.

'Let me tell you,' he says, still enjoying the significance of this decision. 'When Porsche started the Motronic, at one stage they told the customers

they had to switch to the Motronic as well. We refused for a long time because of the financial issues. The other reason was that Porsche said the customers would get only two chips. One was for qualifying and one was for the race.

'This was not a good starting point if we wanted to

John Watson drove with Stefan Bellof at the Fuji 1,000km where Jochen Mass (left) shares a few of the 956's secrets with the Ulster driver.

At Brands Hatch in July 1984, the Richard Lloyd Racing Canon 956 showed all the other private teams the way home. Their advantage came from a new front aerofoil which was said to reduce the car's inherent understeer around the twisting British circuit. Its benefits were disputed by Porsche, but the device was widely copied. (LAT)

By Spa in early September, others were seeking the same 'unfair advantage' that the Richard Lloyd Canon 956 had demonstrated at Brands Hatch. This is the John Fitzpatrick 956.

'We had three different engines. Long-distance, sprint and Le Mans. In the end we learned that the sprint engine was good enough for 24 hours at Le Mans. This was why we had a good result with the fuel, but it wasn't done in one year, you know. It was the result of a lot of testing.'

There was another piece in the Joest master plan that fell into place in late 1983. He hired Domingos Piedade as race team manager. Piedade was an ex-journalist who had turned his hand to driver management, looking after the interests of Michele Alboreto and an emerging Ayrton Senna. He showed his team strategy skills running Gerhard Schneider's BMW touring car team in the late 1970s, before moving to Peter Sauber's sports car team.

be competitive! Porsche continued to do it this way, while we just wanted to see how it all developed. We wanted to make sure it was going to be successful.'

Joest had Kugelfischer build him a special fuel injection pump, with a revised fuel-metering space cam that gave the power required with improved fuel consumption. He continues the story. 'We used all our experience. I think we had many positive points in the engine and the underbody. But it was very hard work. We could not go to the wind tunnel, so we had to get experience by doing [or experiment].

'He always had very good ideas,' says Joest. 'He was good with strategy, driver ideas and race ideas, very good.' Joest compares him to Jean Todt, the contemporary Ferrari F1 team manager. 'Piedade engineered the Pescarolo/Ludwig car at Le Mans in 1984 and he played a very important role in the result.'

Perhaps surprisingly at Le Mans, barely anybody noticed that the Rothmans team was not present in the race. Four cars made the early, break-neck pace. These were the Wollek/Nannini Lancia and the 956s of Palmer/Lammers (in Richard Lloyd's Canon car), Merl/Schornstein/Winter (in the number 12 New

Walter Brun, Hans-Joachim Stuck and Harald Grohs drove this Jägermeister-supported 956 to third place in the 1984 Spa 1,000km. Stuck would establish his name in the Brun car during 1984, paving the way for a Rothmans drive from 1985.

Man/Joest 956) and Schuppan/Jones/Jarier (driving a Kenwood-supported Kremer 956B).

The number one New Man/Joest car, on which so much preparation had been lavished, had a near-disastrous start. Driven by Henri Pescarolo and Klaus Ludwig, it pitted within a few laps with low fuel pressure. The problem fixed, the two drivers began a determined haul back up through the field from 30th place. At this stage their fuel strategy was out of the window. Like so many heroic fight-backs in earlier years, theirs was now simply a race to get back on the leader-board. The effort was soon focused on this one car when the second Joest 956 dropped out at around quarter distance after going off the road.

Into the dark hours and it looked as if the hard work by Lancia was paying off, with the Martini cars leading confidently. But the night took its toll. Both Italian cars dropped away – one with broken suspension and the other missing fifth gear.

Even the steady Jaguars, that had established a strong position early on just outside the top three, ran into problems. John Fitzpatrick's 956B, driven by David Hobbs, Philippe Streiff and Sarel van der Merwe grabbed the lead on Sunday morning and almost immediately, it too stumbled after a storming effort through the night. This handed the lead to the surviving New Man Joest 956B. Despite a major suspension repair, Henri Pescarolo and Klaus Ludwig had clawed their way back to the front. Aided by over an hour's caution period, fuel consumption proved not to be an issue. The delay had been caused during the night, when the two Aston-Martin Nimrods were involved in a frightening accident on the maximum speed Hunaudières Straight. Sadly, the accident claimed the life of a marshal.

Preston Henn chose to run his new IMSA 962 (which he was sharing with Michel Ferté and Edgar Doeren) at Le Mans, but a consistent run had ended after 21 hours on Sunday when the rotor arm broke in the distributor. However, more of this car (962 104) would be heard in the coming years. Henn, meanwhile, switched to his other 956.

For much of the second half of the race, the Jean Rondeau/John Paul Jnr Swap Shop car had run on the same lap as the New Man car, but as happened so often in Group C, a good race was spoiled by concerns over fuel consumption. The American car had had to back-off and Joest had hung on to win by

two laps. Porsche 956s filled the first seven places, with the Wollek/Nannini Lancia next, slowed by its weak transmission.

After Le Mans, FISA saw sense and 'clarified' the proposed changes it had suggested at the beginning of the season. They said the planned 15 per cent fuel consumption reduction would take effect from the

Walter Näher (with headset) talks with Stefan Bellof during a pit-stop at the 1984 Nürburbring 1,000km; Bellof and Derek Bell would win the race.

start of the 1985 season – a year later than planned. They still wanted a complete abolition of the consumption formula, but they accepted more discussions would be necessary. Porsche at least had won that argument, and it wasn't raised again.

The Rothmans-Porsche team took to the tracks with renewed energy after Le Mans. If nobody had missed them in the 24 Hours, then the Weissach team made up for their absence during the rest of 1984. The factory team won every remaining World Endurance Championship race.

The Nürburgring and Spa went to Bell and Bellof, while the German won with John Watson at Fuji. Ickx and Mass won at Mosport, but the team didn't go to Kyalami (along with most of the other 956 teams) because of a disagreement with the organisers over money.

The championship became, predictably, a one-model Porsche challenge, but far from being boring, the sight of a pack of multi-coloured 956s, all with largely the same (200mph/320kph) performance made for great racing.

Running in parallel to the World Endurance Championship for Manufacturers, the World Endurance Championship of Drivers included additional races at Brands Hatch, Imola and Sandown Park in Australia. Considered not so important in Weissach, the Rothmans team did not go to Brands

The Rothmans Porsche team at Spa in 1984. From left to right in this happy group are; Stefan Bellof, Derek Bell, Jochen Mass, Jacky Ickx, Vern Schuppan and John Watson.

Hatch and allowed its drivers to seek temporary drives with other teams.

So while Derek Bell opted to share Al Holbert's IMSA 962 in Portland, Oregon, Stefan Bellof drove with Walter Brun and Jochen Mass in Brun's 956B. Brands Hatch went to Jonathan Palmer and Jan Lammers in Richard Lloyd's 956.

Following through on its Silverstone promise, the Canon car was on top all weekend, being comfortably faster than the Lancias or the Joest and the Fitzpatrick Porsches. This was in no small part from having former Rondeau and John Fitzpatrick manager Keith Greene on the team strength. The Lloyd 956, like Fitzpatrick's 956 at Brands a year earlier, enjoyed something of an unfair technical advantage. Richard Lloyd had been thinking hard of ways to increase the chassis performance of his cars, and in particular, he wanted to kill the understeer on the twisty tracks like Brands.

Peter Stevens – later to work with Tom Walkinshaw on the Jaguar sports cars and with Gordon Murray on the McLaren F1 – put Lloyd's original 956 (chassis 106) through a full programme at MIRA's full-scale wind tunnel at Nuneaton, in Warwickshire. So, at Brands Hatch the Canon car appeared with a front wing and a larger, two-element rear wing.

'We had a huge increase in front downforce,' says Lloyd, 'but we had to balance it with the two-element rear wing. There was a penalty. The drag went up and we paid the price with our fuel consumption, but we thought we'd cracked it on the performance. It was balanced and very quick.'

However, it was not by coincidence that after seeing the changes, the Rothmans cars chose not to follow the trend.

'We had tried that in the wind tunnel before Richard Lloyd did it,' says Norbert Singer, 'and it didn't work! We had also tried it on the 917/10. That [917] nose section looks quite funny now, but we did it with two short small wings and it didn't work,' he says referring to the 1972 Riverside test by Mark Donohue. During the development of the turbocharged Can-Am car, the front wing tabs from a McLaren IndyCar were fitted to the nose in an attempt to cure a similar understeering problem.

'We had seen the same results with Donohue and with our wind tunnel tests – you [simply] spoil the rear wing. The driver has no feeling of absolute

The 1985 Monza 1,000km was the second race for the new 962C. Jacky Ickx and Jochen Mass were classified in fourth place.

numbers, he just knows the difference between the front and the rear.'

The problem came down to a question of aerodynamic balance and that was directly attributable to the rear, not the front wing. 'We tried bigger wings on the 956 in the wind tunnel and it didn't work either. For me it wasn't clear why Richard Lloyd went immediately half a second faster at Brands Hatch. But [then you look at] his basic lap time and he was already slower. He just balanced the car with the front wing. He wouldn't get any more downforce.'

It was no coincidence that Singer did not use a higher-downforce, two-element rear wing. He says that on the 956, the rear wing acted as a trim tab for the behaviour of the whole car. 'With the big wing, it wasn't necessary to add a flap. I think later that we had a flap, which made it easier to adjust, but with the big wing you had to be careful with the tuning.'

The works cars had adopted a very small Gurney flap along the rear edge of the tail, under the aerofoil. This small strip of aluminium had a critical function.

'When it is set very small, it reduces the drag a little bit. If it is set higher, you get a little more downforce at the rear, but you also get more on the nose. I think it was at one of the Spanish circuits [used later], Jerez or Jarama – a tricky circuit with a low top speed, we ran a spoiler of 100mm, just to improve the front. At those low speeds, the drag increase is unimportant.'

Comparison of the lap-times at the Brands Hatch race between 1983 and 1984 tend to support Singer's view of the front wing's effectiveness.

Jacky Ickx's pole time in 1983 was 1min 17.19sec. Palmer's pole time in 1984 was 1min 17.32sec. The latter's time was a 1.47-second improvement over the Lloyd team's best qualifying time from the year before, but it was still 0.13 seconds off Ickx's 1983 best. However, there may be other factors that were weighted in the factory car's favour. Not the least of these was that it was hot and dry in 1984, compared with an advantageous damp, cold day in 1983.

Singer sums up his view of the front wing experiments. 'You get the same effect if you lower the rear wing! But if you do that, maybe you would worry about losing downforce at the rear. When you spoil [the rear wing airflow] from the front, you have better grip at the front and that does reduce the understeer.

It isn't because you have more downforce at the front, it is because you have less at the back.'

Nevertheless, Lloyd's fellow 956 runners were impressed. At Spa, five weeks later and after an Ickx/Mass win in Mosport, Lloyd-style front wings appeared on several other cars. John Fitzpatrick even tried side skirts while many teams were testing modified underbody profiles in an attempt to gain extra downforce.

Whether Thierry Boutsen's pole position at Spa (in 2min 9.63sec) was down to the improved aerodynamics or to the Fitzpatrick car's Goodyear tyres, is unknown, but Jacky Ickx matched the time exactly with his unchanged Rothmans car.

One thing is clear, front wings would appear on 956 and 962s for several years to come, particularly at the tighter circuits. Was this a lemming effect, where the others blindly followed the first adopter? Talk to Richard Lloyd and he will convince you of their value.

Lloyd wasted no time in taking another step forward in his search for the winning advantage. While the others were trying out copies of his front wing at Spa, his team were shaking down a brand-new aluminium-honeycomb monocoque beneath the skin of the Canon 956.

This Nigel Stroud-designed structure otherwise cloned the standard car's components and geometry to pursue improved chassis stiffness. This huge step had been taken after they realised that chassis rigidity was a major influence on the efficiency of the very stiffly sprung ground-effect cars.

At Spa, the new car was quick and qualified fourth. Such was the huge downforce that the double-element rear wing produced though, that in the race it cracked the 'ox-bow', the substantial casting over the gearbox casing that holds the engine sub-frame.

The Lancias had missed both Mosport and Spa, but a single LC2 turned out again for the drivers' round at Imola, but the interval's development had not done them any good and 956s filled the first eight places. Stefan Bellof and Hans Stuck won in Brun's 956 from the very quick, but thirsty, Lloyd honeycomb car. Stefan Bellof had accrued enough points to take the World Endurance Championship of Drivers because of his drives in Walter Brun's 956B.

Bellof would sign for Ken Tyrrell in Formula One for 1985 and because of clashing commitments, his Rothmans-Porsche contract would lapse, although he would re-appear in sports cars during 1985, again accepting drives with Walter Brun.

All Group C cars made after 1 January 1985 had to comply with FISA's new IMSA-inspired chassis regulations. Earlier cars, including the 956, were allowed to run for a further two seasons. Nonetheless, Weissach built a batch of the new, extended wheelbase 962Cs for customers and their own use.

The surprise at the start of that season however, was that the older 956s, into which many customers had put much development effort, were just as quick – if not faster than – the new cars.

When Richard Lloyd's team debuted their new, Nigel Stroud-designed aluminium-honeycomb 956 at Spa in 1984, it was an indication that the stakes were being raised by the best professional teams in a bid to find extra speed. From the first customer 956 deliveries, it was clear that some owners were not prepared to fall in line and have their competitiveness locked into the fortunes of the Weissach team. However, Lloyd was the first to build his own chassis in the search for better handling, improved driver safety and yes, a cheaper option than buying the standard factory item.

The Rothmans team had won the first race at Mugello, but at the next round at Monza, the fastest Porsche in qualifying was the Lloyd car of Jonathan Palmer and Jan Lammers. In the race, a fierce storm brought out the red flag at two-thirds distance and in the middle of a round of fuel stops. Walter Brun lucked into the win with a brand-new 962C, but it was the speed of the Lloyd car that had everybody talking. Until a wheel had come off the car, the Lloyd 956 had been fighting for second place with Joest's 956.

A winter's development had found new speed in the aluminium-honeycomb 956 and a close look at the car revealed that the little Silverstone-based team had been working very hard.

'I think we put their nose out of joint by questioning everything,' says Lloyd of his contact with the engineers at Porsche. 'The car was very good, but as a private entry we were always looking for an edge. It was very frustrating that the factory always had something better. I think the German teams also had more of an advantage because of the language. Their mechanics would mix with the factory mechanics and they would get to hear about all the latest mods.'

In an *Autosport* interview at the time Lloyd said: 'When you buy a Porsche, they don't expect you to tinker with it. But that has never been our policy.'

In 1984, he had hired long-time friend Peter Stevens, then a lecturer in automotive design at the Royal College of Art, and engineer Val Dare-Bryan to bolster his already-experienced race team and begin to develop the 956's chassis and aerodynamics.

On the engine side however, Lloyd remained totally locked into Porsche.

'Everything on that side was done by Stuttgart,' he says. 'On a single engine, we could do practice, qualifying, a 1,000km race and then practice and qualifying for the next race. I think we had about three at any one time. There was always a mental battle about the level of information we were given from Porsche. I remember that we used to sit in the service truck with Gerd Schmid and Jürgen Barth [both of Porsche Customer Sport] and try to get them to release a bit more information.

'At first there was just the 2.6 [litre], but later, there were certain engines for certain circuits – 2.8, 3.0 and 3.2. We spent thousands on engines. We would send a 2.6 back for a rebuild and we could have a 2.8 back. We could do that with the Motronic.' Of course the problem for the customers would be that when they got the 2.8, the Rothmans cars would be running a 3-litre . . .'

The reliance had advantages and disadvantages, especially in the early Motronic days, when the Weissach engines proved to be very sensitive to variations in fuel quality.

'We didn't know what was going on in the Motronic box at first. But it was obvious the fuel spec. was critical. I remember we were running two cars at one stage. One of them was due to go out to Fuji the next day and the other was due to race at Dijon. We did a shakedown at Silverstone with a brand-new engine and after just two laps the engine blew. Eventually they issued all the Motronic customers with new chips and it was OK.'

By hiring Nigel Stroud to design an improved chassis in early 1984, Lloyd wanted to escape the restriction of drip-fed technology improvements from Weissach.

'The standard chassis was wanting in rigidity. Some designers say the chassis should have some flexibility, but we thought with the general dynamics increasing

all round, we should interrogate every aspect, but it was also a financial decision. It would be far cheaper for us to design and construct a chassis that could accept a large majority of the 956's standard parts.'

The Lloyd 956 used an entirely new honeycomb-sandwich aluminium monocoque to improve chassis stiffness and driver safety, together with many other detail changes. The change also overcame the standard 956's tendency to 'age'. The stiffness would degrade over time and hard use as the glue-impregnated cheesecloth Weissach used to fix the aluminium sheets [before riveting] de-laminated. In the USA, such work-hardened 962s would become known as 'flexi-flyers'.

'Nigel designed a brand-new rising-rate front suspension,' continues Lloyd, 'that made for a better ride and lighter steering. We used a different steering rack but used the existing front hubs. The new chassis was designed to accept the standard rear end – engine, transmission and suspension, without any

Richard Lloyd did not rest on his Brands Hatch laurels in 1984 and a month after, Jonathan Palmer and Jan Lammers debuted the Nigel Stroud honeycomb chassis 956 106b. The car would help maintain Lloyd's team as front runners for several years. (LAT)

The start of the rolling lap at the 1985 Le Mans 24 Hours, with the Ickx/Mass Rothmans 962C leading away the Ludwig/ Barilla/Winter Joest 956B, and the two Lancias.

changes.' The chassis was constructed by Bob Sparshott, a well-known English chassis constructor of the time.

'We asked Jürgen Barth what we should call it, and he said call it "106b", as our original chassis was number 106.' The car debuted at Spa in 1984 and as mentioned previously, retired with a broken ox-bow, which is the very substantial casting over the transmission that Stroud had used to mount the centre-strut rear aerofoil.

After Monza there was Silverstone and again, the Lloyd 956 had led the pack until a hub failed. Twice in two races, wheels had fallen off the car. This problem wasn't confined to Lloyd's 956 either.

Loose wheels had become a generic customer 956 problem which spread like a plague at every race at the start of 1985. The Rothmans cars used Speedline wheels and did not suffer from the problem. By Le Mans, teams were being urged by Weissach to use no less than 1,400Nm torque (1,033lb ft), which required a very substantial torque wrench to tighten cold wheels on to hot hubs during a race, but many simply changed to Speedline in a desperate rush to work around the problem in a less agricultural way. Eventually, it was found that there was a design

problem with the interface between the wheel nut and BBS wheels. The solution, which didn't come until later in the season, was to use a larger diameter nut.

The opening races of 1985 promised much for Richard Lloyd. He was optimistic of a good result at Le Mans, even though he had one of his drivers drop out before the event. 'Jan Lammers decided he wanted to race in America, so we filled the hole with James Weaver. But he fitted in well.'

If the Lloyd team (RLR) had attracted all the attention at the start of that season, then perhaps the lowest key appearances came from Reinhold Joest.

The Absteinach team had run only their original 956 (104) in the early races, without substantial gain, but far from taking his eye off the ball, Joest was focusing all of his team's effort on Le Mans. He wanted to win again, and to do that in 1985 he was going to have to defeat Weissach. He kept the previous year's Le Mans winner (chassis 117) out of sight until the 24 Hours, using it as the test-bed for underbody development and engine improvements.

While he had used the mechanically injected engine in 1984, Joest went for the Motronic system in 1985, but the electronics he used were not quite what had left Porsche or Bosch. After the problems with the new engine management in 1984, Joest had 'some friends' (his words) study the system through the first half of 1985, to understand how it worked and then to develop a completely stand-alone chip programming facility.

'That was at our own cost. We had a development going on with the software to programme the EPROMs ourselves. This made it possible in a detailed way to really understand and work on the three-dimensional mapping. 'Nothing was available from Porsche on that, so we developed the software to do it. We could see immediately that the way they were doing it [handing out just two chips – one for qualifying and another for the race], we didn't have a chance to win a race.

'It took us five months and we couldn't do it on the dyno [because Joest didn't have one at the small Absteinach workshops]. We did it all on the racetrack. With this software we could change the mapping four, five or six times in a meeting. This was a big benefit to us, especially at Le Mans. I wanted to win Le Mans. We had the focus on that and we found the way.'

Joest chose to run a 956B at Le Mans in 1985, even though the newer 962Cs were available.

'We stayed with our good car, and the 962 was not as good a car as the 956. It was 180mm (7in) longer, but the ground-effect underbody was much better on the 956 than the 962.'

Another detail to change in 1985 was that the Joest team ran with Goodyear tyres, like several other top 956 runners. This was another carefully considered strategy to find an advantage over the Weissach cars.

'Dunlop were doing all the engineering and testing with Porsche. The Dunlop was a very good tyre, but the Goodyear's feel was completely different. With the Dunlops, you have grip, grip, grip and when that is gone, maybe you have lost the car. With the Goodyear, it is very easy to drive. You feel it immediately. You can turn-in and you get the grip immediately. The Dunlop would grip only up to a certain point and then it was gone. But at Le Mans, I don't think there was any real advantage at this time.'

The stories that these tyres somehow had less rolling resistance and as a result, yielded better fuel consumption also seem wide of the mark.

The other key factor making the lead Joest car a serious contender was its driver team. Remarkably, Henri Pescarolo had decided not to run with Joest. He didn't believe the German team could win two years

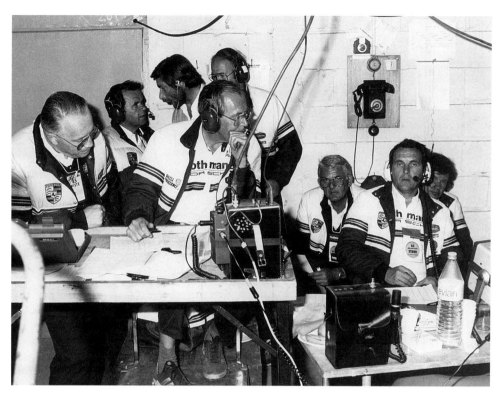

Furrowed brows in the Rothmans-Porsche pits at Le Mans in 1985. From left to right are: Helmuth Bott, Valentin Schaeffer, Jürgen Barth, Dr. Huber, Peter Falk, Paul Hensler, Helmuth Flegl, and at the back, an exhausted-looking mechanic, Kolender. (Peter Falk collection)

in a row and chose to drive with Lancia! Klaus Ludwig would drive with Paolo Barilla (ex-Lancia) with 'John Winter' (the timber merchant Louis Krages) taking a stint on the Saturday evening.

In his top car, Joest would have a Le Mans winner, an ex-Lancia team driver and a home-grown 'find' who, between them, knew exactly what it would take to win the race. Joest remembers he didn't have to give intensive coaching on driving style either.

'We didn't have to talk to them,' adds Joest of his best drivers. 'Normally, the good drivers don't need instruction. Every now and then we would advise them about fuel consumption and we would adjust the pace. Only if we had a new driver would we show him all the difficult (and the good) points.'

Joest's original 956, 104, was driven at Le Mans by Mauricio de Narvaez, Kenper Miller and Paul Belmondo. Both cars were in yellow and white New Man colours.

The return of the Rothmans-Porsche team to Le Mans was no half-strength effort either. The now-usual three cars – all 962Cs – were entered for Ickx and Mass, Bell and Stuck and lastly, the three-driver team of Schuppan, Holbert and Watson. Norbert Singer looked after the lead car with Walter Näher tending the

The Joest team completely wrong-footed the Rothmans team at Le Mans in 1985, being able to run up to two laps more per tankful of fuel than the works cars. The advantage was not just down to optimised engine management programmes.

Bell/Stuck machine. As in 1983, Klaus Bischoff was the crew chief on the third car. All the team cars were running 3-litre engines and all were running 16in wheels. These wheels had a smaller diameter and hence fitted under the low-drag bodywork – unlike the 17in diameter wheels used on the short-circuit cars.

In Wednesday evening qualifying the works cars were very fast. Stuck broke the outright lap record with an average speed of fully 156mph (251kph). With heroics completed, for Thursday practice the team settled into a programme of preparation with the race-specification 2.8-litre engines fitted.

The start of the race was a complete surprise, because after the Lancias had led for a few laps, they backed off to conserve fuel. This was also the strategy of the Rothmans-Porsches, who didn't even figure in the top ten in the early hours. The lead became a three-way contest between the Ludwig/Barilla Joest car, the Palmer/Weaver Lloyd entry and the Brun 956 driven by Oscar Larrauri, Massimo Sigala and Gabriele Tarquini.

What puzzled everybody was that the Rothmans-Porsches were running so slowly relative to the leaders. As James Weaver, driving Richard Lloyd's

956, said to *Autosport* at the time: 'We think we know what we are doing – the car is perfect and we're fine on fuel consumption, but we have that horrible feeling they know something we don't.'

In fact, a half-hour pace car period helped the early pace-setters in their fuel consumption calculations, but there was no getting away from the fact that the leading cars just looked more efficient with their fuel than the Rothmans cars.

'I only wanted to win Le Mans,' repeats Reinhold Joest, his serious face set with the same determination as in 1985. 'After the first pit-stop, Porsche came in, I think it was at least two laps earlier, and after that first stop, Mr Schæffer came over and asked: "What is going on?"'

Joest leans forward at this point to build a little tension into the tale. We can imagine the scene in the busy pitlane, with Joest shrugging his shoulders to Porsche's turbo-engine guru as if to say he was just as surprised.

'Second pit-stop: the same thing!' Joest can't conceal a grin, 'and so we went on like that.'

After only two hours, Jochen Mass brought the

'John Winter' (Louis Krages), Paolo Barilla and Klaus Ludwig enjoy their victory after the 1985 Le Mans 24 Hours. They are joined by Reinhold Joest (at right) as the second-placed team of Jonathan Palmer (holding the outsize bouquet), Richard Lloyd and James Weaver muscle in on the celebrations. (LAT)

number one Rothmans car in with gear selection problems. Several more stops (one to change the whole gearbox) was enough to put that car out of contention.

In the seventh hour, the Lloyd car was delayed in the pits. 'In that race we were delayed by one niggling little problem,' says Richard Lloyd. 'The left-hand temperature gauge went off the clock. We pitted but we couldn't find anything wrong and it didn't appear to be hot.' After several more stops, the temperature sender was just disconnected, but the car fell back to seventh place and had lost a lap.

By midnight the remaining Rothmans cars were in second and third, but still the Joest car seemed to be superior. Then the Bell/Stuck 962C was delayed with a wheel bearing failure and the Ludwig/Barilla 956 extended its lead still further. During the night it ran in company with the Brun and particularly the Lloyd 956, the cars slipstreaming each other for lap after lap on the long straights. The tactic undoubtedly saved fuel and allowed some low-boost running on the engine without significant loss of time, but Reinhold Joest refutes any thought of collusion between the teams.

'No, no. There was never any arrangement.' Nevertheless, running with the Lloyd must have helped? 'I don't remember that, but our car was a lot faster.'

Then the Schuppan/Holbert/Watson 962C was delayed by a failed front wheel-bearing and later, was stopped for good by a broken crankshaft. And to the pleasure of the RLR team, their car was back in second place. It was some four laps off Ludwig and Barilla.

The strong run by the customers was blunted a little when, with just a few hours to go, Walter Brun's leading car retired from third place. Driven by Larrauri, Sigala and Tarquini, the car stopped for good after the engine expired.

The Joest's New Man 956 won by three laps from the Lloyd Canon 956. It was Ludwig's third Le Mans win and 956B 117 achieved a notable back-to-back victory, winning in record time. Reinhold Joest's intense preparation had paid off and he had beaten the factory team fair and square. So had Richard Lloyd. The Bell/Stuck Rothmans 962C was four laps behind him, in third place.

CHAMPION 8 BREW

IF THE FACTORY was pre-occupied with the World Endurance Championship in 1985, then Porsche's representatives in the USA got on with business using the tools that they had been given.

By this time, Alwin Springer had a firm grasp on what was expected of the Porsche flat-six turbo engine and his Andial business supplied most of the 962 competitors in IMSA.

His long experience, first with the 935s, then with Holbert's March in 1983 and later with the development 962, had proved that the requirements for the relatively short (200 to 300 miles) IMSA races were quite different to the Weissach-prepared endurance engine. Nonetheless, it was to that single, long-distance requirement that all new IMSA 962s were delivered.

'The first 962 was a 2.8-litre with the single turbo,' says Springer, 'and we told them beforehand that they shouldn't do that for the United States.'

But the 962s arrived with that engine and predictably, they struggled against the torquey Chevrolet during 1984. It could have all ended there for the 962 in IMSA, if individuals such as Springer hadn't been determined to wring out a more suitable sprint engine.

It proved to be a major development, and he was helped in no small part by Porsche's 'Mr Turbo' of the time, Valentin Schæffer. Further up the Weissach hierarchy, Helmut Flegl, champion of the earlier Can-Am and IndyCar developments, kept Helmuth Bott appraised of the determined, but otherwise largely independent, American effort.

'In those early days the factory would produce an engine that would be bullet-proof,' continues Springer. 'On a scale of one to ten for performance, it would stop at about eight to eight and a half. And what we did was to concentrate on the last point. We worked on getting it up to nine and nine and a half. That was our speciality and I think that's how we made our name. We were very good at that.

'The differences really crystallised out in the 962 days. At that time in Europe, they had the fuel consumption formula and the racetracks there are very smooth, the straightaways are very long and everything is fine. Here [in the USA] you need torque. So getting top rpm and horsepower is not really so critical.

'We didn't have any problems with fuel over here either. We didn't have to do economy runs. So what we did was take an engine, but we changed it completely. It had bigger capacity, different camshafts, different injection and so on. We just brought up the torque and specified it for the racetracks here.'

What set Springer apart from many other engine tuners was that he had a real interest in the new electronic engine management systems. From the beginning of the 962 engine development, he worked to incorporate the Bosch Motronic 1.2 system to the single-turbo, air-cooled engines.

'The development really interested me,' he continues, 'because by 1984 we could bring out the full performance from the engines by adapting the Motronic system.'

There were all kinds of problems adapting the endurance racing motors for the near sprint-race requirements of IMSA. Holbert, mirroring the same tactics used by Reinhold Joest in Europe, ran with a mechanically injected engine through 1984 – but with a capacity of 3.2 litres. It was only at Daytona in 1985 that his car appeared with the Motronic system.

Springer's fascination with the possibilities of being able to almost endlessly adapt and tune what were once fixed engine parameters is still undimmed.

'You could actually put the timing where it needed

to be for each rpm, throttle position and boost, instead of having just one fixed timing with the distributor. That was like a night and day improvement! In Formula One, it had been the thing that had made the turbo engine competitive, because before it had been very difficult. You could lose something on torque and you would gain something at the top end, because we only had one timing point.'

A cutaway view of the early 962 shows the large single-turbo engine mounted over the transmission. The turbo and its cooling would become major development areas on the car.

The Bob Tullius Jaguars gave the 962s a hard time through 1984 and 1985. This is the Hurley Haywood, Chip Robinson XJR-5 on the way to third place at Mid-Ohio in 1985. (Geoffrey Hewitt)

The Löwenbräu 962 appeared to have the 1985 Daytona 24 Hours won until an electrical problem dropped them behind the Henn Swap Shop car. (Geoffrey Hewitt)

The 962's record in IMSA is the stuff of legend today, but the car didn't waltz into the Camel GTP series as the 956 had done in Group C.

The new Porsche suffered from over-expectation of its out-of-the-box performance and under-performance by early customers, even when it came through its initial season.

There had been three cars running from around the middle of 1984. These were Holbert's Löwenbräu car (962 103), Bruce Leven's Bayside Disposal car (962 101) – that Holbert had used until his own car arrived – and Bob Akin's Coca Cola car (962 102). Preston Henn, one of the early customers for the 956 the previous year, would run his 962 104 at Le Mans and later have it shipped back to the USA. He only appeared at the season-closing event at Daytona in November.

These first IMSA customers had been angry at not being considered for the 962's first race in the Daytona 24 Hours in February, but from the moment they received their cars that spring, it was clear it was not the race-ready proposition that they had come to expect from Porsche.

When Akin first ran his 962 at Charlotte in May

1984, the turbocharger diaphragm broke, followed shortly by an exhaust pipe. In the race, the car retired because there were no basic spares to repair it.

Akin was openly critical of the car itself and the workmanship. In a *Panorama* interview he said: 'It has been a little disappointing. Porsche had the reputation for being the home of the off-the-shelf winner, and in my opinion, that is certainly not the case with the 962s that have arrived in the country so far.' He went on to complain about the teething troubles, poor workmanship and the lack of spare parts to support the cars. It wasn't what he expected for what he was paying.

'This car needs a little more custom tailoring for the IMSA series.' Akin added. 'In three-hour races you just drive as hard as you can. Unless you can go an hour and a half, which this car won't do, and the Jags can, you're going to make two stops.'

The fuel consumption issue arose despite the fact that the 962 enjoyed a 120-litre fuel system capacity, compared to the 100-litre system of the Group C 956. It would be one of the areas Springer would address in his work with Motronic. Despite IMSA not being a fuel-consumption formula, fuel usage was still critical.

The matter wasn't helped because all of these early entrants wanted to run the thirstier, but more torquey 3.2-litre engines, rather than the 2.8-litre.

It was the only way they believed they could get on terms with the Chevrolets and Jaguars. It meant adding another 50kg (110lb) to the car's weight to come within the IMSA power-to-weight rules, but it was a penalty worth paying. As Akin said at the time about the Chevrolet: 'It comes out of the hole like crazy with all that torque.'

So this was the height of the mountain that had to be climbed by Holbert in his new role as head of Porsche Motorsports North America, but it was a task, with Springer's dedicated efforts on the engine, for which he found a solution by the following year.

Of the 17 Camel GT Championship races in 1985, the 962 won 16, with the Löwenbräu-supported Holbert 962 winning no less than nine.

The other winners were led off by Preston Henn's Swap Shop 962, who won the Daytona 24 Hours despite his driving team of Bob Wollek, A. J. Foyt and Al Unser Snr suffering from a bout of communal influenza. The hero of the team was

Thierry Boutsen, who drove head-to-head with Derek Bell (in the Holbert car) for long stints during the night. But for much of that race, it had looked as though the Swap Shop car was destined to be second to Holbert's car.

Try as they might, the Mike Colucci-run crew could not contain the strength of the Löwenbräu car. By the time the sun came up over the steeply banked Florida track, the blue and white 962 had built a strong lead, but just when it appeared it was all over, the Holbert car ran into what was first thought to be a fuel problem. It was then diagnosed as an electrical fault. Less than an hour from the end, the persistent Swap Shop car took over and won from Holbert, Bell and Unser Jnr.

In third place at that Daytona race was another 962 that would become a regular, front-running sight in IMSA. Jim Busby, Jochen Mass and Rick Knoop were driving the BF Goodrich 962 (962 106) which uniquely, was running on new, race-versions of that company's T/A radial tyres.

Busby was the latest graduate from the California hot-rod community, and in the coming years would bring a uniquely new outlook to the business of

The Preston Henn 962 refused to give up at Daytona in 1985 and drivers Foyt, Sullivan and Luyendyk were rewarded with a superb win. (Geoffrey Hewitt)

The attraction of Daytona is the ultra-high speed banking, although chicanes have made the turns less exciting than in the days of the 917s. This is the winning Preston Henn 962 after a hard night's racing in 1985. (Geoffrey Hewitt)

Bob Akin's Coke-supported 962 became a regular sight in the IMSA Camel GTP series and won Sebring in 1986. Here it is at Watkins Glen in July 1986. Akin drove with Price Cobb and James Weaver to fourth place. (Geoffrey Hewitt)

winning in IMSA, using all his dragster racing experience in the search for speed. 'We had that one in the bag,' he says cheerfully of the same 24 Hours that Holbert and Preston Henn also laid claim. 'But we were running a trick new Andial exhaust with slip rings in it, and what broke? The slip ring of course!'

Unfortunately for Busby, that Daytona weekend proved very expensive. A second (and brand-new) BF Goodrich-supported car (962 108) was crashed at Daytona. The car was being driven by Pete Halsmer and as Busby recalls, 'he tried an overtaking move on a slower car right in front of where all our sponsors were sitting, and he put the car straight into the wall.'

Busby's other 962 (105) was also crashed by Jan Lammers near the end, but in this case (and in Busby's words), the car folded up and trapped the driver. The two incidents brought to a head Busby's own growing concern about the safety of the basic 962 monocoque.

'We had done a lot of work by then stiffening up the engine bay and the rest of the tub to make them handle better, but nothing to do with safety. So I called Jim Chapman and said I wanted a chassis that would have the stiffness and safety of a Formula One car. I paid for the tooling, and he built it.'

The new Chapman 962 monocoque would prove to be a great success. Even before the first tub was complete, Al Holbert rang Busby to take the car. Busby was reluctant at first to sell any chassis, but as he says today: 'I didn't want to hear about someone getting hurt in a car and knowing that maybe I could have prevented it.'

Holbert, probably anxious to evaluate all his options on the chassis, did a deal with Busby for the Chapman chassis in exchange for parts. Busby would rebuild the crashed 108 with one of the new Chapman tubs and in its subsequent (and equally chequered history), 108B would become one of the most well-known cars on the IMSA championship trail.

Sebring yielded another second place for Holbert after suffering what seemed like a season's worth of mishaps over the race's 12 hours.

The winner was once again Preston Henn (with Bob Wollek and A. J. Foyt driving), completing a remarkable trio of finishes for the Fort Lauderdale team.

The Swap Shop 956 had missed winning Le Mans in June the previous year by just two laps, but they had won Daytona with their 962 the following February and then Sebring in March. In total, this trio of results in the three greatest endurance races of them all has to rate as one of the strongest ever performances by a private team in a 12-month period.

Henn was honoured for his significant achievements in the Porsche when the Swap Shop 962 was later given a place in the Indianapolis Hall of Fame. The string of finishes also highlighted the remarkable versatility of a driver few associate with endurance racing – A. J. Foyt.

The four-times winner of the Indy 500 had won Le Mans with Ford back in 1967, but he won Daytona in 1983 in Henn's 935 and followed it with the string of strong 962 finishes. The Texan might have a reputation for getting a little sore at times, but there was no disputing his unique driving skills.

With the latest Andial 3.2-litre engines producing satisfactory torque, Holbert turned his attentions to the development of the 962's downforce. The IMSA regulations stated that the rear wing had to be within the planform of the rear body, but Holbert raised it further into the airstream to work in cleaner air. This was to clear the now-large hump in the rear body over the continuously reworked turbocharger installation.

Al Holbert's skill at developing the 962 is one of the great features of IMSA in the 1980s. Kevin Jeannette, who in 1985, engineered Bruce Leven's second Bayside car, was on the receiving end of many of Holbert's efforts to seek out the classic 'unfair advantage'.

'Every other guy in those days ran a Porsche and ran it stock. Today, you have to leave the cars stock, but back then the rules said that if it had a Porsche engine in it, then that was about it. Holbert was so good and so keen – and he was a driver too. That gave him an insight that Busby had too. Holbert was the first guy to redesign the pedal assembly. His cars were the first to have the billet bulkhead for the pedals. Now he was pretty close to [chassis builder] Dave Klym in those days and I don't know whose idea it was, but Holbert was the first to notice the problem.

Holbert relentlessly developed his cars to stay with the Jaguars and Chevrolets. This is his HR1 on the way to victory at Lime Rock in 1986. The front wing was an import from Group C. (Geoffrey Hewitt)

then he'd do something else really trick. He'd build his chassis – which was nothing like our chassis – and had much more rigidity. We'd think he'd beaten us because of that, and then he'd have something else on the car. We always got it though. It might not be the next race, but the race after. That was really cool. The problem was he had ten more tricks in the bank! Holbert was the master.'

Perhaps the greatest power test so far for the uprated Andial engine came at the Miami Grand Prix, sandwiched between Daytona and Sebring in late February 1985. This 200-mile sprint could not have been more different to the two classic endurance events that book-ended it.

Holbert and Bell were up against a pair of very strong March-Chevrolets. One, the Budweiser entry, was driven by David Hobbs and 21-year-old Darin Brassfield. Around the street circuit, the Chevrolet had a real advantage, but the race turned into an epic and one which Derek Bell rates as his best driving win in sports car racing.

'I had some of the greatest races in my life against that engine,' he says, referring to the Chevrolet V8, 'but everybody talked about the Miami Grand Prix afterwards as being my race, because it was on TV. I spun twice during the three hour race. Al drove half and I drove half, but mine was the drive!' he beams with a typical driver's modesty. 'Dave Hobbs said afterwards that only Derek Bell could spin twice and win the race! It was between those walls, you know, trying to overtake people, realising there was no room and having to spin out. I didn't hit anybody, I just spun when I realised I was in so deep. The March was the Budweiser car. We were racing in the Löwenbräu Grand Prix and I was in the Löwenbräu car!

'I slipped by Darin Brassfield, who was Hobbs's team-mate. You can imagine the V8 had to be much more driveable around a street circuit. I remember he said that he left me no room, but I still found it. I remember I went down with my wheels right in the gutter on Biscayne Boulevard and won the race!'

The run of wins continued for the blue and white Löwenbräu 962, but as we mentioned earlier, it was not all gloom for the other 962 customers either.

Besides Preston Henn's wins at Daytona and Sebring, Rob Dyson's 962 101 (the ex-Bruce Leven car) was a triple winner (Drake Olsen at Lime Rock,

The 962s proved particularly spectacular on the street circuits. This is the Bob Akin car at Columbus in 1986. Note the tabs either side of the nose – replacements for the nose wing tried earlier in the season. (Geoffrey Hewitt)

'He couldn't figure out that when you gave it a good, hard stomp, it had a soft pedal. He figured out that when you pressed the brake pedal, the whole goddam bulkhead moved! And of course, that led to a big safety improvement too. Then he said: "Let's make an aluminium-honeycomb in front of that which holds the nose on." I think Porsche loved that too. And man! He just smoked the rest of us!

'He'd meet with us every other race and he'd say: "Well guys, we've got lots of new stuff coming" and

Olsen/Bobby Rahal at Road America and Olsen/Price Cobb at Columbus).

Bruce Leven's Bayside car (962 109) took two wins (with Leven and Hobbs at Road Atlanta in April and with Bob Wollek at Sears Point in August). Pete Halsmer and John Morton recorded Jim Busby's first victory with (a Goodrich-tyred) 962 105 at Riverside in April.

The Busby winner was the one bought originally by John Fitzpatrick and was raced at Le Mans in 1984. The 'trainspotters' among us will note that Fitzpatrick put a Group C rear end on this car and he ran it in occasional World Endurance Championship races later that year before trading it back to Weissach. The car was sold at the beginning of 1985 to BF Goodrich to replace the brand-new car (962 108) written off at Daytona. It was 105 that won the race at Riverside.

The only non-962 victory that year went to the Group 44 Jaguar team. The Jaguars had been swamped by the numbers of increasingly very competitive 962s and found themselves struggling to keep up in the development race. The only bright spot for the Bob Tullius team came when Brian Redman and Hurley Haywood won at Road Atlanta.

In 1985, Holbert had nine wins, but he used two chassis. He used 103 until he rolled out his own Holbert racing chassis (962 HR1) at Portland in July,

and the car achieved a first time out victory in the 300km event.

The Holbert chassis, built at his Warrington, Pennsylvania workshops, was a 962 semi-clone and owes more in its justification to Weissach's statement in mid-1985 that it didn't intend to build any more 956s or 962s. Although two homebuilt 'HR' tubs

Once the early bugs were out of the Holbert 962 – and it was fitted with Springer's sprint version of the 3.2-litre flat-six, the car became uncatchable. (Geoffrey Hewitt)

The Jim Busby-entered 962s at Daytona in 1985 ran BF Goodrich's race version of its Comp T/A radial tyre. This is Busby's car. He finished third with Rick Knoop and Jochen Mass. It was an expensive weekend for the Goodrich team.

Wings were a must-have fashion item on the street courses mid-season in 1986. Here, the Bayside Disposal 962 leads the Torno-supported Brun car and the Coke-supported Akin car.

would be built, it didn't mark the start of a cottage industry for Holbert. He left that to two other American chassis builders of note. Holbert's contribution was to inspire the others to search out improvements in the original design.

Dave Klym of Fabcar shared many of Holbert's ideas on how the 962 monocoque could be improved. His extremely well-constructed chassis were stiffer than the factory originals and used machined aluminium blanks for the front bulkhead (instead of sheet aluminium). Klym was given the Weissach drawings for the monocoque. Later, he built replacement tubs that were sold as officially authorised factory replacements. So close were these to the originals, they are said to have used even metric-dimension rivets.

In San Clemente California, Jim Chapman was building aluminium-honeycomb tubs following the same line of thought as John Thompson's TC Prototypes in England. Chapman built a tub for Jim Busby to replace the one written off at Daytona in 1985 and soon found others were knocking on his door with requests for copies.

Today, the subject of a monocoque's authenticity is

guaranteed to get the pulses racing and the lawyers smiling. So many of the front-running cars were crashed, their tubs replaced, and continued to race on the same chassis number that it can be difficult to call any car original. Real confusion sets in if the original wrecked tub was rebuilt at a later date (as has happened in several cases). It's then that the story gets very complicated!

With Holbert running his new 'homebuilt' at Portland in 1985, the existing car, 962 103, was given to Derek Bell. At that race he retired, but two weeks later the team came to Sears Point in California for pre-race testing.

'Oh Crikey!' groans Derek when the subject of Sears Point is raised. 'Did I crash! Yes, a massive crash! And it was the famous Holbert car.

'I had never been to Sears Point and we were on a roll. We had won lots of races that year and we led the championship. Wherever we went we were quicker by then and it was a question of how we were going to win, not if. It was glorious weather and hotter than hell. I remember coming in at ten in the morning and I sort of looked around the track and over the hill. I went round it on a little monkey-bike, but Al said come back at four and have a drive.

'So I got in at ten minutes to five [the circuit closed at five]. I felt wonderful and I thought I knew the way round the track. I slid a bit on my first lap because they'd resurfaced it. Anyway, I came to Turn 11, which is the last-but-one turn with a very fast left and right, and instead of saying to me to do three laps and come in, they allowed me to carry on. So I thought I've got another lap. I'll have another go.

'I wouldn't say it blew my concentration, because I was having a good time. I came down to this turn and I was convinced the corner was nearly flat, and I went through the left-hander and went to turn into the right. As I got into it, the car just wouldn't go round and just slid. I'm not blaming the surface really, but in the heat, the tar was like liquid. And I just suddenly felt, oh shit! The tail didn't go, the whole car just drifted. I kept it in this perfect drift and as I got to the edge – and it is as if I can see it all happening now – I thought the edge will be drier because the air has been at it. But I got to the edge and it just went off, and I had a f'ing great crash that nobody saw! I just hit everything! They rebuilt that beautiful car and that's the one in which we went on to win no end of races.'

As if 1985 had been good, then the following season would demonstrate how effective the 962 had become. Holbert, Bell and Al Unser Jnr won the Daytona 24 Hours in February 1986 and began a roll of no less than 25 Camel GTP victories. The car they drove at Daytona was the rebuilt 962 103 that Bell had crashed at Sears Point, but this race marked a bitter defeat for Preston Henn, the previous year's winner. The Swap Shop car finished on the same lap as the winner after running at the head of the field throughout the race.

'That was pretty hard,' says Kevin Jeannette, who by this time had returned to Henn's team as crew chief. 'We finished second and we had an oil leak. It was leaking so bad and John Shapiro [Henn's team manager] and I couldn't agree where it was coming from. We took the time changing the oil lines and the cooler, but it was in the engine. We lost a huge lead over Holbert. We fixed it and held the lead and then a throttle spring broke.

'Foyt got on the radio and said the throttle is lazy. I think we had a 14-lap lead at that point. He didn't say

he couldn't drive, but that it was hard to drive. We pulled him in, and tried to reset the tension on the second spring that's in there, and when that happened we broke the titanium bolt that held the spring. We sent him back out but he couldn't drive it. So he came in again and I remember AJ was sitting in the car and I jumped in the car with him in it. I hooked a bungee cable around where the spring hooks on to the pedal and I stretched that sucker back right around by the shifter and hooked it on to the safety switch. It probably worked better than the original! But messing around with the car cost us who knows how many laps, and by then we had cooked the diaphragms in the twin wastegates and we had major boost problems. We had to stop again and change both diaphragms. That's when Holbert took the lead. We ended up losing that race by 47 seconds.'

Holbert had done much of the hard work during this race as his team-mates Bell and Unser were affected by cramp. It was a sterling performance by a champion and for his part, made up for losing this race to Henn the previous year. Holbert would take a record fifth IMSA title that year on his way to achieving more wins than any other driver in that competition's history.

After finishing second at Le Mans in 1984, Preston Henn's team won the 1985 Daytona 24 Hours and followed this with victory in the Sebring 12 Hours – one of the most impressive performances by a private race team in modern motor racing. This is the Bob Wollek, A. J. Foyt car at Hendricks Field (Sebring). (Geoffrey Hewitt)

Sebring 1986 went to Bob Akin's bright-red Coca-Cola 962 (with Hans-Joachim Stuck and Jo Gartner) after a battle of attrition with Holbert, Bell and Unser Jnr. The Löwenbräu car limped home third after an incident-filled race, behind Jim Busby's consistent BF Goodrich car.

The competition were now struggling to keep pace with the Porsches. The Tullius Jaguars had begun to fade in 1986, although Chip Robinson and Bob Tullius himself managed to win the final race at Daytona. The Doc Bundy Lola-Corvette looked stronger that year, winning at Road Atlanta and West Palm Beach, while Klaus Ludwig's Ford Mustang Probe always promised much (but only delivered at Laguna Seca).

Holbert, Bell and Al Unser Jnr would win the Daytona 24 Hours again in 1987. They drove the same 962 103 that they used the previous year, to beat Walter Brun's Torno-supported car.

The first year the 962s were forced to run with a maximum 3-litre capacity limit on their turbo engines was 1987 and for this race, Holbert chose to run an endurance version of the 2.8-litre engine (the other top 962 teams all running with 3.0-litre engines).

IMSA President John Bishop was continuously tuning the regulations to ensure that Springer and Holbert could never relax. Every year there were changes to the four GTP engine capacity-to-weight groups (being the normally aspirated and turbocharged groups for two-valve stock-block and four-valve race engines.

IMSA was trying to ease the normally aspirated cars up to a par with the Porsche turbos, but it seemed whenever the stock-based engines found a bit more speed, Holbert (and Alwin Springer) would edge up their own game.

The upside of IMSA was that it had become a seriously competitive championship. The spice in the formula was that the competition was always ready to spring a surprise.

For instance, at the start of 1987 the Electramotive Lola-Nissan ZXT gave a fright to the Porsches by winning the Miami street race. Unreliability would prevent them repeating this result later in the year, but it was a preview for what was to come from the Nissan turbo later.

This would also be the last season for the Bob Tullius Jaguar team and surprisingly, they achieved two wins with the much-improved XJR-7. The following year, TWR would represent Jaguar in IMSA.

Al Holbert stepped back from a full season of driving in 1987. Derek Bell was also unable to do the whole season of IMSA as he was contracted to the factory in the fierce campaign against Jaguar in the FIA World Endurance Championship that year.

So it fell to Chip Robinson to lead Holbert's team and despite winning only three races (including Daytona), he emerged as champion on the strength of a consistent finishing record. That the 1987 season yielded 13 962 wins only goes to show how competitive the other 962 runners were. Price Cobb was a close second in the Dyson car (also with three wins) and Bruce Leven's Bayside team won no less than seven races, but with different drivers.

Holbert's limited season was a product of the growing workload he had from running Porsche Motorsport in North America. In this role, he was demonstrating both political and management skills. Most notably, he defused Porsche's previously confrontational relationship with John Bishop.

Holbert was anxious to work with the IMSA President to promote Porsche as a responsible competitor within Camel GTP. He contributed usefully to the discussions in 1986 on reducing the spiralling speeds of the series.

Porsche had chosen their representative well, even if the man himself was reluctantly facing the prospect of having to cut back on his own racing.

Aside from the IMSA commitment, he had initiated an SCCA Nationals and Trans Am-based 944GTR programme with Atlanta fabricator Dave Klym – who as we have mentioned, was also working with Holbert on building replacement monocoques. But perhaps Holbert's most ambitious plan in these years was that he wanted to bring Porsche back to Indianapolis.

Looked at against the changing backdrop of these other activities, Holbert's achievement with the blue and white Löwenbräu 962 from 1984 to 1987 is remarkable.

Another winner during this time was Alwin Springer and his Andial business. The change to a 3-litre maximum capacity, with a 930kg (2,050lb) minimum weight (it had been 943kg/2,079lb) had barely registered as an issue and through the late 1980s, Andial became the surrogate home of the Porsche racing engine in North America.

The continuing success of the Porsche turbos (in particular) would prompt IMSA to revise its rules again for 1988, but nobody could complain IMSA wasn't working. The 16-race series was drawing huge crowds wherever it went and that is in no small part down to the large number of well-run 962s that could turn out, race after race, coast to coast.

Across the Pacific Ocean, another sports car success story was being written. The Japanese Sports Car Championship, run to the Group C format, had struck a chord with the enthusiastic Japanese motorsport fans. Like IMSA, the fields were not all Porsche, but contained an interesting selection of alternative manufacturers. The Japanese economy was in an unstoppable upsurge of health by the mid-1980s and there was big money waiting for those overseas drivers and teams willing to mix oriental adventure with their racing.

In its first year, 1983, the series was limited to just the Suzuka and Mount Fuji circuits, but the five-round series drew huge crowds. This popularity, in turn, attracted influential national sponsors and provided a stage for developing new local drivers.

The Japanese championship may not have been the hotbed of Porsche development that was the WEC and IMSA, but the racing was no less competitive or exciting.

After formative seasons in 1983 and 1984, the series attracted many of Japan's own manufacturers into racing. Mazda, Nissan and Toyota would step up their activities on the international scene after testing their competitiveness against the 956s at home. The number of Group C 956s (and later the 962C) rose steadily through the 1980s.

With the Rothmans-Porsche team no longer needing his regular services for the FIA championship (he would be asked back to drive the odd championship race, and annually for Le Mans until 1988), Vern Schuppan renewed his relationship with the Nova team of Ryouichi Inose (now an influential Porsche collector), and Moto Mariwaki.

The 1983 championship had proven to be a fairly easy task for Vern and Naohiro Fujita to win. The Trust (a Japanese after-market car accessory business) 956 was even fitted with a Le Mans long-tail body throughout, but it was the only Group C Porsche in every race, and after winning the first championship, Vern Schuppan continued to build on his contacts in Japan in the following seasons.

Vern Schuppan shared this Trust-Iseki 956 in Japan with Keiichi Suzuki in 1985 and 1986. (LAT)

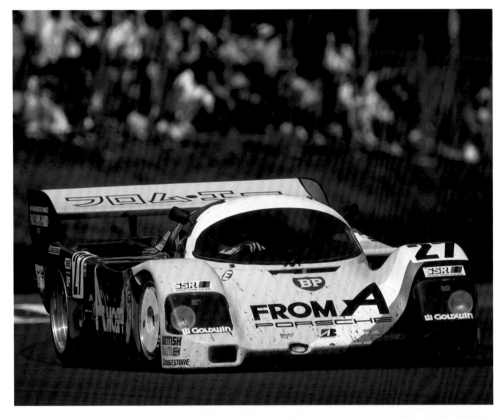

Chassis number 108, one of the original batch of customer 956s, that Schuppan and Fujita used to win in 1983, was replaced in 1984 by a new chassis for Schuppan and Yoshimi Katayama.

Nova ran two 956s that season and the Ricky Chiba-owned Advan-backed car driven by Kunimitsu Takahashi and Kenji Takahashi would win two races to Schuppan's three.

A third 956 – the ex-Preston Henn chassis 103 – joined the series in July, but was later written off at Fuji.

For the World Endurance Championship round at Fuji in September that year, Schuppan and Hans-Joachim Stuck drove the Trust car to a good third place behind the two Rothmans cars. Stuck's drive in the Nova-Trust 956 consolidated his already strong reputation. The German driver would appear alongside Derek Bell in the Rothmans team the following year.

Japan was a principal market in the Pacific rim area for Porsche and the emergent Japanese Sportscar Championship would open up a lucrative profit centre for the customer sport department. Gerd Schmid from Weissach became a frequent visitor to the Japanese series.

Nova ran this From-A supported 962C in the 1987 Fuji 1,000km for Hideki Okada and John Neilsen. The pair finished ninth. (LAT)

Kunimitsu Takahashi won the Japanese Sportscar Championship in 1985, 1986 and 1987 for Nova Engineering. His co-champion driver in the first two years was Kenji Takahashi (they are not related). This is their dominant Nova Engineering Advan-Alpha-supported 962, chassis number 111. (LAT)

'Porsche support from Gerd Schmid worked very well,' recalls Nova Engineering's Moto Moriwaki. 'Nova has dealt with so many companies over our 30 years, but I tell you, my friend Porsche was excellent at all times. I don't know whether that was down to Gerd or Porsche, but the support was first class.'

The 1985 season proved to be the Takahashis' year in the first 962 seen in Japan. Trust set up their own team (taking an unimpressed Schuppan with them) and it fell to the Nova-Advan- (known as Yokohama outside Japan) backed car to easily win the championship from Schuppan's troublesome Trust-Iseki car.

The find of these years was Kunimitsu Takahashi. 'He had been a motor cycle racer,' says Moto Moriwaki, 'and he was the first man to put the Japanese flag on the centre pole [of the podium]. Later he joined Nissan as a works driver. He was the kind of driver who could drive anything. He had lots of natural talent and was very fast. That would sometimes make a lot of problems for his co-driver, because he liked the car set up in a particular way. Fortunately, we found this out early on and we set the

car for the co-driver. But Kuni could still do the same times as on his own settings!'

By 1986, the lucrative Japanese scene was attracting more interest from international drivers, and more cars, but the Takahashi pair repeated their championship win, with once again, Kunimitsu Takahashi taking the drivers' championship. He and the Nova team would make it three in a row in 1987. Also by this time, 962s were proliferating in Japan. Besides the Nova-Advan car, two other Nova cars were turned out in the colours of From-A (a recruitment newspaper).

The Japanese championship was demonstrating what IMSA had already proven, that sports car racing, even if the cars are the same, can be very exciting if the spectacle is right. The big difference between IMSA and Japan was that the latter races tended to be much longer – normally 500-mile or 1,000km events. It said much about the patience of the Japanese enthusiast!

National enthusiasm in the championship was pumped up by the home manufacturers – Nissan, Toyota and Mazda increasing their efforts, and as a result of the significant money available, European interest in the series was growing continuously.

Mauro Baldi and Mike Thackwell drove Richard Lloyd's 962 106b (seen in the unfamiliar colours of the Matsuda Collection) to third place in the September 1987 Fuji 1,000km. This podium placing crowned perhaps what was Lloyd's strongest Group C season, which included winning the lucrative Norisring event. (LAT)

The first lap of the 1989 Fuji 1,000km and Porsches are the most numerically popular make. Leading is the Alpha Cubic 962 of Totani, Nagasaka and Lavaggi which finished 14th. (LAT)

Joest won the 1986 Fuji 1,000km, but it was Kremer – backed by the Japanese Leyton House corporation – who were the first to enter a team continuously in the championship, in 1987.

The two highly rated European customer teams both found Japan a source of significant reward. 'Japan was unbelievable,' recalls Reinhold Joest. 'We are talking about another time completely. It was very

easy when you had a good team with good drivers to get good results, and that made it very easy to get very good sponsorship. At this time the Japanese paid a lot. We did three seasons with three different sponsors. It was good – good enough to have the right budget that we needed for the whole season.'

Vern Schuppan seized the opportunity to start his own team in Japan during 1987. He bought 962 003, the 1986 Le Mans winner that had been crashed by Hans-Joachim Stuck at the Nürburgring later that year.

'I was driving for Trust in Japan,' says Schuppan, 'and Rothmans there approached me about setting up a team. I went back with a proposal that involved that particular car. I set up my own operation and carried on driving for Trust for another two years. That was 1987. In 1989, we bought another car – the Takefuji car – and ran that as well. It wasn't planned, it was just one of those things that came along.' Schuppan would demonstrate that he had a very good (and much-envied) line into the Weissach team. As he established his operation in Japan, he acquired not only 003, but 005, 008 and 009 as well.

Car 009 was the same one that Bell and Bellof had used to win the WEC in 1984. 'It was just a practical way to form a race team and have good cars – cars that were ex-factory. After a few years, the 956 would become fairly flexible and it wasn't just because of the monocoque, the underbody loosened as well. You only realised it when you drove a new car, because that would handle so much better. That's why I bought ex-factory cars. They had been completely refurbished and had stiffer chassis.'

Derek Bell and Geoff Brabham took the Rothmans-sponsored 962C to sixth place in the team's debut race at the Fuji WEC race that year. It was no coincidence that only well-known names appeared in Schuppan's cars.

'If you were running in Japan and dealing with Japanese sponsors, they didn't care how talented the guy was, as long as he had a big name. The hardest thing was finding somebody who had a name and who would satisfy them. Derek was huge and he had the runs on the board.'

If 1987 had marked the transition from the 956 to the 962C in Japan, then 1988 was when everyone went to 3-litre engines. Such was the increasing competitiveness of the Toyotas in 1987, it was feared that they would be on top consistently the following

season. But fortunately for the Porsche runners, the SARD-run cars disappointed with poor reliability. That the WEC round at Fuji was won by the TWR Jaguar XJR-8s only served to stir up the variety. The From-A backed Nova Engineering 962C of Hideki Okada and Stanley Dickens won three out of the five championship races and captured Nova's fourth straight title.

Kuni Takahashi won the newly renamed All Japan Sports Prototype Championship in 1989 driving the Nova-Advan 962 and, despite only winning one race - the Suzuka 1,000km, and with Stanley Dickens. The other three races won by 962s went to three different teams: Harald Grohs/Akihiko Nakaya won the March Fuji 500km (in the From-A Nova 962); Vern Schuppan/Eje Elgh (in the Omron Schuppan 962) won the April Fuji 1,000km, and Masanori Sekiya won the July Fuji 500km (in the Leyton House Kremer car). The SARD Toyota managed to win the October Fuji 1,000km and gave a hint that maybe the team were beginning to understand their car.

The second place in the championship did not go to any of these, but the consistently driven Trust Engineering 962, RLR.203 (a Richard Lloyd Racing chassis).

The championship was now extremely lucrative and several new teams from Europe increased the number of 962s on the grid. Walter Brun landed sponsorship from the Alpha Construction concern, bringing Frank Jelinski, Henri Pescarolo and Oscar Larrauri over to race. Briton Tim Lee-Davey, a regular competitor in the WEC also appeared with Desiree Wilson and Marukatsu backing. Many of these teams introduced their Japanese backers to Le Mans.

The 962C did not win a single race in Japan during 1990, despite very serious entries from at least six Porsche teams. The most consistent performances came from George Fouche and Stefan Andskar in the Trust-Nisseki 962C and the new combination of Stanley Dickens and Will Hoy in the Alpha-Taisan 962C. Toyota and Nissan fought out the five-race championship with Toyota taking two races, and Nissan three.

The story was the same in 1991, with Nissan and Toyota dominating the results, but even these were second best to the rapid TWR XJR-14s when they appeared at Sugo for the final round of the championship in November. Once again, the Trust Nisseki 962C of Fouche and Andskar was the best-placed Porsche, but by this time, the top Porsche teams were already changing to more modern equipment.

After nine seasons of racing, the Japanese sun had finally set on the 962C. The 956/962C record in that country is spectacular (as is the long record of Nova Engineering with the Porsche coupés) and rates as the most consistently successful career for any car in any international championship. The first win had been in April 1983 and the last at Suzuka in December 1989. In this $6\frac{1}{2}$-year timeframe, the 956/962 had won no less than 31 Japanese sports car championship races out of a total of 35, and this excludes the WEC races at Fuji.

Tiff Needell and Derek Bell drove the Richard Lloyd Racing 962 200 at the Suzuka 1,000km in April 1989. (LAT)

CASTING SHADOWS 9

Despite increasing competition from both the existing customer 956s and Jaguar's new XJR-6, the 962C won the World Endurance Championship for a fourth consecutive time for Porsche in 1985. This is Derek Bell on his way to victory at Brands Hatch. (Rothmans International)

WHEN STEFAN BELLOF had joined Tyrrell for 1985, his place had been taken by another happy-go-lucky, but supremely talented German, Hans-Joachim Stuck.

The 34-year-old Stuck was the son of the famous pre-war Auto Union driver, Hans Stuck. Hans-Joachim had first made his mark in the German touring car championship with BMW and with Jochen Mass, had won the 1972 Spa 24 Hours. He had graduated to Formula Two (with Mass) with help from BMW and on occasional runs in the works Marches in 1973, had made a strong impression.

Nevertheless, his credentials for endurance racing were not that obvious. In the annual *Autocourse* round-up, Ian Phillips noted: 'despite his limited single-seater experience, [he] was always very quick but tended to be hard on the car and rarely finished.'

By the following season though, Stuck was right on the pace. He led the works March F2 team in his Jägermeister car and with March, made his debut in Formula One. He was favourite for the F2 title that year, but he lost it to Patrick Depailler at the final round.

He had done enough to stay in F1, but he never seemed to settle. After March came Brabham, Shadow

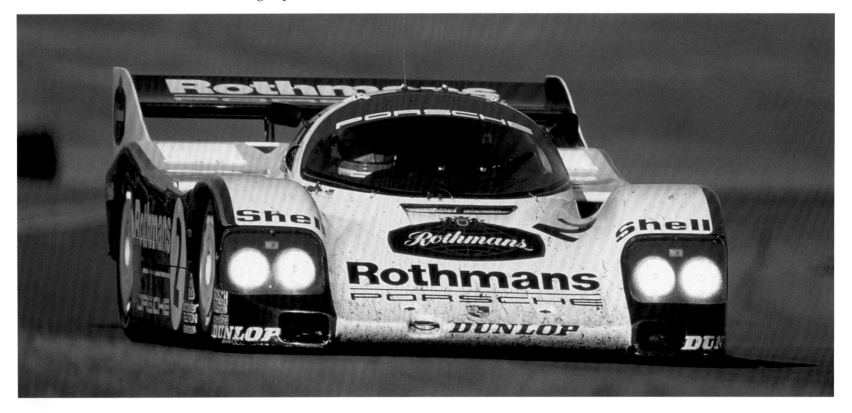

and finally ATS. After 79 starts and 29 World Championship points, he looked for new frontiers in 1980. He joined Peter Sauber's sports car team after winning the previous year's BMW Procar Championship in an M1.

In 1983 and 1984, he drove Walter Brun's 956s occasionally in the WEC. Notably, he had shared with Bellof to win the 1984 Imola 1,000km race. Stuck was also German and in Germany in particular, achieved instant publicity for being the son of a famous father.

By the time he came to Rothmans-Porsche, he was completely familiar with the 956. He was partnered with Derek Bell and through 1985 the pair became the new class act in the factory team.

It pointed to a remarkable consistency and a new-found maturity in Stuck. The German driver went on to become a cornerstone of the Porsche motorsport team, covering countless miles of testing as more competitiveness was coaxed out of the cars.

'I don't think anyone did as many miles in a 956 or 962 as I have done.' He says. 'I knew that car like I knew my pyjamas! I had the opportunity in testing and the races to do so many thousands of miles. It gave me so much experience in the car.

'Those cars had so much grip. They make a Supercup car today look like a toy! Even a GT1 car – that has very high speed on the straight, but almost no downforce compared to those Group C cars.'

Following two second places before Le Mans, Stuck and Bell's first win would come at Hockenheim in

Walter Brun's cars steadily improved their competitiveness through 1984 and 1985, winning at Imola in 1984. The eye-catching Jägermeister 956 made a photographer's life that much easier. (LAT)

Hans-Joachim Stuck fitted into the Rothmans team seamlessly. The German driver would become a superb ambassador for Porsche. (Rothmans International)

A happy-looking Porsche crew at Hockenheim in July 1985 – before the fire accident in the race. (Peter Falk collection)

July. But the race isn't remembered for this, but more that it marked the beginning of a grim series of events that would eclipse all the other achievements of 1985.

The Autodrom can get very hot in mid-summer. The stadium area is a natural sun-trap and when the endurance championship visited there for the ADAC 1,000km in July, the race took place in conditions that wouldn't have disgraced the Sahara Desert.

The ambient temperature was said to be at least 30° Celsius (86° Fahrenheit) and inside the cars, it went way beyond that. With two wins already that year, Jacky Ickx and Jochen Mass had maintained their position as the leading team in both the Rothmans team and the championship. This was despite increasing competitiveness from their team-mates Bell and Stuck, the Kremer's 962C driven by ex-grand prix drivers Manfred Winkelhock and Marc Surer and the Brun 962s of Bellof/Boutsen and Larrauri/Sigala. Brun's growing strength is measured by the fact he ran three cars at this event, the third being for himself and future F1 star Gerhard Berger.

In conditions of searing heat, the race immediately became a fight between Jochen Mass and the Kremer and Brun cars. When Jochen Mass brought his Rothmans 962C in for the car's first stop, the refuelling hose went on before the vent bottle. It was a critical timing error. Peter Falk, who was standing in the Rothmans pit, takes up the story.

'This was the car that Mr Singer was looking after [as crew chief]. The man with the fuel hose went in first. It was a matter of just tenths of seconds, and the vapour pressure in the tank blew back through the fuel hose and into the big tank [of the gravity refuelling rig]. It was quite full. Immediately fuel came out of the breather and splashed down. The car was nearby and the initial ignition was caused either by the hot turbos or exhaust pipes. We are not sure.

'There was a feeling that maybe there might have been a cigarette or something else smoking in the pit. That I don't know, but it was like an explosion. I was standing two metres away and I was OK. But Mr Singer had to go through the fire with two mechanics.'

While the car was singed but OK (it retired later for other reasons), several of the team's pit crew were not so lucky. Most injured was Norbert Singer, who was transferred to the special burns hospital in Ludwigshafen. Singer would spend weeks in hospital with very serious burns to his face and body.

'Mr Singer was very hurt. I had to go to three hospitals after the race. The two other mechanics were not very burned' and they were home by the next weekend. But Mr Singer was in and out of hospital for about five years.'

While the mechanics had been wearing flame-proof overalls, Singer was in his normal shirt and slacks. Later in the race, virtually the same thing happened to one of the Kremer cars, when the fuel-vapour pressure actually split the fuel bladder. However, nobody was hurt in that blaze.

By the next event – at Mosport Park in Canada – there was an update to the Porsches that enabled a pressure relief valve to be fitted to the fuel tank's bladder. The Hockenheim race had continued despite the infernos, and rewarded Derek Bell and Hans Stuck with their first win together.

However, the feeling of gloom that would hang over this season, took on new intensity after the championship visited Mosport. In that race, Manfred Winkelhock lost his life driving the 962 in which he had won earlier in the season at Monza.

Winkelhock crashed during the 1,000km race in early August, the unforgiving Canadian track claiming

the popular German at the 140mph (225kph) Turn 2, a sweeping downhill left-hander.

'It wasn't 100 per cent clear what happened,' says Peter Falk, 'because of course, the Goodyear tyre people will say it wasn't their tyre and Kremer would say it wasn't my car. As far as we know, and as far as we can make a conclusion – we saw the car and we saw the tyre – for us it was quite clear that the tyre failed.

'Everybody was very upset, because he was a Swabian [a native of the Stuttgart region]. He lived locally to us and we knew him very well.

Sadly, however, there was more to come. The next race at Spa wouldn't be remembered for Lancia's win – a major success after trying for so long – but for its incidents.

Jonathan Palmer had the luckiest escape of the season during qualifying. The strength of the honeycomb RLR 106b was proven emphatically when Palmer had a tyre suddenly deflate as he was going through the super-fast left-hand sweep before the new Stavelot Corner.

'I was sitting in the Rothmans motorhome talking to Jacky Ickx,' says Richard Lloyd, 'and I remember

Hans-Joachim Stuck and Derek Bell took their first win together at Hockenheim in 1985, in part making up for the frightening accident in the pits that had befallen the team earlier in the race.

Peter Falk's race summary of the 1985 Mosport 1,000km shows clearly what he believed the reason was for the accident – Reifenschaden VR – a blown front-right tyre, and his appreciation of the Dunlop Denloc safety tyre.

making some comment about how good our car was. That was when he said: "Haven't you heard?"

'It was never proven, but all the indications were that Jonathan had the right-front tyre deflate very fast. He went straight into the barrier at 45°. It was a huge accident. The steering column stopped an inch from his eyes, it was a phenomenal impact, and I don't think he would have survived if the honeycomb hadn't concertina'd to absorb the energy.'

Palmer broke some bones in his foot and leg and was out of racing for several months. Remarkably, Lloyd would have a new Canon car on the grid at Fuji just a month later, for his sponsor's home race.

On lap 77 of the race at Spa, Stefan Bellof in Walter Brun's 962 and Jacky Ickx in the Rothmans car made hard contact at Eau Rouge. In the huge accident that followed, Bellof was grievously injured. The young driver who had made such an impression at Porsche after a wild first year and then followed that with the Drivers' Championship in 1984, died later from his injuries. His death had a profound effect on the Weissach team

A full-time Formula One drive with the Tyrrell Racing Organisation in 1985 meant he was unable to do all the FIA endurance races and perhaps surprisingly, he left the Rothmans team to drive occasionally for Walter Brun.

Manfred Jantke became close to the Giessen-born driver while he was at Porsche.

'He was the most exceptional driver, on talent alone, that I have met. He wasn't so young either [he was 27 when he died]. I never met anyone who laughed so much. He liked to laugh loud and he was a very noisy person! He had enormous confidence in his abilities, yet he wasn't a big mouth, but you could also feel he was able to do better than anybody else – including Jacky Ickx. Jacky was the big chief then.

'But Stefan just knew [he was better]. He was at that level and he could do a little bit more because he was younger. He wasn't a calculator, he was just a natural driver.'

Peter Falk agrees with that view. 'The only way he could drive was well, woof! Even in a normal car on normal roads – woof! Only flat out!'

Falk's pairing of Bellof with the hugely experienced Derek Bell in 1983 had produced lap records, but broken cars. The low point had been the Nürburgring, where Bellof crashed out of a strong lead (and almost certainly lost Derek that year's Drivers' Championship). Despite his new partner's sometimes fraught induction into endurance racing, Derek led Bellof by example rather than instruction.

'In those days you didn't do that,' he says on the subject of coaching. 'I know I'd been around for 12 or 13 years, but it was a new team. And we were no spring chickens either – I must have been 40 by then – but I don't think I would have dreamed of trying to tell Stefan [what to do].

'I didn't say anything to him. I might have made a few jokes in the hope that something might have sunk in, but mainly I was just disappointed [when something happened]. Do you know he came up to me after the crash at the Nürburgring and he said he was sorry. I said it wasn't necessary to say that.

'I would never say: "What the f' do you think you were doing?" But you might say that today, because it could keep you alive. Nowadays, I would talk to him, but I sort of left it to Porsche then. They were so pumped up about his lap times.'

A more mature Bellof had been seen in 1984 – perhaps the earnest post-race discussions with Peter Falk and Helmuth Bott were having some effect, but the mentoring influence disappeared with his departure for Tyrrell. Driving occasionally for Walter Brun brought him head-to-head with the best sports

'I don't think I would have dreamed of telling him what to do,' says Derek Bell of his 1984 partner, Stefan Bellof. (Rothmans International)

The start of the ill-fated Spa 1,000km at Spa in 1985. The Bellof/Boutsen 956B is behind pole man Riccardo Patrese's Lancia, while the Ickx/Mass 962C is behind the yellow New Man 956B.

RENNEN: 1000 KM SPA   X WM-Lauf
DATUM : 1.9.85   Nicht-WM-Lauf

Streckenlänge: 6.94 (km)   Wetter: TROCKEN
Einsatzfahrzeug: 962.004. Fahrer: ICKX / MASS   Start-Nr.: 1.
        962.003.   BELL / STUCK   2.

Ersatzfahrzeug: 962.002.   1 T

Ergebnisse Rennen: 1. WOLLEK/BALDI/PATRESE LANCIA RD Fahrzeit: 5:00,23,42
(ABBRUCH)   2. BELL/STUCK 962   122   5:02,27,86
              3. LUDWIG/BARILLA 962 JÖST   121   5:02,22,35
              4. PATRESE/NANNINI LANCIA   121   5:01,34,21
              5. BRUNDLE/THACKWELL JAGUAR   120   5:02,09,45
              6. WINTER/QUEZ/WEIDLER 962 JÖST 120   5:02,09,78

Trainingszeiten: 1.
                2.
                3.
                4.
                5.
                6.

Schnellste Runde
Rennen: MASS 2.10,73 MIN

Probleme:

Ausfallursachen: Nr. ① UNFALL RUNDE 78   km bis Ausfall:

RENNVERLAUF: UNFALL BELLOF/ICKX IN EAU ROUGE 78. RUNDE
       → ICKX LAG SEIT EINIGEN RUNDEN DIREKT
          VOR BELLOF IN FÜHRUNG, ALS DIESEN
          IN EAU ROUGE AUS DEM WINDSCHATTEN
          HERAUS ZU ÜBERHOLEN VERSUCHTE

Fahrzeugdaten
Motor:
Getriebe:
   Übersetzung: 1.:   2.   3.   4.   5.
           KT   Differential

Fahrwerk:
   Federn: vorn   hinten
   Dämpfer: vorn   hinten
   Stabilisator: vorn   hinten
   Felgen: vorn   hinten
   Reifen: vorn   hinten
   Misch.:   vorn   hinten

Bremsen
   Bremszange   Kolben Ø   Belag
   Bremsscheibe   Bremskraftverteilung

Sonstiges:

The race summary for the Spa 1,000km in 1985, with victory going to the Wollek/Baldi Lancia after the race was stopped just past the five-hour mark.

car driver of the time, Jacky Ickx. For a young charger like Bellof, it was essential to be seen to overcome the Belgian ace and the 1985 endurance racing season developed into a big grudge match between the two drivers.

'The competition between Ickx and Bellof was bad for us,' says Peter Falk. The internal rivalry had developed through 1983 and 1984 because Bellof always wanted to go as fast as possible in the races.

The fuel consumption restrictions of Group C meant he couldn't do that, and if there was to be a factory car that acted as the 'hare' in a race, it would be team leader Ickx's that was always chosen. That wound up Bellof.

'They were not friends, absolutely not,' adds Falk with some disappointment.

Derek Bell confirms there was no love lost between the two drivers. 'There never is between a star and an up-and-coming star. I was always in the middle and I didn't really give a shit as long as we could win races. It didn't bother me. I guess that's the difference between me and those sort of guys.'

Nobody disputes that Stefan Bellof made an error of judgement in trying to overtake Jacky Ickx going through the second part of the very fast Eau Rouge Corner at Spa. The twisting curve plunges left into a fold in the Ardennes hills before leaping steeply right uphill towards the very fast left-hand sweep known as Le Raidillon and the long straight towards Les Combes. Without question, Eau Rouge is one of the most difficult and challenging sections of racetrack to be found anywhere in the world.

It was about halfway through the 1,000km race. It was a warm, dry September day and Ickx and Mass had established a narrow lead over Bellof and Boutsen in the Brun 956B.

'There was a camera in Ickx's car and it was all recorded,' continues Peter Falk. 'Four laps before the crash there was a pit-stop for both cars. Ickx came out just before Bellof, and for four laps, Ickx was just ahead.

'Bellof couldn't overtake him on the straight after Eau Rouge – that's normally the only place to overtake – but he couldn't get past him. So we watched it for four laps. The line Ickx took into Eau Rouge was exactly the same. We measured them [the split-times] later with the computer, they were exactly the same. And it was the same on the lap when the crash happened.

'Many people and journalists said that Ickx moved to the left and blocked Bellof. That was not true. His line was absolutely the same. He had to go to the left side, otherwise it was impossible to go through Eau Rouge, and Bellof was well, without a brain. He tried to go past Ickx on the little bit after the left-hand curve. He was to the left of Ickx's car and you could see the tyre marks on the left side.'

'It was such a naïve overtaking manoeuvre,' adds Derek Bell. 'You could not believe it.'

Both cars speared off the course. Bellof's 956 hit the outside barrier at undiminished speed (some say at more than 170mph/274kph). Ickx glanced off the Armco on the inside of the bend, and in an instant the two cars were destroyed, with hungry flames eager to consume the wrecks. Ickx struggled out and rushed to Bellof's aid. Although the fire was put out quickly, Bellof was fatally injured. He died later in the course's hospital.

'I have my own opinion,' says Manfred Jantke, 'and

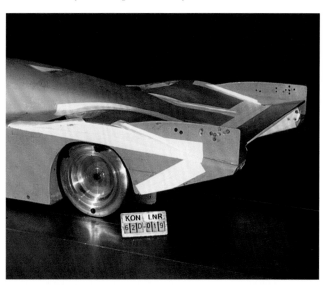

These three photographs from Norbert Singer's files show that the aerodynamics development did not stop during 1985. Teams like Joest and Lloyd discovered a measurable advantage that year, particularly in the efficiency of their underbody ducts, so generating more downforce.

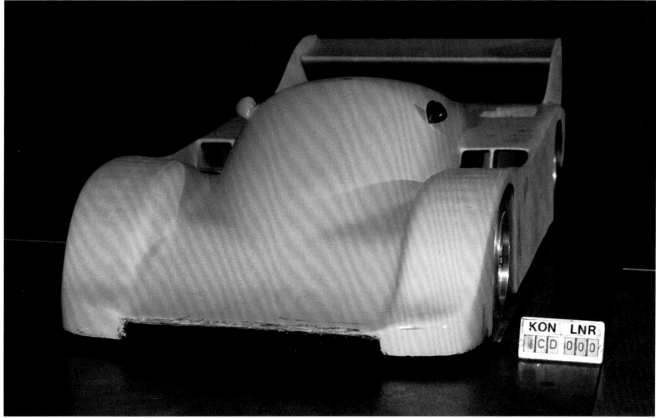

Top left: This view shows a more deeply sculpted nose being evaluated on the 962.

Top right: Using 17in wheels permitted narrower tyres for the same contact patch (and so allowed wider underbody ducts), but the taller wheel assembly interrupted the airflow over the top body to the rear wing.

Bottom: The wind tunnel testing was a continuous process as the 962 was developed to full competitiveness.

By late 1985, the castor built into the front suspension of the 962C had increased to 9°. The large red ducts bring cooling air to the brakes.

I know Klaus Bischoff [crew chief on the Bell/Bellof car in 1983/84 and a close friend of the Bellof family] doesn't agree with it.

'I know that Stefan was extremely positive and optimistic at the time we had this thing between Ickx and Bellof. When they raced, Stefan was quicker than Jacky.

The front of a Weissach 962C shows the brake and clutch hydraulics, plus the windscreen washer bottle.

'It is my opinion that Stefan wanted to pass Jacky in front of everybody. He didn't want to pass him anywhere else. He wanted to pass the king of Spa there, so that everybody could see it. I think that is what led to the accident.'

The crash undoubtedly had an effect on Jacky Ickx, who even before the race had been considering his future in motor racing. Jantke remembers the deep feelings that surged in the gifted Belgian driver's mind.

'Jacky was very emotional. If you met him you wouldn't expect that. This accident was at a point in his career when he was thinking whether he liked it or not. He was so deeply shocked. It was definitely not his fault, not at all. It was Stefan's mistake. But Jacky was hurt so much, he didn't like racing so much afterwards. I think it led to his retirement when it happened.'

At the end of the season, the 40-year-old Jacky stepped out of the team leader's shoes at Rothmans-Porsche. He was content to reflect on a 20-year career that had given him eight grand prix wins, 181 Formula One World Championship points, six Le Mans victories and countless more endurance championship wins. He is blunt about his reasons for quitting.

'I wasn't good enough any more,' he says reflectively today. 'There is a time for everything. I gave the best I could and I reached the point where I couldn't do it any more. There were many reasons. It used up so much time and my quality of life. I think it is a good thing not to hang around when you don't feel like doing it any more.'

In that busy year then, both Stefan Bellof and Manfred Winkelhock, two German drivers who were enjoying full-time drives in Formula One, died in Group C Porsches.

Looking past the personal tragedy of the losses, the deaths of these two emergent drivers was a body blow to German motor racing, which had not seen any serious grand prix challengers since Graf von Trips in the early 1960s. Germany would have to wait until the 1990s for a new champion.

The very serious accidents at Mosport and at Spa (and including Palmer's fortunate escape), all within the space of a month, frightened Formula One team managers to such an extent that many banned their drivers from any further participation in endurance racing. At the time, this affected among others, Thierry Boutsen, Stefan Johansson and Gerhard Berger.

Lancia was awarded the victory at Spa, despite the race only running for five hours. But tragedy aside, it was a deserved victory for the Martini team after so much effort. Sadly though, time appeared to be running out for the Italian team.

When Ricardo Patrese snatched pole position at Brands Hatch in late September, it seemed his intended audience was more the company's senior management than the paying spectators, as the team was now struggling to stay alive. The race then went the usual way, with the two Rothmans Porsches (led by Bell and Stuck once more) heading the results with the two Lancias third and fourth. It was a lot better result for the Italian cars than could have been expected one or two seasons previously, but the writing was on the wall.

1985 had highlighted the fact that although the pretty Dallara-built coupés were achieving a level of reliability, their Ferrari engines always seemed to be one step behind the Porsche flat-six.

Despite significant development, the Lancias never found enough consistency to meet the delicate balance of power, fuel consumption and reliability that Group C demanded.

At the end of the year, and faced with having to design a new car for the revised regulations, the Italians made plans to bow out. Their campaign in endurance racing had covered four years and the results had been patchy. Most importantly, they had failed to win Le Mans, even in 1984 when the Weissach team had declined to run.

Norbert Singer has his own view on the lack of success by a team he greatly respected. 'Lancia was much more competitive than the results show. They had the Ferrari engine and the horsepower numbers you heard were, well, far above ours. When you saw the testing and qualifying times, they were pretty fast. Unfortunately, they never won Le Mans and I think they only won two or three world [manufacturers] championship races.

'Sometimes you include all your ideas and you get everything in [to the car]. You can be fast and reliable, but you need a little luck, and they didn't have that – or they didn't have the experience for Le Mans or whatever. It has happened to us.'

In retrospect, 1985 was Lancia's strongest season. The much-improved LC2 benefited from new Michelin radial tyres and more refined aerodynamics.

The 3-litre Ferrari V8 now used Weber-Marelli engine management and wherever the Martini cars appeared they were usually in the running for pole position, and reliability was much-improved.

As a post-script on the Italian cars, a single factory-entered Lancia was entered for the first two races of 1986, but after failing to widen the number of cars run by customer teams and the unfortunate death of one of the team's key development engineers, that was the last time the Martini team was seen in Group C. Cesare Fiorio directed Lancia Corse's resources towards rallying, and in so doing, he opened the door to welcome success for the Italian team.

But if the Italian threat receded as 1985 came to a close, then the final races produced a very serious new challenger. At the Mosport Park race, two new Jaguar XJR-6s made their debut, run by Tom Walkinshaw Racing (TWR). The TWR Jaguars brought British Racing Green back to top level sports car racing and would take up the manufacturers' battle with Porsche with an intensity not seen before in Group C.

The British manufacturer's flame had been ignited in the early 1980s not by any home-grown effort, but by American Bob Tullius. The Group 44 XJR-5 was immediately competitive from its IMSA debut in mid-1982 and won four races in 1983, with designer Lee Dykstra maintaining a continuous development programme from the outset.

FISA's about-turn on the Group C regulations early in 1984 had allowed the IMSA cars to run at Le Mans that year. The Tullius cars ran as high as sixth and seventh before retirement ended the run on Sunday morning. However, internal Jaguar politics began to engulf the enthusiastic Group 44 team.

A year earlier, Jaguar's chairman, John Egan, had announced that Tom Walkinshaw would represent Jaguar in the European Touring Car Championship, and it soon became clear that the ambitious Scot had plans beyond the company's XJ-S sports cars. By the end of 1984, Walkinshaw had taken over the endurance racing programme.

TWR turned their backs on the Tullius chassis and engaged Tony Southgate to design a state-of-the-art composite monocoque. The XJR-6 used the then-current Formula One practice of sandwiching aluminium-honeycomb in moulded carbon-fibre/Kevlar skins.

The line-up in the pits
before practice at the
December 1985 Selangor
800km – the first World
Endurance Championship
race to be held in
Malaysia. (Rothmans
International)

It was light, and in the era when sports cars were making the most from ground effects, very stiff. Like the Dykstra XJR-5, the revised two-valve, 6.2-litre V12 – now good for around 650bhp – was carried as a stressed member and featured a beefy Hewland transmission further developed by March Engineering.

The speed of the TWR Jaguars was immediately apparent at Mosport. The cars qualified in third and fifth place on the grid, behind the two Rothmans cars. In a race overshadowed by the tragedy of Manfred Winkelhock's accident, Brundle, Thackwell and Schlesser brought one car home to third place, again behind the two dominant Rothmans 962Cs.

At Spa the best finisher had been the Martin Brundle/Mike Thackwell car that finished in a careful sixth place. Brands Hatch had witnessed a loud and very excited reception for the home-grown team, but despite all-star driver pairings, both cars retired. The problems continued at Fuji, but the Jaguars, like most of the Porsches, did not race after first an earthquake and then a typhoon at the Japanese circuit. TWR's debut had been low key, a learning exercise, but few doubted the British team would be back with renewed force in 1986.

Given everything that had happened in 1985, it was easy to overlook the Rothmans-Porsche team's outstanding achievement of winning a fourth consecutive World Endurance Championship. Despite the defeat by Joest at Le Mans, the ever-improving competitiveness of teams such as Kremer, Brun and Lloyd in the World Championship, the Weissach team had still emerged on top.

Technically, it had been a very challenging year. Perhaps the most immediate concern had been the susceptibility of the Porsche flat-six turbo engine to variable fuel quality while, of course, eking out the maximum power and minimum consumption.

It took the Rothmans team some time to come to terms with the 15 per cent reduction in fuel resources available for each race in 1985, and evidence points towards fuel conservatism being the major factor in the defeat at Le Mans.

Weissach seemed to struggle at times in juggling parameters such as engine capacity and compression ratio to achieve a reasonable race pace, without running out of fuel. There were other concerns that challenged the Weissach engineers though, over the winter of 1985–86. Norbert Singer was incapacitated from the painful burns incurred at Hockenheim. Porsche's chief race engineer would be out of action for many months and the team sorely missed his guiding presence.

After the tragic accidents of 1985, there was a growing customer concern over the crash safety of the 956 and 962 chassis. The initial response from Weissach was to say (rightly) that both fatal accidents

that year would have been non-survivable in any car. But the crashes did induce a sense of introspection within the team. Various detail improvements were introduced, particularly around the footbox, but Weissach chose not to get into further chassis development or embrace either aluminium-honeycomb or carbon-fibre manufacture. In fact, in a surprise announcement Weissach let it be known that it did not have plans to build any more monocoques at all.

The chassis business would be picked up eagerly by a small group of fabricators around the world. These included Atlanta's Dave Klym (who in time would become the factory's preferred supplier), Jim Chapman in California and Britain's John Thompson and Richard Lloyd. In turn, these manufacturers introduced their own interpretations of how to improve the passive safety of the basic monocoque.

Over the winter of 1985–86, Porsche focused its attention on the semi-automatic Porsche Doppel-Kupplung (PDK) transmission. This was a major development project with intended applications in both road vehicles and racing. The project team was headed by transmission expert Rainer Wüst, but the development was a puzzling one for those outside Porsche. Racing cars with automatic transmission had never achieved consistent results and there was nearly always a weight penalty. With the entry of Jaguar, several commentators suggested Porsche should be guiding their efforts towards finding more speed.

In the view of engineering head Helmuth Bott, racing was the perfect place to develop pieces that might be used on future Porsche road cars. Therefore, that winter would witness a maximum effort to get the hitherto troublesome transmission raceworthy for the coming season.

The PDK name referred to its novel twin-clutch design, but in reality it was a state-of-the-art pre-

The Mosport Park race marked the debut of the TWR Jaguars. Here Martin Brundle leads the two Rothmans cars. (LAT)

The new Porsche Doppel-Kupplung (PDK) transmission proved itself in need of significant additional development during 1985.

selector gearbox that offered the driver power-on sequential gear selection (by means of a front-back lever beside the steering wheel). But while PDK offered two-pedal racing on the move, a conventional clutch was needed for starting.

The driver could pre-select downshifts approaching a corner, leaving him to focus on braking and turning while the electronics looked after the shifting at the correct engine revs. It was intelligent, in that if the driver pulled back on the lever to select three downshifts under braking, but by making the third change would over-rev the engine, the control unit would only make two shifts.

The upshift was manual, being controlled by the driver simply by tipping the lever forward. The twin-clutch arrangement allowed full power-on upshifts, theoretically giving the car an advantage over a manual-shift gearbox. An LED panel advised the driver what gear he was in and what was pre-selected.

In theory, PDK was a good idea but the execution was let down by the materials and electronics technology of the time. Drivers reported that the shift was fairly abrupt, which will have increased the demands on the components. The transmission added a full 25kg (55lb) to the weight of the 956 and compromised fuel consumption.

The first few seasons of exposure for PDK were not auspicious. The test bed car was 956 003, which had won Le Mans in 1983. This was fitted with an experimental gearbox and made a rather low-key appearance at the season-ending Kyalami 1,000km race that year.

It was run as a third Rothmans entry with Al Holbert and Vern Schuppan, two of the drivers that had won in France, but even the well-known mechanical sympathies of these two were unable to keep the 956 going. After an unimpressive run, a faulty ignition coil is said to have finally stopped the car after 143 laps.

Further development continued but the gearbox was not seen again in a race until Imola in September 1984, when Jacky Ickx and John Watson endured a torrid experience as the unit repeatedly failed. It broke twice in practice and the car lasted but two laps in the race.

There was much work to do and the PDK was not seen again for another year until September 1985, but at Brands Hatch, Holbert and Schuppan managed to bring the car home fifth, for its first World Endurance Championship finish. As his team-mate Hans Stuck later found, Schuppan discovered the automatic Porsche had many advantages.

'I think the PDK was the most fantastic technical development I experienced during the whole of my driving career,' says Schuppan. 'When it worked you could just concentrate on the driving, and it wasn't really any slower. I remember at Brands I was following Stucky and as I came out of Clearways, I could see his car going up the hill to Druids – and we went on like that for lap after lap, staying at the same gap. I don't think the weight bothered the car, and if the reliability had been there I would have preferred it.'

But by this time, some of the other drivers were getting fairly stressed-out at having to drive the auto-transmission cars, especially when drivers' championships were at stake. It seemed to them the PDK development was going nowhere and all the while, Porsche were obviously facing the prospect of formidable opposition in 1986.

At that point, and considered with the benefit of twenty-twenty hindsight, the development of PDK in racing appears to have been a distraction rather than leading to any real benefit. Strongly backed by Helmuth Bott, the project therefore went ahead despite a mixed reception from the drivers. Norbert Singer though, remains convinced of the project's value.

'PDK was, in principle, a very good thing. At that stage, that was what we knew and the effort we could do. (I think) it was too early. You can compare it with the introduction of ABS in racing.

'I remember my first race where I was responsible for that on the 917 in 1971, where we tried to race with the ABS. Years later, when I talked to the people – it was Teldix in those days – they said it was far too early. We tried to do things mechanically that electronics should do – as there were no electronics in those days. It was similar with PDK.

'The double-clutch system is a lot of mass and energy. When you use a carbon clutch, it is much easier and effective. But in those days there was no carbon clutch. When you do it with normal heavy clutch material, you run into problems.

'We did do a very successful test [of the principle]. It was faster, but it was not really as reliable as it should have been. Later, we did some development for other customers with carbon clutches and it was much lighter and better. In principle the idea was good, but it was far too early. Mr Bott's idea was that we should put it in the racing car and the development would go much faster. Of course, it went faster, sure, but it was a big effort.'

Perhaps most importantly, there is the implication that in devoting so much effort to developing PDK, other improvements aimed at keeping the cars winning in future years were overlooked. Singer accepts this. 'Yes, [for instance] a new chassis and maybe a new engine,' he concedes, 'yes.'

PDK would take a much higher profile in 1986 – the 956/962 family's fifth season at the top of international sports car racing.

Jacky Ickx at an early stage of the ill-fated Spa 1,000km in September 1985. (Rothmans International)

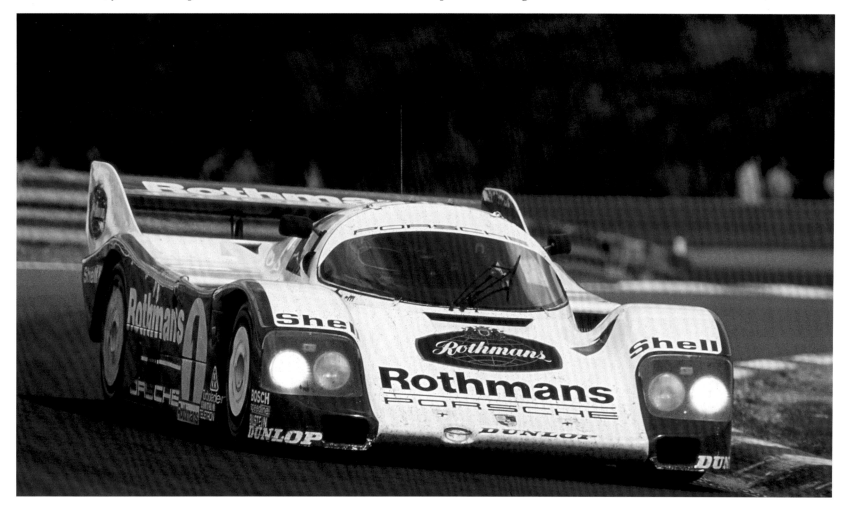

THE CAT GETS ANGRY

Reinhold Joest was unable to make it three wins in a row for his 956 117 at Le Mans in 1986. Ludwig, Barilla and 'Winter' retired while one lap ahead, following the prolonged night-time period behind the safety car. (LAT)

WHEN JAGUAR ANNOUNCED in September 1984, that Tom Walkinshaw Racing would run a full WEC campaign, including Le Mans, the tremors could be felt around the world.

The team's sprint racing skills were recognised as second-to-none and their endurance capability was proven in 1984 with a win in the Spa 24 Hours. The XJ-S campaign in the European Touring Car Championship had given TWR's engine development team, under Alan Scott, a complete under-standing of every strength and weakness of the basic two-valve V12.

Nevertheless, it was an obvious starting point that TWR should begin their WEC programme with one of Lee Dykstra's well-developed XJR-5 IMSA chassis. Indeed, one of the cars was evaluated in England (and driven by Derek Bell) early in 1985 – when the Porsches were at the height of their superiority. Bell reported the car to be sound, but not as good as his regular 956.

After a full evaluation, TWR went back to a clean sheet of paper. Tony Southgate drew a brand-new carbon-fibre monocoque car, calling it XJR-6 and continuing the 'XJR' branding started by Bob Tullius.

Meanwhile, Alan Scott's team began again with the V12. The engine used many TWR and Cosworth-fabricated internals with the basic Jaguar castings. The result was a 6.2-litre two-valve V12 that delivered around 640bhp. This would rise to 6.5-litres and 700bhp during 1986.

The two TWR cars debuted at Mosport Park in August 1985, running as green-painted Jaguars and without third-party commercial sponsorship. A hugely popular British debut followed at Brands Hatch (hinting at the massive support the team would have at Le Mans in the coming years), but the two season-closing races in Fuji and Shah Alam were disappointing. However, after the brief contact with their new adversary, Weissach faced the fact that in the following season, they would be dealing with a formidable competitor.

The Silk Cut cigarette brand became Jaguar's title sponsor for 1986, with the cars changing colour from predominantly green to the sponsor's purple and white.

'We knew they would try again,' says Peter Falk. 'They were there in 1985, but they were not competitive enough. We knew they would be back in '86 and that it would be very hard for us. We had to develop our car more and we did that.'

What is surprising is that faced with such a strong competitor, and after four very successful seasons with the old chassis, they didn't consider a new car.

'Yes!' laughs Falk, 'I think Mr Singer had some ideas for a new car, but we didn't have the budget. It was very hard to convince the Board to give us the budget for a new car when the existing one was still winning. We couldn't convince Mr Schutz [Porsche's then-CEO] that we needed one or two years to build a new car. We couldn't say to him that we needed to build a new car now for 1988.'

In fact Schutz, a German-born American, was thinking about a new IndyCar rather than a new endurance racer.

The PDK transmission achieved its first win at the 1986 Monza Supersprint. The winning 962C of Stuck and Bell leads the Massimo Sigala, Jesus Pareja, Walter Brun 962C and the two TWR Jaguars at the start of the race.

Thierry Boutsen and Frank Jelinski won the Spa 1,000km in September 1986, on the way to earning Walter Brun that year's World Sports Prototype Teams' Championship. (LAT)

Bob Wollek joined the Rothmans-Porsche team in 1986 to (very ably) fill the gap left by the retiring Jacky Ickx.

'He wanted to [do an IndyCar] and so did Mr Holbert,' continues Falk. 'Mr Singer and I said to Mr Bott that we didn't want to do that. We had enough to do already and we wanted to do worldwide races, not just American races. We also knew it would be very hard because the Americans have years and years of experience and we had nothing. We knew it wouldn't be very good to start with.' But despite their protests, the IndyCar programme went ahead and there was no new sports car.

What shocked Weissach at the start of the next season was just how good their opposition had become. The Rothmans cars had played on their bullet-proof reliability in earlier years, as a means to beat both Lancia and their own customers in the long-distance races. Now, in the new-format World Sports Prototype Championship (WSPC) for drivers, there were three new 'sprint' races of around 350km (217 miles) and the short (180km/112-mile) Norisring money race.

These short races not only challenged the value of the 962C's extreme durability, but also the policy of using older, more experienced drivers rather than young hot-shots.

Besides Jaguar and Porsche's own very determined customer teams, there was another challenger in the form of Peter Sauber's revitalised sports car team.

Sauber had changed from BMW to Mercedes power the previous season and for 1986, he had won sponsorship from the Kouros cosmetics company. The Mader-developed, turbocharged 5-litre V8 matched the Jaguar's 700bhp, but to begin with, the C8 chassis did not appear to have as much downforce as the 962C. However, drivers Henri Pescarolo and Mike Thackwell were more than capable of getting the results.

With so much competition and being denied the budget to build a new car, or even significantly revise the 962, Weissach planned a very focused 1986 campaign. They would concentrate all their resources on winning Le Mans and use the other races of the WSPC primarily as a development workshop. This latter policy would generate some considerable dissent from certain of their drivers.

The trimmed 1986 development budget was focused on making the PDK a race-worthy system, justifying its continued use on the basis that this was the automatic transmission of the future for Porsche production cars.

There was also a new driver on the Rothmans team that year. Following Jacky Ickx's retirement, the choice of Bob Wollek was almost automatic. By 1986, Wollek had two championship titles in the Deutsche Rennsport Meisterschaft (DRM), had won the Daytona 24 Hours twice and the Sebring 12 Hours once. His two years at Lancia in 1984–85 had brought a much-needed maturity to that team's brat pack of grand prix sprinters. The 41-year-old Wollek had shown that he was as fast as the youngsters, but had the maturity to get the fragile Lancias to the finish. It is not difficult to understand the confidence the Weissach team had in pairing him with Jochen Mass.

PDK became a regular feature on the Rothmans cars in WEC events in 1986, irrespective of the challenge presented by the customers or Jaguar and Sauber. Here, a PDK-equipped car is about to give journalists the ride of a lifetime at the Nürburgring.

Hans-Joachim Stuck watches as Derek Bell guides their 962C out of the crowded Le Mans pitlane early on Sunday morning, June 1986. Variable weather conditions made all the finishers look as if they had survived a war – which sometimes is a good description of endurance racing. (Rothmans International)

Reinhold Joest demonstrated that his team still had the measure of the fuel issue when Klaus Ludwig and Paolo Barilla led in the double Le Mans-winning 956 until its clutch had failed. In this last season of its eligibility, chassis 117, now in yellow and grey taka-Q colours, was showing the 962s that it was far from obsolete.

At Silverstone, both Rothmans 962s were fitted with the PDK transmission, but as a result of continued worries about fuel usage, Weissach fell back on to the 2.65-litre engine for the race. By complete contrast, and even after their fuel consumption problems at Monza, TWR debuted a four-valve 6.5-litre V12, and a revised car that was much-improved by more-efficient ground-effects.

The Jaguars were completely dominant in England, the winning car finishing two laps ahead of Bell and Stuck. Mass and Wollek retired with transmission failure.

There was now real pressure on the Weissach team to perform at Le Mans in 1986. Not only did they not want Reinhold Joest to achieve a hat-trick of wins, or indeed for any of the other nine customer entries to win, but it was clear they would have to face up to very determined efforts from both Jaguar and Sauber.

TWR entered three XJR-6s (back with the proven two-valve V12), while Sauber sent two Mercedes-powered C8s. Without a doubt, this was the strongest opposition Porsche had faced at Le Mans during the Group C period – and arguably, ever.

Only the Rothmans 962C driven by Vern Schuppan and Drake Olsen had the PDK transmission and this car retired after just 41 laps – with transmission failure after Olsen spun just after Indianapolis. Vern recalls a discussion he had with factory mechanic Klaus Bischoff, while he was sitting in the car waiting for the start of the Saturday morning warm-up. 'Klaus came over and said we should try to break the car, because 009 [with the manual gearbox] was ready to go and the car had been qualified well-up the grid. The Supercup-prepared 962C was being used as the spare car and had all Weissach's latest sprint modifications. Suffice to say that the PDK survived the warm-up – but only 41 laps of the race. Schuppan was transferred to the Wollek/Mass car.

The very fast pace soon took its toll on the pretenders to Porsche's throne. Both Saubers were out before the evening, while all three Jaguars failed sooner or later. Strangely, considering the Silverstone

Given the much-increased threat from the other teams, the first race of the season at Monza produced a surprise. Bell and Stuck were able to take a fortunate victory in the new Supersprint ahead of the de Cesaris/Nannini Lancia LC2-86 and the Schlesser/Brancatelli Jaguar.

The fuel consumption regulations made a farce of the race. Both the Lancia and Jaguar ran into serious consumption problems towards the end, and even Bell and Stuck had to cruise to the finish. This marked the first, and only WSPC victory, for the PDK transmission. The Rothmans car was also running a 3.0-litre engine in this race for the first time, this capacity having been used only for qualifying in 1985.

performance, the British cars were not able to run at the pace of the leading 962s. It suggested the team had enjoyed considerably better fuel consumption at the British race.

The Ludwig/'Winter'/Barilla Joest car was intent on making it three victories in a row, but Bell, Stuck and Al Holbert had other ideas.

The contest raged into the night, but would be influenced by Jo Gartner's awful accident in the Kremer 962C during the early hours. The pace car was out for a full 2½ hours and when news of the Austrian's death reached the pits, the race took on a very sombre mood. It was during this enforced slow-running period that the Joest car's engine seized – almost certainly influenced by the long delay.

'At this time, we didn't have a thermostat in the water system,' says Reinhold Joest. 'Ludwig was

behind the pace car for two hours maybe, and the engine cooled down too much. A bush in the oil pump came out and the bearing went – well, it didn't go, because it wasn't there! I think we had a one-lap lead at the time, but the engine was finished.'

When the race restarted Bell, Stuck and Holbert had an eight-lap lead over Warwick, Cheever and Schlesser. The last Jaguar to survive then had a tyre explode, destroying its suspension.

Bell's Le Mans victory was his fourth, but Gartner's death cast a long shadow over the result.

Hurley Haywood drove for the Bob Tullius Jaguar team in IMSA from 1985 to 1987 and he drove the third XJR-6 at Le Mans for TWR in 1986. The car retired after just 53 laps with failing fuel pressure, but as a driver with experience of the first 956s, then both the Tullius and TWR Jaguars and later, the 962s, he is

The Vern Schuppan/Drake Olsen 962C was the only Porsche fitted with the PDK transmission at Le Mans in 1986. The car lasted just 35 laps before Olsen spun and then suffered a shaft failure in the transmission. (Rothmans International)

in a unique position to comment on the merits of all these 1980s prototypes.

Hurley had been a strong factory driver for Porsche in the early 1980s, and had won with the Rothmans 956 at Le Mans in 1983. All the drivers had found the first 956s very physically demanding to drive, particularly because of the heavy steering. When, later that year, he had broken a leg at Mosport, Hurley faced a painfully long rehabilitation. More importantly, he found he did not have the strength to push down the 956's heavy clutch.

The Tullius Jaguar used a Hewland gearbox. Apart from starting, the driver did not have to press the clutch to change gears, and Hurley needed an easy car to drive. His good working relationship with Al Holbert led to an introduction to Bob Tullius.

'It was a serious crash. I had to wait until my leg healed up and it took a very long time – two years to really get the thing back together. I had five operations.

'Al Holbert told Bob Tullius after I had hurt myself that the smartest thing he could do was to hire me. Al and I had had some great battles in Porsches up to

then and he was a gentleman. That's how I got my job with Jaguar.

'Jaguar said that in their cars I didn't need the clutch and so I drove for them for two years before going back to Porsche.' The Tullius Jaguar was an easy car to drive compared to the 956, but when the IMSA 962 arrived, it struggled to stay on their pace.

In 1986, he was drafted into the TWR squad for Le Mans, but he was unimpressed with the XJR-6 compared with his regular IMSA car.

'It was like a truck in comparison! They were not particularly nice to drive. That first engine was just so big. It wasn't so sweet-sounding as the Tullius V12s either. Walkinshaw's V12s were very throaty, more like a V8 sound. And just the whole team, the whole atmosphere [wasn't so good].

'We [Haywood and Brian Redman] were on loan to Walkinshaw by Tullius. By that time word had kind of filtered down that Walkinshaw was going to take Tullius's place in the United States. There were a lot of hard feelings and it wasn't really conducive to an enjoyable weekend.'

Hurley would find himself back in a 962 for 1988

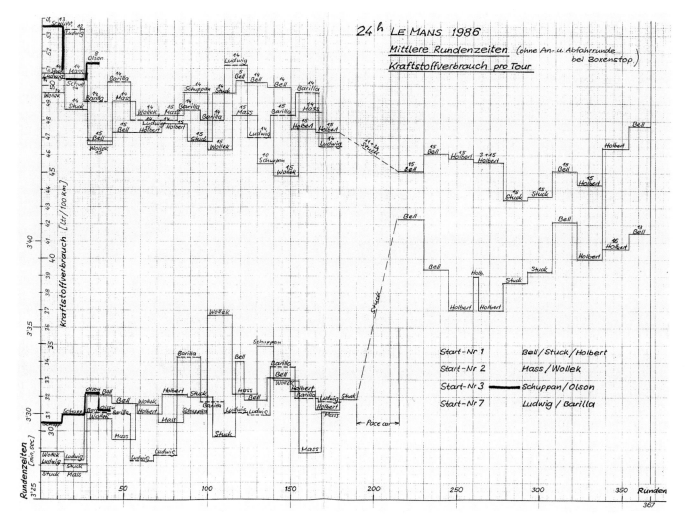

24ʰ LE MANS 1986
Mittlere Rundenzeiten (ohne An- u. Abfahrrunde bei Boxenstop.)
Kraftstoffverbrauch pro Tour

Start-Nr 1   Bell / Stuck / Holbert
Start-Nr 2   Mass / Wollek
Start-Nr 3   Schuppan / Olson
Start-Nr 7   Ludwig / Barilla

Lap time and fuel consumption analysis of the Rothmans team cars at the 1986 Le Mans. Two lines are shown for each car (with the Schuppan/Olsen trace halting after just 35 laps). The top line for each car is the average fuel consumption (in litres/100km), while the lower line is the average lap time. Note how the Bell/Stuck car's times rise during the pace car period and their fuel consumption falls.

and by this time, the Porsches were easier to drive. There were also several outside concerns building 962 chassis.

'The early 962s were kind of flexible and the chassis by the other builders were much stiffer.' But he had no concerns about the safety of the original factory chassis.

'I had some pretty good wrecks in them and I'm still sitting here! I saw a lot of guys wreck them – they were pretty stout automobiles.'

He cannot recall any specific differences between say, the John Thompson-built 962 chassis and the Dave Klym version. 'The Klym chassis was a very good one. It was very stiff and we were pretty much all thinking the same way that the stiffer the chassis, the better the car. So all the late chassis that were built outside the factory were all very stiff.'

To complete the comparison, Hurley is also able to define the differences between the Group C 962C and the IMSA 962. 'I just remember the Group C cars were a little easier to drive, a little less brutish. With the single turbo, you've got lag questions and you've got big spikes of horsepower. The twin-turbos made it much softer, and the softer it is, the easier it is to drive.

'There were some aerodynamic differences between the two cars and I usually only drove the Le Mans Group C cars. You didn't have the stick or the road-holding that the Stateside 962s had because we didn't race on tracks like that. So for me the IMSA cars always had tremendous amounts of downforce, the tyres were bigger and they just had much better roadholding.'

After Le Mans in 1986, the flavour of the WSPC changed, the races moving towards the ever-improving

TWR Jaguars. First there was the Norisring 100 Miles, previously a round of the German national Supercup, but now included in the International Championship for Drivers.

Porsche entered a special lightweight 3-litre 962C (962 005) for Hans Stuck in this event, recalling its effort years previously with the 'Baby' 935. The car was entered in Blaupunkt colours in deference to this being a continuing round of the German national championship (in which Blaupunkt supported the factory Porsche entry).

Derek Bell was released by Weissach for the race, but leading the championship (with Stuck), he looked around for another drive. Bell tells the story in his usual colourful way: 'I had a call from John Fitzpatrick. He said he could help me with the points. He said he couldn't afford to pay me, but he said I could drive his car. When I think about it now, it was bloody good of John. So I get to the Norisring – and Stucky's there with this special Supercup car. It had this trick shit, super-duper, rocket-ship engine – a wonderful car. It was a world championship race, but you only needed one driver. So (I believed) it was being engineered that Stucky was going to win the championship, and me, being Derek Bell, I'm prepared to say Stucky deserved it. He was a star. I was disappointed because I was going to lose the championship because I couldn't get it together. Then Fitzy offered me the drive.

But in practice, things did not go quite as Derek would have wished. 'Well, Stucky was on pole and I'm in 16th! We had all sorts of trouble with shocks and springs. I never found out why we weren't quick there, and in the race, we're thundering round and I'm having a pretty lonely time.

'Then I go past the pits and I notice a big crowd around one of the pits. I came around again and I see it is Stucky's car. Next time round, he's still there, and I thought that's bloody great! There's no way I'm going to finish in the points. So that was it. I finished 12th and Stucky was 15th.

'But at the end of the year Stucky and I were equal on points. I thought that's very fair and bollocks to Porsche trying to scam it! Then they turned around

The Weissach team did not go to the Brands Hatch 1,000km in 1986, so Bell and Stuck rented Reinhold Joest's double Le Mans-winning 956 – including the services of Joest's driver Klaus Ludwig (getting out of the car). Although the 956 had the legs on the factory cars for most of that season, at Brands it suffered with a fuel pick-up problem. (Rothmans International)

and said you came 12th and he came 15th at the Norisring, so you beat him!

'It was really a shot in the arm. It was poetic justice really, they were trying to get Stucky the world championship. But to be fair, Stucky was doing the Supercup and they only had one car. So it was funny that at the end of the year I should get it.'

As in previous years though, Weissach was really only interested in the Championship for Constructors in 1986. By this time they were also running down the sports car campaign to release resources for the IndyCar project. Derek and several others in the factory driver team had to freelance a few times to stand any chance of being in contention for the drivers' title.

Bob Wollek drove the rebuilt Richard Lloyd 956, 106b2 at the Norisring, but was disqualified after not observing a black flag. He continued the arrangement at the next race – the Brands Hatch 1,000km, where Bell and Stuck drove for Reinhold Joest.

With the assistance of Derek's manager David Mills, they raised enough sponsorship to drive the double Le Mans winner (956 117). 'We got the sponsorship from

Rothmans, Autoglass and Shell, perhaps £10,000, £12,000 or £15,000 from each one,' says Bell.

This very special 956 was fitted with the higher-specification 2.85-litre engine that was being used by the leading customer teams at this time.

Derek Bell (right) and Hans-Joachim Stuck ran into fuel consumption problems at the tense 1986 Spa 1,000km. The race was won by the Thierry Boutsen/Frank Jelinski 962C of Walter Brun. Bell and Stuck had to slow down, which also let the Warwick/Lammers XJR-6 into second place.

Hans-Joachim Stuck pressing on at the very wet Nürburgring 1,000km, and passing the March-Porsche 85G of David Leslie and Richard Cleare. Stuck's race did not last long.

Jochen Mass's race at the 1986 Nürburgring 1,000km was cut short when he was accidentally rammed from behind by an unsighted Hans-Joachim Stuck. Mass had slowed behind the pace car, which had come out to calm the field after an earlier accident.

'We had run against that car all year and it had been so fast. We knew it was better than our factory cars. It had been developed around that one chassis, whereas every time we went out, we had new stuff.

'That was the PDK year and here we were going to have a manual gearbox. We knew the car was strong and we knew it was fast. So we got to Brands and we had a fuel pick-up problem all weekend! We had been praising the car and it had been blowing our doors off in lots of races. When we get the chance to drive it – and we've raised the 30 or 40 grand to do the race – the car didn't run that well.

Stuck had taken pole position, but in the race they had no answer to the Lloyd 956 (now in Liqui-Moly colours), driven by Wollek and Mauro Baldi. In complete contrast to Silverstone, niggling problems kept the competitive Jaguars out of the results. This was to summarise the Jaguar story in 1986.

A very wet Nürburgring 1,000km event (on the 'Neue' course) was stopped at 22 laps when both Rothmans cars (the 1986 Le Mans-winning 962 003 and 962 004) were taken out in a major crash in zero visibility.

'There was a lot of fog,' recalls Peter Falk, 'the pace car had just come out and Stuck was a little behind. The fog only seemed to be at the start and finish area. It was a little bit too late for me to warn him that the pace car was out. He crashed at the Castrol Esses, the corner after the pits at the new 'Ring. There was the pace car and behind it were Mass and the others, and then Stuck came past at full speed and crashed into Mass. Both cars were destroyed.'

Many cars could not or would not take the restart for a shortened, three-hour race. After another annoying problem for the Warwick Jaguar (this time failure of the air jacks), the Thackwell/Pescarolo Sauber took a surprise victory for the Swiss team.

If Porsche were scaling down their effort by the end of 1986, that didn't stop their drivers getting worked up over their own championship. By the final round in October at Mount Fuji Derek Bell's anxiousness to win the championship was at full pitch.

Derek Warwick in the Jaguar may not have won any more races after Silverstone, but the Silk Cut driver had whittled Bell and Stuck's lead in the drivers' championship to nothing by Fuji.

So Bell was none too impressed when his Rothmans car appeared sporting the unreliable PDK transmission and a development ABS system (taken from the 959 project).

'Oh yes, my bitch at Fuji – that was over having the PDK system. I remember saying there will be 25,000 or 40,000 people here tomorrow and they'll all be saying that bloke Bell is a right old tosser! Look at him cruising round at the back – because we weren't going to go fast.

'You can't expect the public to understand. The PDK was a brilliant system, but not in a long-distance race! It didn't often last long in a 1000km. Stucky and I won at Monza, but that was only just over 200 miles. We broke driveshafts regularly with the PDK. That was what happened in Malaysia in 1985.' Another driveshaft broke in practice at Fuji and it was where Derek says he fell out with Professor Bott.

'I remember every time I walked past the racing truck, there was this standard gearbox in the back and I remember thinking that is the world championship sitting up there and I've got to drive this other thing. Nobody else in the team seemed to be shouting about

Bell was amazed to find his car was fitted with the PDK transmission for the final, crucial event at Fuji in 1986. In the race, a driveshaft broke and he and Stuck lost 17 laps while a replacement was fitted. Nonetheless, the drama would have no effect on the result of the race or the championship. Here, while the mechanics tear the rear of the car apart, Norbert Singer consoles a patient Stuck. (LAT)

it. Even Stucky never said to me: "Derek, we must go and sort these people out". He seemed to accept it.

'But I'm not like that. I had an extra 100lb [45kg] on the back from the PDK and 50lb [23kg] on the front from the bloody ABS! 'I'm going, "I don't believe this!" and I'm shouting and screaming at people.

'Eventually Peter Falk called up Bott. The next day he came back and said that he had told Professor Bott that we were not happy. So he said take off the ABS, but that was when I said my unfortunate words on the television. We were on pole and when the race got going, Stucky collided with a smaller car. It damaged the undertray, so he came in. But they said he should continue and we were working our way up to a good placing. I helped with that and later, I was absolutely exhausted from the heat and humidity.

'Up comes this guy from Sky or Eurosport and he asked me what I thought of it all. As I said, it was a really tough drive, Stucky starts to go out of the pits and I hear this terrible noise from the car. He had broken another driveshaft. I said: "I don't f'ing believe it! That was the world championship!"

'I said: "Porsche are always doing a development of something and it drives me up the wall." I said that surely they want us to beat Jaguar?'

But after the race was over, the Drivers' Championship was given to Bell and Stuck because the Weissach lap-scorers had spotted that the Warwick/Cheever XJR-6 had been awarded one too many laps. The observation by the Porsche timers was accepted by the Japanese race organisers and gave Thierry Boutsen and Frank Jelinski second place over the Jaguar. The amended result denied Warwick the WSPC drivers' title and also secured the teams championship for Walter Brun.

The race was won by Joest's 956 117, the veteran 956B going out with a championship victory and confirming its position as possibly the most famous Group C car of them all.

Unfortunately for Derek, his outburst was shown in Europe the next day.

'Later that year I received an invitation to the Porsche Cup presentations and I was asked if I would like to take lunch with Professor Bott. When I walked into his office, there was one table and two chairs. It was a stark, small and private restaurant, and he said: "Herr Bell. Nice to see you. Before we eat, I must say how disappointed I was in what you said." And I thought, "oh no!"

'I said I was so sorry. He said everything Porsche does has to be a development. I said I understood, but that it was very difficult when I was a racing driver and want to win races. I'm sure he respected that, and I respected him.'

Despite the new threats, 1986 turned out to be as successful as ever for Porsche. Le Mans was won and only two races were conceded to other makes. But 1987 would be a different story, and the lack of focused performance development began to tell on the 962C.

The first four races of 1987 – at Jarama, Jerez, Monza and Silverstone – all went to the TWR cars. It appeared Porsche's reign in Group C was over. Were Weissach losing their motivation?

After five consecutive constructors' championships (four to the Rothmans team and, in 1986, one to the Brun team), Peter Falk says his job was as interesting as ever, but it was not all Group C.

'I had been involved from 1983 with the Paris–Dakar [rally] and a little bit with the Formula One project. The engine guys that built and developed the [TAG] engines were in my department.' Then there was the IndyCar programme.

'In 1987 [for the 1988 season] we had to make the whole car, not just the engine. We were full. We had to make the monocoque, so we had enough work.'

It was perhaps no surprise that Jaguar stole the initiative in Group C that year.

'I went to him and congratulated him,' says Falk after seeing Tom Walkinshaw's cars win the early races. 'It showed us our engine was at an end and we couldn't do anything. We had no budget to make a new engine.'

Porsche decided they were not going to overcome the Jaguars in the remaining short races and made plans to withdraw the factory team after Le Mans.

'We thought that a new engine with a big displacement would be best, like the Mercedes and the Jaguar. We knew that was better, but not everyone in the factory wanted to hear that.'

To some extent this was because there was so much experience within Weissach on turbocharging, but there were also personalities involved.

'Mr Mezger was very involved with the IndyCar project and he was also never really interested in Group C. He had his [engine development] department and he decided to do the Formula One

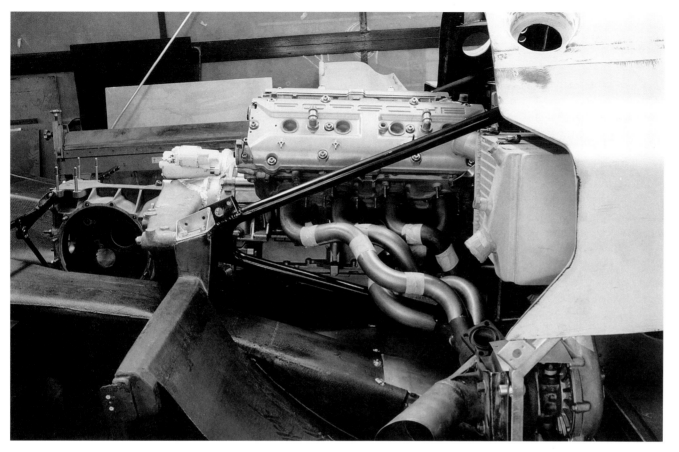

These two photos of the
962C with a 928 V8
engine demonstrate the
extent of the studies into a
new car at that time.
Sadly, the project would go
no further. Note that
thoughts were of a mildly
turbocharged installation,
along the same thinking as
the Mercedes engine in the
Sauber.

The 928 block has been
coupled to a regular 962
transmission and
packaged within the two
underbody ducts.

engine first and then the Indy engine. There were one or maybe two guys to work with Mr Schæffer and myself. We talked very openly about this problem.

'We were very glad when Mr Kremer came and said he had put a 928 engine in a Group C car and asked us if we could do some further development on it. But Mr Bott apologised and said we had no money, no budget, although that would have been the best way.'

Kremer had built a mock-up of the 928's V8 engine in the back of a 962, but without support from Weissach, he was unable to take the idea further.

With a very limited budget therefore, development for 1987 centred on a revised front suspension, a lightened PDK semi-automatic transmission and a more-reliable version of the 3-litre full water-cooled engine. Three new 962Cs were built in Weissach over that winter, two for the WSPC races and a new lightweight car for Stuck to campaign in the five German Supercup races.

At TWR's Kidlington, Oxfordshire base, another winter of development by Allan Scott had enlarged the V12 to no less than 6,995cc. The near-720bhp engine delivered both torque and reliability. There were detail revisions to Tony Southgate's carbon-fibre chassis (now called XJR-8) and for the first time, there was a dedicated car for Le Mans the XJR-8LM. By any

Derek Bell and Al Holbert together at Le Mans in 1987. With Hans-Joachim Stuck they would win the race for the second consecutive year – but it was hard work!

measure the 962C, even with the heavily tuned 3.0-litre engine, would have struggled to stay on terms with the Jaguar package.

In early June 1987, and after four straight defeats in the preceding WSPC events, there was a mood of grim foreboding in the Porsche camp about the next race – Le Mans. But against the odds, the race would turn into a tour de force for the ageing Porsche.

First, Weissach's normally clockwork-like preparations did not quite go with the usual precision. Peter Falk takes up the story. 'In 1987, Hans Stuck crashed one of the Le Mans cars at Weissach. We had four cars – three cars for the races and one spare. He drove all four cars and he crashed Mass's car. We said to him: "Hans, you don't get a new car, you get the third car – it's an old one." He's a very nice guy so he replied: "No problem," and he drove the old car.'

As a result, only the three remaining 962Cs (002, 008 and 006) appeared for what would be Rothmans last race with Porsche. They faced three Jaguar XJR-8LMs and two Sauber C9s in a contest that looked weighted heavily towards the now-dominant British team.

'Then in practice,' continues Falk, 'Price Cobb crashed another car (002 with the PDK transmission), so we had only two cars for the race.' However, the factory effort was supplemented by three cars from Walter Brun, two from Reinhold Joest, two from Kremer and one from Britten-Lloyd.

Nevertheless, the customer Porsche attack also had its problems. An over-lean engine management programme (or perhaps suspect fuel) destroyed several engines during qualifying.

As at Monza, the long periods at wide-open throttle had exposed the fragility of the now-highly tuned Porsche flat-sixes. Even early in the race – indeed before the first hour was up – both Joest cars were out as was another from Kremer. Within two hours, three Brun cars had retired: two eliminated in accidents and the third by engine failure. As if this was not bad enough, the Mass/Wollek/Schuppan factory car failed.

'After one hour,' Falk says, 'Mass came in and said "engine trouble". It was the same thing – because of the fuel. So for 23 hours we had only one car – Stuck's car.' The failures triggered frantic efforts to find a new chip for the engine management that would ensure the remaining cars' survival, and after some high-speed development work, a new, less-demanding engine management chip was hurriedly programmed for all the surviving Porsches.

Only two 962s seemed to escape the problem – the works car of Stuck, Bell and Holbert, and the BLR entry for Palmer, James Weaver and a relocated Price Cobb.

'Normally in this type of race you are calculating fuel consumption in miles per gallon or kilometres per 100 litres or whatever,' says Falk. 'In a time race like Le Mans, we calculate how many litres per hour they had to consume at the limit. If we had used more than – I think it was 106 litres per hour – we had to slow down. If it was less than that, we could go faster. These calculations were absolutely destroyed if we had rain, a pitstop or if there was a pace car. Then you could go faster.'

During the night there were several long pace car periods. The weather deteriorated and the sole-surviving factory Porsche and the Jaguars became involved in a tense struggle. At one point, this rivalry so alarmed the ACO's officials that both Falk and Walkinshaw were summoned to the race steward's office. 'In the night,' recalls Falk, 'Tom Walkinshaw and I got the order to come to the steward's office. Tom and I walked up the pit-road side by side, while out on the track, our cars were flying side by side – it was an incredible race. In the office, Alain (Bertaut) said to us in a very loud and angry voice, and standing in front of his steward colleagues: "Your cars have overtaken another under the yellow lights. If that happens again, I will take them out of the race. That is all!"

'Tom and I went down the pit-road again side by side. He said: "Alain is crazy!" I answered: "Maybe, but he would never destroy such a fine race".

'On the Sunday morning I was standing in front of my pit computer. My eyes were red. I was tired, dirty, unshaven and I didn't smell all that good! But then Alain came over. His eyes were bright and he was smiling, very clean, well shaven and fresh. He said: "Sorry about that during the night, but I had to do it because of my colleagues! He wished me good luck, turned and walked off briskly in the direction of Tom's pits, probably to say the same thing. That was Alain. He is a really nice guy.'

The pace car periods had given the leaders some breathing space. As usual, the race was claiming a steady toll. Walter Brun's only surviving car, driven by Uwe Schäffer, had a massive accident in the Porsche

Curves during the night. Then a superb run for the BLR car came to an end when a fuel line detached at top speed on the Mulsanne Straight. The resulting fire left the car in a very sorry state.

The most serious incident happened to Win Percy. He had a frightening high-speed crash on the Mulsanne

Peter Falk's race summary for the hard-won 1987 Le Mans 24 Hours. This would be Porsche's last Le Mans win with the 962.

RENNEN: 24 h LE MANS   X WM-Lauf
DATUM: 13./14. 6. 87.   Nicht-WM-Lauf

Streckenlänge: 13.535. (km)   Wetter: ~~Trocken~~/Feucht/Trocken
Einsatzfahrzeug: 962 006.   Fahrer: STUCK / BELL / HOLBERT..... Start-Nr.: 17
     962 008..   MASS. / WOLLEK............. 18
     961 01..   METGE / HALDI / NIEROP..... 203
Ersatzfahrzeug :....

Ergebnisse Rennen: LAPS
1. STUCK / BELL / HOLBERT .. 962. Fahrzeit: .. 354
2. LÄSSIG. / YVER. / DE. DRYVER .962 .. 334
3. RAPHANEL / OURAER / RESOUT. 962 COUGAR .. 331
4. FOUCHE / KONRAD / TAYLOR .962 .. 326
5. CHEEVER / BOESEL. JAGUAR .. 324
6. SPICE / VELEZ / DE. HENNING .. SPICE C2 .. 320

Trainingszeiten:
1. WOLLEK......... 3.21,09. MIN...
2. STUCK......... 3.21,13
3. CHEEVER......... 3.24,36
4. BRUNDLE......... 3.24,68 .... JAGUAR
5. LAMMERS......... 3.24,90 .... JAGUAR
6. RAPHANEL......... 3.25,21

Schnellste Runde Rennen: THACKWELL (SAUBER-MERC.) 3.25,4 MIN

Probleme: REIFENTEST WEISSACH : 962 007 UNFALL STUCK (FZG. IRREPARABEL BESCHÄDIGT)
1. TRAINING MITTWOCH : 962 002. UNFALL COBB. (FZG. ABGEBRANNT.)

Ausfallursachen: (18) MOTORSCHADEN NACH 17 RUNDEN km bis Ausfall: ....

RENNVERLAUF: NACH DER 1. RENNSTUNDE SIND BEREITS 1 KREMER-962, 2 JÖST-962 UND EIN WERKSAUTO (MASS) AUSGEFALLEN (KRAFTSTOFF-QUALITÄT)
DAS LETZTE ÜBRIGGEBLIEBENE WERKSAUTO NAHM IN DER NACHT BEI NIESELREGEN (STUCK FUHR 3 TURNS AM STÜCK) DEN JAGUAR 1 VOLLE RUNDE AB UND LEGTE DAMIT DEN GRUNDSTEIN ZUM SIEG.

Fahrzeugdaten   962   961
Motor: .. 3. LITER. WASSERGEKÜHLT. ε 9.0:1 / 2,85 LITER. LUFT/WASSER ε 8.8:1
Getriebe: ~~SCHALTGETRIEBE~~..........
   Übersetzung: 1.:........ 2.:........ 3.:........ 4.:........ 5.:........
     KT........ Differential ....

Fahrwerk:
   Federn: vorn ....   hinten ....
   Dämpfer: vorn ....   hinten ....
   Stabilisator: vorn ....   hinten ....
   Felgen: vorn ....   hinten ....
   Reifen: vorn ....   hinten ....
    Misch.:   vorn ....   hinten ....

Bremsen
   Bremszange ....   Kolben Ø ....   Belag ....
   Bremsscheibe ....   Bremskraftverteilung ....

Sonstiges: ....
....

*Stuck/Bell and Holbert
duplicated their 1986 win
again in 1987, the Porsche
defeating a very strong
attack from the TWR
Jaguars in a race run
throughout at sprint pace.*

in the third XJR-8. His car rolled, but fortunately he (very) narrowly escaped injury to himself.

Because of all the accidents and resultant safety car periods, Peter Falk was able to instruct his drivers to turn down their turbo boost and save fuel. It gave the leading Porsche enough margin to keep the surviving Jaguars at bay.

'This was Stuck's work during the night,' recalls Falk, 'to push and push, and to push them down.'

When Martin Brundle's Jaguar retired at dawn, Stuck, Bell and Holbert were able to maintain a very substantial lead through Sunday. They finished no less than 20 laps ahead of the Obermaier 962C of Jürgen Lässig, Pierre Yver and Bernard de Dryver.

'This was a very hard 23 hours for us,' laughs Falk today, 'and I don't mean only for the drivers! It was a very good race for us.'

This was a race Porsche hadn't expected to win, but that made the ultimate victory all that much sweeter. It was a fitting thank you to long-time sponsors Rothmans, who made their last appearance with Porsche at this race.

The only other notable win for a Porsche customer

in the shorter races of the WSPC that year came at the Norisring. This race was split into two heats of just over 100 miles each.

Britten-Lloyd Racing (Richard Lloyd's team name now reflecting the new interest of John Britten) had rebuilt their car after it had been comprehensively burned out at Le Mans two weeks previously. The team were given one of the factory's hot 3.0-litre engines and as two drivers were needed, the car was driven by Mauro Baldi and Jonathan Palmer.

Baldi drove a storming first race to beat Stuck's factory 962C. The Weissach car retired in the second heat and gave Palmer an easy run to gain first overall, despite the second heat going to Bob Wollek. Wollek's Joest car was later disqualified for having a fuel capacity which was just over the permitted maximum of 100-litres. This was an honest enough mistake as tank capacity on the Group C cars was managed by adding or taking out little plastic balls, and it was all-too-easy to get the number of these required mixed up.

Porsche used the Norisring to announce that it had decided to withdraw from further participation in the

The cockpit of the 962 had become very full with gauges and controls by 1987. This is the PDK-equipped version with steering wheel-mounted push-buttons and a digital display to tell the driver which gear was selected.

WSPC that year. The decision assured the championship for Jaguar.

Fuel quality, as well as fuel consumption, had been a major headache for all the top teams in 1987. At that time, Formula One was rife with special fuels and although octane-enhancing additives were banned in Group C, there was no shortage of interpretations as to what constituted a standard fuel.

'The FIA perfectly described the requirements for octane number and vaporising point,' says Peter Falk. 'We were allowed to go outside of the paddock and take fuel from a normal petrol station. Normally you would go to the petrol station in the paddock. I remember there was some trouble with Walkinshaw because he went outside and took his fuel from Esso or Shell or something like that. OK, we did the same later, but we didn't know what happened with Walkinshaw's drums. It was the same with Fiorio [of Lancia] too!'

Falk is sure Lancia stayed within the rules. 'We know Lancia didn't [use additives] because we had proved that! We were in Monza and we noticed that Lancia didn't go to the fuel station and that they had brought their own drums.

'We wanted to know what was in those drums, so I said to Mr Schæffer to try and get some. So he took a big pan, that we used for cleaning parts. He went to the park behind the Lancias and he found one of the mechanics. He asked if he could have some fuel for cleaning. And he gave him some! So we had some fuel and we had it analysed,' he laughs, 'but it was OK.'

During this time, Weissach had more than its fair share of blown engines. The engineers were pushing the limits of the compression ratio and ignition timing in an effort to stretch fuel consumption, but detonation had become a serious issue.

'The nearer you could come to that point [where detonation occurs],' says Norbert Singer, 'the better the fuel consumption you get. If you go beyond that point, you get a burned piston.'

Falk says he doesn't know if other competitors were using banned [octane-enhancing]) additives such as toluene, but to quote an old English proverb, 'there is no smoke without fire'. The FIA moved to legislate on fuel at the start of 1987. Toluene and all aromatic additives were banned, and the fuel octane number was restricted to 97.

Peter Falk with Tom Walkinshaw in 1987. Walkinshaw would win the World Sports Prototype Championship with the Silk Cut Jaguar team, but the Rothmans team denied him from winning at Le Mans.

The issue did not seem to be too much of a concern at the slower tracks such as Jerez and Jarama at the start of the new season, but when the cars came to the high-speed Monza, there were big problems.

Eight 962 engines were destroyed, including those of Joest, Brun and Britten-Lloyd Racing. There was uproar from the customer Porsche teams, who believed the commercial-grade fuel available in the paddock at Monza was sub-standard.

'It was written in the regulations that you had to use normal pump fuel that you could get from a gas station,' continues Norbert Singer.

'I knew somebody who could check fuel samples. He was from an institute where they can do that. He took samples in Spain, in Jerez. He took a sample of a normal fuel in the city. There was a gas station outside the circuit and there was a gas station in the paddock. He took three samples and they were all from the same company – and they were all different results!

'We asked the question what they meant by normal, standard fuel. Lots of people realised that standard fuel doesn't mean anything. You take Aral or Shell or BP, and everybody says: "Ah! They could be different!" A Shell in Stuttgart is different from a Shell in Munich or Weissach or wherever. It wasn't defined. So people started to think they could put a little extra in and this would help the fuel consumption. You can adjust the engine to that – the compression ratios and that sort of thing – and in the end you gain a lot.'

But of course the risk is that the engine will suffer damaging pre-detonation – the fuel will ignite like in a diesel engine as it compresses on the firing stroke, and this is what happened at the high-speed circuits such as Monza.

'It was detonation and there was no knock sensor in those days,' says Singer. 'Afterwards, I would drive to the races in a 944 car that had a knock sensor. We got some equipment connected to it and we used Weissach fuel as a baseline.

'We would try the race fuel – and this is something Mr Falk liked to do [at this point Singer rocks with laughter] – and we would check that. But it wasn't so easy.

'He had to run flat out – it was on normal roads – but then he would have to be on the brakes at a certain speed and at certain revs, so he could check the knock. Then he could see whether the local fuel was the same or less quality than what we had. If it was less, we had to reduce the ignition timing, and we did that at every track.'

'We prepared a 944 engine with variable ignition points,' says Falk. 'We put racing fuel into that car and drove it on public roads around the circuit so that we could find the earliest ignition point. Then we had a measure for the quality of the fuel. 'From that we could programme the Motronic. There was a big variation of the octane number from circuit to circuit and from the paddocks to the outside.'

It was this 944 that saved the Rothmans team at Le Mans in 1987. After Vern Schuppan's Rothmans 962C dropped out with a burned piston, he was grabbed for some additional duties. He was installed in the 944 with an engineer bent over the car's computer and told to drive flat out on the roads around Le Mans. The engineer worked out the correct engine mapping for the quality of fuel being supplied in the pits and on their return, duplicate chips were installed in the surviving cars.

The fuel controversy blighted the season for many teams and the problem wasn't really resolved to everybody's satisfaction until this new chip became freely available.

PICKING UP THE PIECES

11

AL HOLBERT EXPERIENCED a significant change in the competitiveness of his opposition during the 1987 IMSA season. While the Löwenbräu took a second straight victory in the season-opening Daytona 24 Hours, the blue and white car would only win three times during the remainder of the season. This included one win at Lime Rock for Holbert himself, and two for the team's new recruit, Chip Robinson, at Portland and San Antonio (with Derek Bell).

Nevertheless, Robinson won the Camel GTP Championship by finishing consistently rather than taking multiple wins. It was the third straight year that Porsche had won the IMSA GTP Championship of Makes.

Robinson's single solo win fell some way short of the performances of Jochen Mass (four wins) or Bobby Rahal (three wins) – team-mates in the Bruce Leven-owned Bayside 962s. Price Cobb in the Rob Dyson-entered car also took three wins in 1987, Cobb winning the Porsche Cup North America for the second year.

Like the better European 956 teams before them, the best IMSA customers had found ways of staying

Al Holbert, Derek Bell and Al Unser Jnr took their second consecutive win at Daytona in 1987. This is Derek in the 1986 race where the team made up for the disappointment of the previous year. In the closest Daytona finish ever, they finished just ahead (on the same lap) as the Preston Henn 962. (Geoffrey Hewitt)

on nearly level terms with the Holbert 962, and despite the near-domination by Porsches, the Camel GTP championship had never been more popular with the fans.

'There wasn't a factory car as such,' says Derek Bell, 'and as far as the crowds were concerned, you had the Löwenbräu Porsche, the Budweiser Porsche and the Coca-Cola Porsche all fighting each other. You had all these people and the crowds, the fans, loved it. It was so much bigger than in Europe – and you know Rothmans promoted it really well – but in America, the whole thing was to the public. They'd say: "There's the Bayside car!" or "There's Bobby Rahal in the Budweiser car!" You had this tremendous following.

'It didn't matter that they were all Porsches. It was bloody good racing. Even when the Jags and the Ford [Probe] came in, they had different noises but they all looked much the same. It was like F1, if they'd been in one colour you would have had a hell of a job [spotting the difference].'

At the racetracks, the new Porsche Motorsport North America support operation had been built up from nothing by Holbert, since the 962 had appeared in

early 1984. In those early days, customers had been knocked out of races by not having access to the smallest of spare parts, but by 1987, the huge support truck that attended every Camel GTP race had parts to build at least two full 962s. A second truck supported the Trans-Am and 944 production championships. The support operation was headed by Peter Schmitz, who maintained a flourishing business both selling, and in the case of engines, leasing, components to the teams.

In terms of engine development, the programme was entirely home-grown. With only two or three staff assigned to sports car engine development worldwide, Weissach's Valentin Schæffer was fully stretched to help Alwin Springer's IMSA programme. But nonetheless, Springer had built a substantial operation and was supplying the engines for a large majority of the front-running 962 teams, and the Andial name appeared on all the IMSA-winning Porsches. The task was made much more difficult because IMSA kept moving the goal-posts in a bid to give the non-Porsche opposition a chance.

In 1984, the capacity limit for forced-induction, production-based engines had been a maximum of

Mauro Baldi, Brian Redman and Bob Wollek looked set to win the 1988 Daytona 24 Hours for Jim Busby until the car collided with a Jaguar XJR-9. Damaged bodywork was enough to let another XJR-9 through to win by a lap. (Geoffrey Hewitt)

The Baldi, Redman, Wollek 962 leads the Rob Dyson-entered 962 driven by Dyson himself, Price Cobb, James Weaver and Vern Schuppan at the 1988 Daytona 24 Hours. Following is one of the Jaguars and the Walter Brun 962 driven by Massimo Sigala, Oscar Larrauri and Gian Franco Brancatelli. (Geoffrey Hewitt)

3.57-litres with a minimum weight of 900kg (1,985lb). By 1987, this had been teased down to a maximum of 3-litres with a minimum weight of 930kg (2,051lb).

In the meantime, various attempts had been made to give both normally aspirated, production-based engines and racing engines more of an opportunity.

The Tullius Jaguars took advantage of the maximum capacity increase in 1986 to stretch the Jaguar V12 from 6-litres to 6.5-litres, but the cars were handicapped by an increase in minimum weight from 900kg to 943kg (2,079lb). The bad news for the Group 44 team was that Springer was able to find more from the Porsche turbo to meet that improvement.

For 1988, Tom Walkinshaw Racing was planning to enter IMSA with a full 7-litre V12, but these hopes were dashed when IMSA froze the capacity limit and only relaxed the minimum weight in the normally aspirated class to 930kg. The new TWR Jaguars rolled out that year with just 6-litre engines.

For that season, IMSA made a big effort to cut the advantage of the turbocharged engines. Forced-induction engines had to adopt an inlet restrictor of 57mm, this being placed within 50mm of the turbo's inlet air compressor.

The organisers also saw the coming of the four-valve, all water-cooled Porsche engine and they decided they did not want it. They did not ban it as such, but dictated that it should run with 36mm restrictors, a 3-litre maximum capacity and a minimum car weight of 953kg (2,062lb). Subsequently, and after much negotiation, the restrictor size was relaxed slightly.

Placing restrictors on a turbo engine was a completely new variable of which Porsche had little experience. Norbert Singer recalls the time, a little later, when the FIA asked Weissach to comment on such devices. 'It was quite complicated. I remember we did a test and it worked so-so. On the dyno, you can run at stable revs. Then we ran it on a car and well, it showed it wasn't so bad. We could work with that.'

With Porsche marking time on its sports car programme in Weissach, Don Devendorf's IMSA

In 1988, Derek Bell and Chip Robinson drove the Holbert 962 in the gold and white colours of the Miller Brewing concern. This is Robinson on the way to second place at the July Watkins Glen race. (Geoffrey Hewitt)

Nissan team perfected a device that would give them a winning advantage in 1988 – an electronically controlled wastegate.

This ensured that even if the top-end power was reduced, in the mid-speed ranges, engine torque remained virtually as it had been without the restrictor.

By this time, Andial had changed away from the factory-specified KKK turbocharger to the US-made Garrett AiResearch products. 'That was a very simple decision,' says Alwin Springer. 'The KKK people [in the US] didn't have a lot of experience. The Garrett people are like, 20 minutes away from us [in Santa Ana] and they were on the ball. They would work closely with us to get a turbo that was matched to the engine, its mapping and everything else. KKK would just supply the turbo and say that's it, have a good time!'

The introduction of restrictors tested the knowledge of everyone involved in the IMSA development.

'It took us a long time – and even today – to understand what the restrictor did to the turbo's performance. It hit us cold. But on the other hand it hit everybody else cold. Don Devendorf from Nissan actually out-foxed us. He had it under control and was steps ahead of everybody, both on the electronics and controlling the boost.

'That was the main thing. It was so simple. There's a point as the revs build when you get maximum boost and then it falls off. When the airflow through the restrictor gets to sonic speed, nothing works any more. You could see it because the horsepower would flatten off and the turbo rpm and the exhaust temperature would go up and up. What you wanted to do was to have the boost come up as fast as possible and then come down, because if the airflow got to that sonic point, it would kill everything. So you would stop your rpm at about 8,000, and with the normal wastegate, with springs, you couldn't do that. That was Devendorf's advantage. He did it electronically. He had a good chassis combination and he knew how to get the power on the ground and the engine to produce more torque. He had electronic wastegates in '84, and all credit to him.'

After, three straight years of IMSA domination, 1988 did not look promising for Porsche. While Holbert began to spend more and more time developing the new IndyCar programme, the sports car team struggled. Holbert Racing now ran their self-built HR chassis in the white and gold colours of Miller beer,

but from the very first race, they had a steep mountain to climb.

While seven Porsches filled the first nine places of the 1988 Daytona 24 Hours, the new IMSA Jaguar XJR-9 was first, with another in third. But it would prove to be a false dawn for Jaguar.

Porsches won in Miami and Sebring – the latter going to Bruce Leven's consistently competitive Bayside Motorsports team of Klaus Ludwig and Hans-Joachim Stuck. Then, at Road Atlanta, the new Electramotive Nissan ZXT claimed its first victory – from a Jaguar.

The Nissan, with drivers Geoff Brabham and John Morten, then proceeded to take eight straight wins in 1988. While Brabham took the Camel GTP drivers' title, Porsche salvaged the Makes Championship solely by weight of points-scoring finishes further down the order.

Bosch reacted immediately to Nissan's technological advantage, and the Porsche factory cars ran similar devices at Le Mans in June 1988. The new Motronic release – 1.7 – was made available to customer IMSA

After Jaguar had broken Porsche's run of victories at the Daytona 24 Hours in 1988, the British team were (just) unable to repeat the feat the following year. Bob Wollek, Derek Bell and John Andretti staged another very close finish – a little under a whole lap ahead after 24 hours of racing. (Geoffrey Hewitt)

By 1989, the Busby 962 was on its third chassis (and known as 108C) and had been extensively developed. Most noticeable were the considerably remodelled rear body aerodynamics – the work of Roman Slobodinskyj. (Geoffrey Hewitt)

teams from shortly after this, but the 962s were never able to get back on terms with Nissan. It was a time of great frustration, as Derek Bell remembers.

'America is the biggest market in the world for any manufacturer,' he says, recalling Porsche's position in IMSA by the end of 1987. 'For someone who was going to buy a Porsche, IndyCar racing or F1 racing meant nothing. Porsche history has always been sports car racing, and in America there was such a tremendous fan base for real road racing. We were always getting 40,000 to 50,000 and right up to 100,000 people at some races. It was a big show. Jaguar was in there and Mazda and Toyota. We had one hell of a show going with good TV and big prize money. It was like $40,000 for a win and then if you won three races in a row, you picked up another $60,000 from the Camel pyramid. It was real entertainment, but Porsche were not aware at all of what was happening in sports car racing in America

'By 1988, they didn't know what to do next. That was when Al said we needed a new car, that we were getting beaten. But Porsche said they couldn't afford it. I think they said it would cost

something like $16 million, and Al said he would do it for $1.6 million.

Sadly, the plans were blown apart on 30 September, when Al Holbert was killed. His light aircraft crashed near Columbus, Ohio. Holbert, then 41, had won more IMSA races than any other driver (49) and had won the title no less than five times. He had won numerous SCCA Can-Am races, competed in CART and had won the Le Mans 24 Hours three times. This deeply religious and devoted family man was a very severe loss to the motorsports world in general, but doubly so to the Porsche community in North America.

It was an event that was to change the life of Andial's Alwin Springer. 'Al Holbert was, first of all, a very honest and open guy,' he says. 'He was sincere. When he said we do it this way, you didn't need a contract or anything. You could take his word for it. He was a very good leader. He could show people that he could do something and then he would expect it from you. He was high on expectations, but always very fair, and as a personal friend, I lost a very good one.'

By late 1988, Andial was deeply involved in the Porsche Motorsport North America headline programmes, both IMSA and IndyCars. Their facility in Santa Ana was expanding. 'We had one building where we did the street [tuning parts] and the racing. In 1987, we wanted to go into IndyCar racing and Holbert made it clear that we would have a customer focus and we would do the engines. So we bought the second building right beside the existing one and we turned that into a race shop.'

But when Holbert died everything came to a stop. 'It was a little tough. We wanted to build a new car [for IMSA] and we were talking to Weissach about taking the Indy engine and converting that into a [sports car] engine. There was a study, but maybe because Al died, it somehow died. Nothing happened. 'After Al's death, the whole programme pretty much came to a stop.'

Derek Bell also recalls the vacuum.

'He was going to build his own car. The day he died he came up with a model – an eighth-scale model – and he said to me that this was the car we were going to drive the following year.'

'We had all the plans made,' echoes Springer. 'I saw the drawings. We were going to build the car in England and we hoped that we would get the Indy engine developed into this. Weissach would have done that. They would have done the basics and we would have taken over. It would have been a new chassis with all Holbert's experience.'

Bell continues. 'Helmut Flegl [who, in late-1988 had taken over the role of Porsche Sports head from Peter Falk] came over after the accident and asked what we should do. There were so many questions that needed answers, like who was going to put the team [for 1989] together and who was going to run it. We needed Al because he was so technically knowledgeable.

'I felt I had to do something to keep the team going. But I didn't live in America. I should have taken the bull by the horns and got a really good engineer to run the project and carry on, but I think Porsche said they were going to close down the team. I had the greatest admiration for Al of any person that I have driven with. He was so calm.'

Porsche Motorsport began a relocation from Holbert's Warrington, Pennsylvania base to the PCNA headquarters in Reno, Nevada. Both PR head Bob Carlson and parts head Peter Schmitz moved to Reno. However, the IndyCar team remained in Warrington with Flegl overseeing the hiring of Penske's Derrick

Alwin Springer emerged as Porsche Motorsport's front man after Al Holbert's untimely passing. Springer was a reluctant leader, but would guide Porsche's sporting interests in North America during the 1990s and beyond, with great sensitivity. (Geoffrey Hewitt)

Walker and Newman-Haas engineer Tony Cicale for the relaunched effort.

The sports car support would also take a new direction. By this time, Andial had consolidated their support of the 962 customer racers in IMSA, but were still only supplying engines. It was left to individual teams to drive forward chassis development – and in particular aerodynamics.

Holbert had tried hard to get IMSA to reduce the volume of the underbody air ducts in all IMSA cars for 1989, because the new water-cooled engine was wider than the old air/water unit. Unfortunately, the proposal came rather too late and the 962s battled on as before.

After Holbert's death, Jim Busby's BF Goodrich operation emerged as the preferred team for any development pieces from Porsche. By 1989, Busby's principal chassis was a significantly reconstructed 962 that dated back to 1985 (chassis 108). This brand-new chassis had been written off at Daytona in 1985 and as 108B emerged after a rebuild with a new Jim Chapman honeycomb monocoque that Busby himself had commissioned. Bob Wollek suffered a huge accident in 108B at Sears Point in 1987. Many put the Frenchman's survival down to the honeycomb structure of that car. But 108 surfaced again, and as 108C, with another Chapman tub and driven by Wollek, Redman and Baldi, it finished a close second to Jaguar at Daytona in 1988.

This car then embarked on a substantial development process, driven principally by Busby's renowned mechanical engineer Roman Slobodinskyj (who had designed the Indy 500 pole-winning Eagle in 1972, the novel 'laydown' Offy of the mid-1970s and the 1980 Interscope-Porsche P6B chassis). Combined with the substantially improved Goodrich tyres, Busby's significantly reworked 962 became a thorn in the side of the dominant Jaguars and Nissans.

This by-now famous car sealed its position in the record books when Wollek, Bell and John Andretti won the 1989 Daytona 24 Hours. That event was also notable for the official retirement of the late Holbert's championship-winning Löwenbräu 962 103. Holbert's pit crew ran a final tribute to their boss in the form of the second Miller/BF Goodrich car (962 119) for Mario and Michael Andretti.

The winning 962 finished only a few minutes ahead of the TWR Jaguar after stirring drives from all the drivers involved. Wollek and Andretti would triumph again at the West Palm Beach track in April.

Sadly however, the two victories did not begin a trend that the Goodrich/Miller car (or any other 962) could maintain against the still-dominant Nissans and TWR Jaguars.

By this time, the hard-worked 108C's appearance had been substantially updated. Apart from its distinctive gold and white Miller Beer colours, Slobodinskyj had remodelled the tail, using the now-popular centre-strut aerofoil mounting. But where the engineer found an advantage over other IMSA 962s was by mounting the (two-element) wing much lower and closer to the rear body than before, so that its effect actually helped draw air out of the underbody ducts. Large, rear side-panels to the car's tail section gave this high-downforce car a completely unique look. Slobodinskyj would also revise the nose section and cooler outlets on this car, substantially improving its overall downforce.

The success of the Busby team led the factory to loan them the lightweight 962 that Hans-Joachim

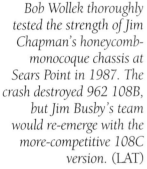

Bob Wollek thoroughly tested the strength of Jim Chapman's honeycomb-monocoque chassis at Sears Point in 1987. The crash destroyed 962 108B, but Jim Busby's team would re-emerge with the more-competitive 108C version. (LAT)

Stuck had used for the German national Supercup sprint series in 1988, but chassis 009 did not find favour with Busby's team.

So much development had been directed into 108C, that it was like starting again with 009. The factory chassis was found to be too flexible, compared with the very high stiffness of the Chapman tub and this reflected a complete contrast to the set-up of the European 962s. IMSA 962s tended to run far softer suspension with a much-stiffer chassis than the Europeans'.

By this time, Weissach had also announced that it was unlikely that a replacement car for the 962 would be constructed until 1992. The Indy project was in full swing and there had been a decision to focus what small budget there was for sports car racing on the existing 962. Another factor however, was a changing climate in IMSA.

In early 1989, John Bishop had sold out to a new organisation, who had declared an intention to move towards the FIA's new F1-rules sports cars by 1992. By favouring 3.5-litre racing engines, the outlook for Porsche's flat-six, and the 962, did not look good.

Springer had begun development of the four-valve, full water-cooled engine from the middle of 1988 in a bid to come to terms with the increasingly superior competition. The engine used two smaller turbos and there was significant discussion with IMSA over the size of the restrictors. IMSA initially wanted a restrictor size of just 36mm, but relented to 38mm. The new engine ran with Motronic 1.7, complete with electronically controlled wastegates.

Since the engine was largely the same as that used at Le Mans in 1988, Springer had to begin again by adapting the long-distance, fuel-efficient motor to the sprint conditions and high torque requirement of IMSA.

The water-cooled engine still wasn't on the tracks by mid-summer and by August, Jaguar had introduced its new XJR-10 carbon-fibre chassis with a new V6 twin-turbo engine. Nissan would respond with its own new engine.

IMSA variety in 1989 was further widened by the entry of All-American Racers with the Toyota 88C. Dan Gurney's team began a learning year with a rapid 2.1-litre four-cylinder turbo, prior to their first victories in 1990.

For Andial – and their customers – getting the Porsche twin-turbo engine competitive was becoming

The Busby 962 after a night's hard work, here driven by Bob Wollek. This view shows the very low position of the rear aerofoil. Note the movie camera in the cockpit. (Geoffrey Hewitt)

By 1990, the 962 was largely outclassed by the Electramotive Nissans. This is the Dyson 962 of James Weaver and Scott Pruett at the Miami Grand Prix. They finished third behind two Nissans. (Geoffrey Hewitt)

an urgent requirement, but unfortunately, IMSA's new owners didn't appear to share the same opinion.

In trying to please the newcomers to the Camel GTP Championship, the IMSA seemed to make sure the Porsche twin-turbo was mandated out of competitiveness. Despite the punitive restrictors however, the 962's resilience became a feature of these later years. The car just kept popping up in the results.

Meanwhile, with fading prospect of a new sports car, Porsche Motorsport North America (outside the largely Weissach-run IndyCar project) struggled to recover from the loss of Al Holbert.

'It was an organisation without a leader,' says Alwin Springer. 'Helmut Flegl approached me to take over Porsche Motorsport in North America and from there we made a start.

'In 1990, I took over the helm of Porsche Motorsports in the United States, but as a consultancy

business. At that stage, I didn't have a reason to quit Andial. I had a good partnership and they [Porsche] had to show me first why I should quit. They pushed me, but I said I wanted to make 20 years [with Andial]. That was 1995. At that point we gained financial control and by the beginning of 1997, we said OK, and we took it over.'

Jim Busby switched to Nissan for 1990 and as a result, Rob Dyson's 962 took over the title as most-developed IMSA 962 to date, with revised aerodynamics and suspension.

The highlights included Bob Wollek's pole position for the opening Daytona 24 Hours in Bruce Leven's Bayside 962. He, Sarel van der Merwe and Dominic Dobson, would finish third behind two Jaguar XJR-12s. The only win in a year dominated by the Electramotive Nissans was achieved by the Dyson car, driven by James Weaver, at the September Tampa race.

The victory was welcome, but the reality was that the 962 had become outdated. Springer knew that the only real solution was a new car, and with Group C in disarray, this was unlikely.

'From 1989, you could see the car couldn't really handle it any more,' says Springer. 'The other guys advanced and we couldn't do it.'

When the Porsche business went into steep recession worldwide in 1991, there was no question of a new car or engine. 'We were down,' adds Springer with a finality.

But, as several determined team owners would prove in the coming years, the 962 was not quite finished in North America.

In the 1988 Group C World Sports Prototype Championship, the TWR Jaguars won six races to Sauber's five. With huge amounts of mid-range torque from the XJR-9's 750bhp V12 and the mildly blown Mercedes-Benz V8 in the Sauber, good for at least 700bhp, there was not a lot of opportunity for the Porsche 962. With the WSPC events getting shorter and being staged at more and more of the made-for-TV tracks, the principal engine requirement was instant torque – and lots of it.

There was no direct Weissach involvement in the wider WSPC in 1988, except for Le Mans. The team that received the closest support was Joest Racing, although general customer support in 1988 was as strong as ever.

'We had a really good friendship with Mr Singer and Mr Falk,' says Reinhold Joest. 'We could compete at

the track over the weekend, but when we had technical problems, I could go there and talk very openly. They helped us a lot and maybe we helped them. When they were not so involved themselves they would use us to try and develop some things. We still had some good ideas.

'We changed the bodywork to the single-wing system and the car was immediately two seconds faster. We talked all these things through and Mr Singer said we could check the car in the wind tunnel. His services were for free, but when we tested in Weissach, we had to pay – always!'

Nonetheless, it was a bleak year in 1988 for Porsche Group C teams hoping to stand on the podium. The only major victory was in the non-championship Kyalami 500 for Bob Wollek, Frank Jelinski and Wayne Taylor in a Joest 962, and even this was in the absence of Jaguar.

All the customer teams from the previous year entered cars in 1989, and there was a new face in the form of Jochen Dauer. Dauer had bought up the John Fitzpatrick cars at the end of 1986 and had been competing in the German Supercup and European Interserie championships in 1987 and 1988.

Accepting the importance of the Japanese market for its production car sales, Weissach sent a single car

to Fuji in October for Klaus Ludwig and Price Cobb to drive. They were only able to finish second behind Cheever and Brundle's XJR-9 however.

Ludwig had been leading when he believed a brake disc had broken. The resulting pit-stop revealed nothing was amiss, but by this time the Jaguar was past. It rubbed salt in the wounds of a season when Porsche could do little about the advancing opposition.

The one race in 1988 that Porsche tried very hard to win was Le Mans. It was the final show-down between Weissach and a TWR Jaguar team desperate to win the famous race after two defeats in 1986 and 1987. The brief from their Jaguar masters to the British team could only have been: 'Win at all costs'.

It was one of the more memorable 24 Hours in recent times. The race was run in fine weather, save for a brief rain shower on Sunday morning. The crowds were huge and the racing was run at grand prix speeds throughout.

Five TWR XJR-9LM models were entered. Three were run by the regular WSPC team and two by Jaguar's IMSA team manager Tony Dowe (and driven by US-based drivers).

For the first time in seven years, the factory Porches were not carrying Rothmans colours. Three cars were

Hans-Joachim Stuck tests the factory 962C at Weissach in preparation for the 1988 Le Mans. In seven seasons of racing, it is remarkable how little the exterior of the car has changed, and in the long-distance endurance races, it barely seemed to matter.

prepared in the colours of Shell and Dunlop, with Stuck, Ludwig and Bell in one car; Wollek, van der Merwe and Schuppan in the second, and Mario, Michael and John Andretti in a third. All were conventionally bodied long-tail 962Cs (010, 007 and 008 respectively).

There might have been an air of finality about this Weissach entry, but it was very serious and much preparation had gone into the visit to France.

Most notably, the 962's 3-litre all water-cooled engine received the Motronic 1.7 engine management, which included Bosch's first attempt at electronic control of the turbochargers' wastegates. This improved the mid-range torque, which was seen as a critical shortfall to the Jaguar and Mercedes powerplants.

Supporting the factory cars were eight private 962Cs from the leading customers. All were running the older Motronic 1.2.

What was noticeable about the customer entries was that a majority were using aftermarket chassis on their cars, particularly the aluminium-honeycomb version from TC Prototypes, the Northampton

The Wollek, Van der Merwe and Schuppan 962C retired from the 1988 Le Mans 24 Hours just before dawn.

enterprise run by John Thompson (and in which Tony Southgate had an interest).

Joest hedged his bets by running one standard factory chassis and an improved version of a Thompson chassis. He recalls he wasn't all that impressed with the British tubs.

'We had a lot of problems with it. Later on the chassis was not stiff enough, so we changed the whole underbody to a steel plate. Then it was stiff enough.'

Hans-Joachim Stuck repeated his startling Le Mans speed and claimed pole position with a stunning 3min 15.64sec lap, an average speed of 154.76mph (249kph). In the process, his 962C was recorded at 241mph (387.8kph) on the newly resurfaced and non-chicaned Hunaudières Straight. This speed nearly equalled the 246mph (396kph) best set by the long-tail 917s back in 1971. The three factory Porsches started 1-2-3.

Stuck went into an early lead at the start but was soon overhauled by the charging Jaguar of Jan Lammers. After three hours, Porsche's lead car, now driven by Klaus Ludwig, ran out of fuel at

Indianapolis. Ludwig had to coax the 962C round to the pits on the starter. He had been expecting the fuel reserve light to come on during his in-lap, but the fuel pump was unable to draw the remaining eight or so litres from the tank.

'He wanted to do a lap more, as was usual for him with Joest,' explains Peter Falk. 'He thought that because he could do it with Joest, he could do it with Porsche! But it didn't work that time!'

'We had trouble later on with this car, when we found we couldn't drain the tank. Later, beyond the halfway point, we had to refuel after six, seven or eight laps. Normally we can do ten or eleven. So we had at least one or two pit stops more than usual. There was a little filter to clean the fuel, not a fine filter but a bigger filter [like a mesh], just before the fuel pump. It wouldn't pick up all the fuel.

'It was very, very difficult to change the filter with the fuel tank in the car, but two mechanics came to me and said it was impossible to continue if we were getting only eight laps per tank. They asked to try to change it.

'I had to decide because there was a risk the car could catch fire [in the pits]. But they did it, and it worked. We were getting 12 laps again.

'On the last lap when we were [running with] Jaguar, Ludwig told me on the radio that he had misfiring and he wasn't sure if he could get back to the pits. He had to change to the reserve – and that was not normal! – so maybe this [new] filter was also full of contamination. Perhaps when this had happened to him the first time, the filter was already full. I don't know.'

Falk believes that debris from the fuel tank blocked the filter. 'It had been a new fuel tank, with new rubber.'

Ludwig's first stop cost the leading Porsche two laps. It left the Wollek, van der Merwe and Schuppan 962C head-to-head with the leading Jaguar. When Lammers was pushed from behind by Jesus Pareja's Brun 962, the Jaguar had to pit for repairs and Porsche led again.

At midnight, it was the Wollek car in first place by a full two laps, followed by the Lammers Jaguar and the Andretti Porsche, but just after 3am the Wollek Porsche was out with a failed water pump. The Andrettis were also slowed when a turbocharger had to be changed on their car.

By this time, the Watson/Boesel/Pescarolo XJR-9 had also retired with a failed gearbox and the same

problem had seriously delayed the Sullivan/Jones/Cobb car.

Out of this carnage, the Stuck, Bell and Ludwig 962C clawed its way back on to the same lap as the leading Jaguar by dawn. Appropriately, it was Ludwig who led the Porsche charge.

Sunday morning witnessed one of the finest duels Le Mans has ever seen, with the Lammers, Dumfries and Wallace in the leading XJR-9 trading first place with the Porsche. But it appeared the Jaguar was slightly better at using its fuel allocation and the Porsche was being forced to stop earlier because of the fuel filter blockage.

Meanwhile, the Brundle/Nissan Jaguar retired. The other Jaguar, driven by Daly, Perkins and Cogan, was embroiled in a struggle with the leading Joest Porsche of Dickens, Krages and Jelinski, but these two cars could only watch the leaders from a distance.

Lammers brought the Jaguar in to change a cracked windshield, while the Porsche was being badly slowed by the blocked fuel filter. Both cars remained on the same lap, with the Jaguar holding about a minute's

The 1988 Le Mans 24 Hours came down to a duel between the 962 of Hans Stuck (here), Derek Bell and Klaus Ludwig, and the Jaguar XJR-9LM of Jan Lammers, Johnny Dumfries and Andy Wallace. The Jaguar won by a single lap. (LAT)

advantage. A brief rain shower allowed Stuck to close the gap, but the margin widened again when the Porsche's filter was changed. This cat-and-mouse game went through the whole morning and into the afternoon. Porsche was not able to close the gap any further, and there were a lot of 'ifs' in this, one of the greatest Le Mans races ever, but it became Jaguar's race. Both cars finished on the same lap.

As an aside to the 1988 Le Mans 24 Hours, there remains an intriguing unanswered question. Among those I have spoken to in the course of researching this text, there has been a consistent reference over the actual amount of fuel some cars used to get to the flag.

There is an implication that perhaps the playing field might have been more level for some than others.

From the beginning of Group C, the fuel allowance at Le Mans had been just 2,210 litres. Year after year at Le Mans the allowance had repeatedly altered the character of the race as teams struggled to stay within the allowances. Thankfully, the original plans to reduce the fuel allocation by 15 per cent had finally been scrapped altogether, and it was clear the teams needed a higher, not lower, allowance to ensure a good race. Peter Falk made a proposal to Alain Bertaut in 1985 and from 1986 the allowance was increased to 2,550 litres (561gal), but monitoring the amount of fuel used by each team was a very difficult task. At Le Mans, an ACO pit official was assigned to each car and throughout the event, a record was developed of how much fuel was being taken from the pit garage fuel tank. This is done by reading the gauge on the side of the tank. In theory, this ensured that the car used only its legal fuel allocation, but even the new limit gave the teams a big fuel consumption problem and inevitably, some spotted a loop-hole.

Group C cars have two fuel fillers, one for fuel entry and another for venting the tank as fuel is added. When a car comes in for refuelling, the vent bottle goes on first, followed by the filler hose, but if the vent bottle already contains some fuel, it goes in before the 'official' fuel. The result can be to effectively increase the amount of fuel available to a specific car.

'Yes,' says Norbert Singer, 'I have no proof, but I am pretty sure. I saw some teams and I really saw how they do it, and it's amazing because you had to concentrate so much on that.

'I'm not going to mention a name, but when they prepared for a pitstop, the mechanics came out, the wheels came out and the guy with the fuel hose came out. And [it was at a time in the race when] nearly the whole field was coming in at the same time, so the pit road was very crowded.

'You had to concentrate [on the one team]. Then the cars started arriving – in front and behind – with lots of dust and noise, and I realised the man with the vent bottle wasn't there.

'In front they are preparing everything – the guns, the wrenches and so on. And suddenly the car comes in and the guy with the vent bottle just comes out of the pit and the fuel is in, and nobody could check, but I could see it was full-up! Completely full! The fuel was going back and forth and you could see. After the refuelling and he has taken off the vent bottle, there should normally be two or three litres [overflow], but when the car came back in for refuelling [next time] the bottle was completely full. You could hardly see the fuel slopping around [at the top]!

'Let's say you get 1,000 litres for the race and on the fuel station you see that you put in 80 litres or 85 litres, and with the vent bottle you get the extra fuel. At the end of the race you can afford to make another pitstop and run as fast as you can.

'The procedure is the same for all the races. You have the fuel meter and the steward writes down what you have taken, say 90-something litres or whatever. You have a little left over in the vent bottle and that is taken off the total. He writes [say] 99 litres minus five, and that's the official sheet showing you had 90-something litres. Officially, the vent bottle was meant to be in a certain place which had to be marked and the steward can look at it every time. Of course he can look and there might be five litres left, but when the car comes in, there's another 10 in there!'

The fuel for such top-ups of a leading car would be readily available within a large team, particularly if there had been early retirements, or even if there had not. A look at some vent bottles from 1984 onwards reveals that some teams covered the sides with stickers to make it very difficult to see what was inside. Others even painted their bottles completely!

Singer was not alone in expressing his disappointment over the fuel bottle loophole.

The story goes to show that the stakes in motor racing are very high and that some will go to any lengths to win. The phrase 'unfair advantage' is no stranger to motor racing and to some, unfair, means just that.

A KIND OF MAGIC

12

'I HAVE THAT LITTLE FILTER at home in my workshop,' reflects Peter Falk, of the part that cost Porsche [on the road, anyhow] the 1988 Le Mans 24 Hours. 'It is on the wall. If we had won that race against Jaguar again, then maybe we would have been given more opportunity to do more races in Group C. But in that year we had a change of Board and Mr Branitzki became the chief. He was excited by Le Mans, but he was also a financial man.'

The Weissach racing team was permitted one last outing, at the Nürburgring at the end of September. It was the final round of the German Supercup, as the national sports car series was called at that time.

Hans-Joachim Stuck drove the 850kg 962C (007),

complete with PDK transmission and a very hot (10:1 compression ratio) engine. The fiercely contested Supercup had run since 1986 (replacing the earlier Deutsche Rennsport Meisterschaft) and was hugely popular in Germany for its excellent promotion and good prize money.

Stuck's entry in the works car had been a feature for the past two seasons, but in 1988, he had to contend with the very rapid Sauber-Mercedes C9 of Jean-Louis Schlesser. In so many ways, it was the final show-down between the old endurance campaigner and the best of the new generation of sprint racers.

Porsche made a big effort for the final race at the 'Ring and against the odds, Stuck drove a typically

The 1988 Nürburgring Supercup race was the last event for the Weissach race team with the 962. Here, Hans-Joachim Stuck keeps ahead of a determined Jean-Louis Schlesser in the Sauber-Mercedes.

Peter Falk's race summary for Weissach's last official entry with the 962C – at the Nürburgring Supercup race in September 1988.

accuracy. We did everything step-by-step and very carefully. This was as much for the engineering as for the organisation and the workshop. We tried to make our mistakes only once and not repeat them. There was a part of the workshop that was full of parts that had failed, so that the mechanics could see every day what was bad.

'It was a pleasure for me to see the cars that we made running as we wanted them, that drivers were doing what we wanted (well, mostly!), and then I would say there was the fascination of trying to be better than the others.'

If Porsche had been able to stay directly involved in racing after 1988, Falk has no doubts that a new car and engine would have been required. There has been much talk that the Indy V8 engine might have been suitable, but he says not.

'A chassis was prepared but we never fitted the engine. The Indy engine wasn't good for endurance racing because it was too small [at 2.65-litres] and didn't have the right characteristics for Group C. It was Mr Bott's desire, but I don't think this would have been the right way to go. The better way would have been to install the 928 engine – which the Kremers suggested and Sauber-Mercedes actually did [using their own large-capacity V8]. But Mr Bott would not give us the money to develop this.'

While Weissach focused on the Indianapolis programme in 1989, the professional customer teams were far from finished in the World Sports Prototype Championship (WSPC).

This series was thrown into transition in 1989 by the FIA as they tried to align the championship's appeal (so they thought) with grand prix racing. They created a new class for 750kg, normally aspirated, 3.5-litre prototypes and so that their new cars were not eclipsed by the old campaigners, pushed up the Group C minimum weight to 950kg (2,095lb). The new cars were able to use 'free fuel', while the older Group C cars had to continue to use commercially available fuel, which from 1988, had been increased to 98.7RON. Equally disappointing was that the new owners of IMSA expressed every intention of trying to align their series with the FIA's new direction.

The FIA also determined that there was little appeal in the old-fashioned 1,000km endurance race format for their new world of high-tech sports cars and they introduced a universal 480km distance. Competitors

storming race to win. It was a symbolic high note with which the Weissach race team ended the most successful chapters in Porsche's racing history.

Asked what made the Porsche racing team so strong in the 1980s, Peter Falk replies: 'I would say

had to register for the whole series and would be fined $250,000 for each non-showing. It is no small wonder that many private teams chose to find something else to do.

For several years, Daytona, Sebring and Le Mans had worked together under a group title called the Endurance Triple Crown, and with the FIA and IMSA seemingly determined to change the whole philosophy of sports car racing away from their endurance format, in the coming years these classics stood together while the sports car scene deteriorated into confusion.

The start of a period of very poor relations between the FIA and the ACO began in 1989. Le Mans was not included in the WSPC that year for expressing dissent over the restrictive proposals being made by the FIA, although in fact, the suspension was more to do with a spat between the FIA and the ACO about television rights. Even the French Government became involved during 1990 as the threats bounced backwards and forwards.

In an argument that reflected the myopia of CART and Indianapolis in later years, the failure of the FIA

and the ACO to agree a compromise completely under-estimated the importance of this one race (and for that matter the independently run Daytona and Sebring events) to motorsport as a whole. In the coming years, the widening chasm between endurance racing and F1-style sprints would bring sports car racing to its knees.

In a late 1988 issue of *Christophorus* (Porsche's external magazine), motorsport press officer Jürgen Pippig said: 'Retirement of the factory team doesn't mean Porsche sports cars will disappear from Group C. To the contrary, Porsche will be represented more than ever by a line-up of professionally-operated customer teams. All the material gathered in Weissach will be passed on to customers.' And there was a large number of those.

Brun, Lloyd, Kremer, Obermaier and Dauer all maintained or increased their activities in the WSPC, with many having broader visibility in the USA and Japan. New names in 962Cs included Salamin Racing and Tim Lee-Davey. With so much continuing interest from teams running the ageing 962, it was difficult to believe that Porsche were the uninvited guests at the

When Weissach withdrew from direct participation after the Nürburgring Supercup meeting in 1988, the Joest team gained preferential support in the continuing development of the 962. This is Bob Wollek at the Nürburgring in 1989.

FIA's new party. What the large number of 962s proved however, was that they were still the backbone of sports car racing – it was a fact that seemed to be missed completely by the men in blazers.

Vern Schuppan believed an opportunity existed in the wake of the factory team's withdrawal to supply replacement chassis to those teams still racing the 962. The Australian was basing his expansion on possible Weissach interest in his new Nigel Stroud-designed carbon-fibre 962 monocoque. The Stroud-designed Schuppan chassis was first used by Tim Lee-Davey at Spa in 1989.

'I thought it was potentially quite a good business,' says Vern, 'because I thought here we were, seven or eight years on from the first 956 and still running an ally tub. The cars were becoming more and more desirable to collectors, to the extent that you would buy a new 962 and it would be worth more money than you paid for it. I had the idea that not only would running a carbon chassis improve the handling, making the thing a bit more state of the art, but somebody could buy a brand-new car and swap all the hardware over to one of my tubs.

'That way you could keep the old chassis and you didn't risk writing it off. We used the old 962 005 as the buck. It did all sorts of jobs. I remember it was quite a difficult job as carbon-fibre is thicker than the original aluminium.

'Porsche were going to buy tubs from me and they actually supplied me with all the blueprints, and after we were well advanced on the first one, they did an about-turn and decided to build more tubs themselves. They were just the regular aluminium tubs, and it was at a time when quite a few people were dabbling in it. That certainly mucked it up for me.'

Richard Lloyd persevered with Nigel Stroud's original aluminium-honeycomb design and for Le Mans in 1989, the team had built a second chassis (962 RLR.201). Lloyd sold several cars, including one to Rob Dyson for IMSA and another to the Trust Nisseki team in Japan.

The Kremers had worked with John Thompson to develop both aluminium and carbon-fibre replacement monocoques for the 962. The CK6 series had made Kremer almost independent of Weissach when it came to chassis development and the team had

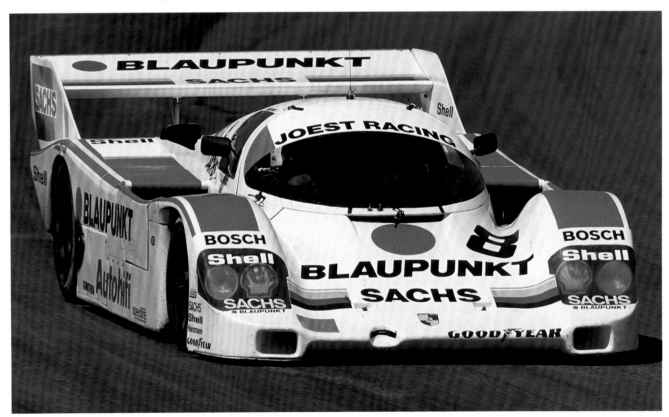

The Weissach-suppported Joest 962C of Bob Wollek and Frank Jelinksi sprang a surprise win at Dijon in May 1989, re-igniting enthusiasm at Porsche for sports car racing, albeit briefly. (LAT)

experimented with monocoques in both aluminium and carbon-fibre (the latter using riveted carbon panels). Both were claimed to be lighter than the standard chassis. Bernd Schneider won the Porsche Cup in 1990 by competing with a Kremer CK6 carbon chassis in the European Interserie Championship.

However, it was Reinhold Joest who expected to benefit the most from Weissach's departure from direct racing involvement. With a nod from Porsche's new research and development head Dr. Ulrich Bez, Joest started work on a new race facility at Wald-Michelbach, not too far from the compact premises at Absteinach.

'Bez told me to make the engine department bigger. He wanted to bring all the engines to our factory.' It was a major investment for Joest, taken on the implication that his team would take a direct role as Weissach's new motorsport representatives.

For the 1989 WSPC, Joest gained support from Blaupunkt, who had been a strong supporter of both the works cars and Joest's own team in the German Supercup.

When the Sauber-Mercedes scored a 1-2 at the opening round in Suzuka, it appeared the die was cast for the rest of the season. Nobody paid too much attention to the Supercup sprint race at Silverstone after that, because Sauber was not present, but at the head of four 962s, Bob Wollek had shown that Reinhold Joest's team was still a force to be reckoned with.

Just a week later, Wollek and Frank Jelinski underlined their Silverstone speed by taking a surprise win at the next championship race at Dijon-Prenois in eastern France. Against the cream of Mercedes, Jaguar and all the others, the form-book had been turned on its head.

It had come down to tyres: the Joest Porsche was running on Goodyears, while the Saubers used Michelins. On a deteriorating, hot surface, Wollek took the lead half an hour into the race and Jelinski maintained it. The Joest 962 was right on the pace of the Saubers, and ahead of a suffering Jaguar. As the race progressed, this was turned into an advantage as the Porsche's Goodyears proved to be the better rubber.

To underline that everything was not lost for the Porsches, the Richard Lloyd 962 200, driven by Derek Bell and Tiff Needell, finished fifth (behind a Toyota) after various niggling problems.

Oscar Larrauri, Walter Brun and Jesus Pareja-Mayo had the agonising misfortune of their car failing with only a few minutes of the 1990 Le Mans 24 Hours remaining. At the French race, to be classified as a finisher the car must cross the finish line under its own power, but Pareja-Mayo had no choice but to leave the car with a broken engine just past the Mulsanne Corner even as the marshals were putting away their flags. They would have finished second, splitting two TWR Jaguars. (LAT)

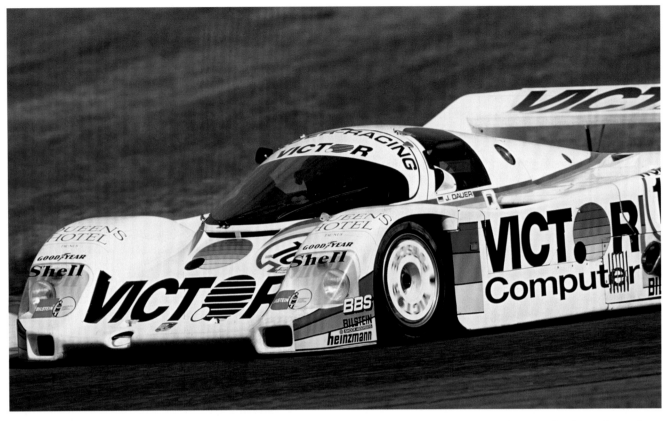

Jochen Dauer had purchased John Fitzpatrick Racing's 962 cars at the end of 1986 and after two seasons in Supercup and Interserie, entered the WSPC in 1989.

The Dijon victory caused all kinds of questions to be asked in Weissach. Reinhold Joest remembers the discussion with some considerable poignancy, as he was already being given the impression that his role with Porsche was going to expand.

'This was the highlight for Bez. He said: "Look! We are the Porsche factory and we can go with Joest and win together!" The idea was to do one year with the 962 and then the following year produce a new sports car.'

Norbert Singer was given time to support the Joest effort and a limited development project focused on the improvement of details. 'We received a small budget when Joest won the Dijon race against Mercedes in 1989,' says Norbert Singer. 'Some people in Weissach began to think that the 962 might be competitive again, but it was down to a problem with their [the Mercedes'] Michelins.

'Afterwards Mercedes changed to Goodyear, but some people said that with a little bit of money we could improve the car and still win. The first thing we did was to get more downforce.'

Perhaps noting the effectiveness of aerodynamicist Peter Stevens's work on the Richard Lloyd cars, the Joest cars adopted revised rear bodywork with a separate rear aerofoil. There were other detail improvements: 'We moved the water pump at the base of the engine to a higher point and that allowed us to have a wider underbody duct. There were some four or five people involved in getting these things done. OK, Joest didn't win any more races, but we improved the car quite a bit.'

But he very nearly did win. At Le Mans 1989, the Joest Porsche almost caused a major upset. The all-star crew in the leading Joest car was Bob Wollek and Hans-Joachim Stuck and these two kept the best 962C in contention throughout. What surprised everyone was not that the Porsche eclipsed the best Jaguar XJR-9LM (which finished fourth), but that the Joest car had the speed to run ahead of the now works-backed Sauber-Mercedes.

During the night the Joest car pulled out a one-lap lead over Peter Sauber's best C9 driven by Jochen Mass, Stanley Dickens and Manuel Reuter (all seasoned ex-962 drivers!), but this was lost when a coolant hose split. Sauber-Mercedes were able to move their other car up to second when the Joest car was further delayed

by a slipping clutch, but Joest was third and Jaguar, on whom so much expectation had been placed for a back-to-back victory, were fourth. Joest's second car, driven by Henri Pescarolo, Claude Ballot-Lena and Jean-Louis Ricci finished sixth just behind the other surviving C9, which had been crippled near the end of the race by a broken transmission.

Wollek and Frank Jelinski continued the respectable results in the WSPC that year by splitting the Sauber-Mercedes at Brands Hatch and at Spa while Harald Huysman and Oscar Larrauri drove Walter Brun's 962C to second in the final round in Mexico.

Against all the odds, Reinhold Joest took second place in the Teams Championship behind Sauber. This accomplishment is measured by the fact that behind him were Walter Brun (third) and then the TWR Jaguars and Nissan Motorsports (Europe).

Dijon proved to be a one-off victory for the Porsches, Mercedes winning every other race in the championship – and Le Mans. Nevertheless, the Weissach management was still enthusiastic and a budget was found to continue the arrangement with Joest and the 962C into 1990.

The trade-off was that it meant throwing away the only measurable performance advantage over the Saubers – the Goodyear tyres. 'We were winning with Goodyear and we went back to Michelin!' recalls Joest, 'and Mercedes-Sauber changed to Goodyear!'

Joest attended a press conference at Weissach around this time and was given a preview of Bez's future ideas for motorsport.

'You know these ideas were not bad. This was [Porsche] coming back to sports cars. They wanted to do this and have Mr Flegl in the USA with CART. Dr Bez made a contract with us for the season, but,' and Joest takes a deep breath as he recalls that 1990 season, 'it was the biggest disaster of my life.'

'So Joest had to leave Goodyear,' reflects Norbert Singer, 'and he had always been a Goodyear team, but he wanted some support from Porsche. We said OK, but because this was a deal Porsche did with Michelin, he had to change.'

The change proved to be problematic for the 962C. 'Oh yes,' smiles Singer, 'the Michelins were completely different. Today, we would say they had typical Michelin handling. They always had radials with very

Vern Schuppan began to develop his own 962 chassis from 1989, but in the meantime he acquired several very competitive ex-Weissach chassis to earn his team's keep in Japan. This is 962 008 at the March 1989 Fuji 500km, previously the Dunlop car that the Andretti family had driven at Le Mans in 1988. At Fuji, Schuppan and Eje Elgh finished second. (LAT)

flexible sidewalls. It gave pretty good grip, but it wasn't so precise – there was some movement there. The Goodyear gave the same grip, but felt more rigid.'

It was a poor decision. With the more-developed 962C, using brand-new monocoques (built by Dave Klym in Atlanta) and the latest 3-litre factory engines, the cars were quick, but fatally handicapped. The first race at Suzuka brought a 16th, then at Monza a fifth, and Silverstone a fourth – and it was Walter Brun's cars – running on Yokohamas – that became the major Porsche force in the WSPC.

At Le Mans, the 962 proved the value of a car built for the purpose. Brun, Oscar Larrauri and Jesus Pareja put on a classic 962 demonstration of maintaining a consistent pace and letting the fancied Nissans and Jaguars fight it out – and suffer the consequences. Jonathan Palmer highlighted the type of year Joest was having when he suffered a massive accident in qualifying on the Mulsanne Straight, between the two new chicanes. Thankfully, he was unhurt.

In 1991, Reinhold Joest turned his back on Group C and set up a race shop in the USA. He started as he hoped to continue, with a win at Daytona that February. Car 962 129 was driven by 'John Winter' (Louis Krages), Frank Jelinski, Henri Pescarolo, Hurley Haywood and Bob Wollek. (Geoffrey Hewitt)

The Joest 962 at Daytona shows that motor racing isn't always a non-contact sport. Joest's IMSA campaign with the 962 would yield consistent results, but only one more win. (Geoffrey Hewitt)

Through the night the Brun Porsche had stayed in the top two and was always in contention for the win. By the last hour the car was one lap down on the leading Jaguar. With what were expected to be just three more laps to do, the Brun Porsche expired at the Mulsanne Corner in one of the most heart-breaking DNFs of recent times.

Two or three months after Reinhold Joest had signed the contract with Porsche for 1990, R&D head Dr Ulrich Bez had flown to Japan and signed a contract with the Footwork organisation. Porsche were going to build an engine for Formula One. By the end of that season, it was obvious that the Stuttgart company had taken on too much.

'At the end of 1990,' recalls Joest, 'the factory said they were finished with racing. It was just too much for them to do sports cars, CART and Formula One.'

The decision came just as Joest had finished moving into the spacious new facility at Wald-Michelbach –

designed to accommodate the much-discussed integration of his and Weissach's race activities.

Joest's team picked itself up for 1991 – and returned to Goodyear tyres. He turned his back on Europe and set up a new IMSA team, beginning another chapter in his team's predictably successful story. Joest opened his account with a victory in the Daytona 24 Hours that year, beating the class-leading Nissans run by Don Devendorf on durability. There were no wins in 1992, but in 1993, the Joest team scored a 1-2 at Elkhart Lake.

From its introduction at the start of 1984 to the last win at Elkhart Lake, the IMSA 962 had achieved an incredible 54 Camel GTP wins.

The negative result of all the FIA's pressure on the ACO was that the Hundaudières Straight on the Le Mans circuit had been disfigured by two chicanes in 1990 – and they had not prevented Palmer from having his frightening accident. The positive side was that after the 1990 race, work started on a brand-new

On his way out to the 1992 Daytona 24 Hours, Vern Schuppan's Japanese backers effectively withdrew from his ambitious road car project, crippling the business. Nevertheless, at Daytona, the Schuppan team 962 came good and only a broken brake caliper denied them the win, the car finishing third. (Geoffrey Hewitt)

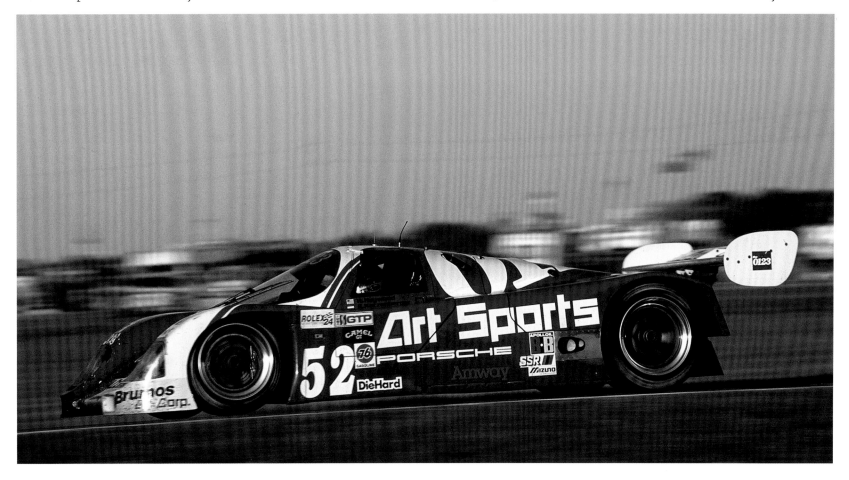

pits complex in a bid to update the facilities to those more in line with the FIA's expectations. Nevertheless, the ACO was not about to exclude the core of those regular competitors from its big race as the FIA moved towards an all F1-style sports car series.

Despite the FIA's protests that only the new-generation cars should run, the ACO kept the door open for the older Group C cars, but it was made as difficult as possible for them. By this time, the 962s were having to run a minimum weight of 1,000kg with a host of other restrictions.

The best-placed 962 at Le Mans in 1991 was again run by Reinhold Joest, this time driven by Hans-Joachim Stuck, Frank Jelinski and Derek Bell. The car finished seventh, 15 laps behind the winning Mazda, a trio of Jaguars, a Mercedes and another Mazda. It would have been higher but for a coolant leak.

This was the last year that the old Group C cars were allowed in the WSPC, or as it was called from 1991, the Sportscar World Championship. The F1-rules series itself only lasted another year – just long enough for Peugeot to get some publicity value from their hugely expensive sports car programme. During 1992 and 1993, sports car racing in

Europe effectively died, the racers gathering in beleaguered groups to race tame 911 Carreras and French Venturis.

Of the 'new generation' of racers from 1988, Mercedes and Jaguar had disappeared after achieving their objectives. Neither built replicas for customers to race, and in IMSA, the loathed German cars (the 962s) had merely been exchanged for the loathed Japanese cars.

IMSA's new direction was a mad policy, given the spectacular success of the series just one or two years earlier. It seemed as if sports car racing worldwide was intent on shooting itself in the foot with an Uzi.

In the really dark days of 1992 and 1993, the turbo cars faced FIA or IMSA-inspired punitive weight (and at Le Mans, fuel restriction) penalties compared with the fashionable (but sparse) normally aspirated full-race machines.

But there was a spirit at these big races that recalled Kevin Costner's *Field of Dreams*. The organisers knew that their survival depended on keeping the races open, in a sense it was a case of 'if you build it, they will come'. What that meant was ignoring the governing bodies regulations and keeping the doors open for all-comers, including the old 962s.

And they did come. At Daytona in 1992, Hurley Haywood, Eje Elgh, Roland Ratzenburger and Scott Brayton brought one of Vern Schuppan's 962s home third. At Sebring, Reinhold Joest's 962 also made it to third (Larrauri, Sigala and Gianpiero Moretti) despite problems on all the team's cars with water leaks, again.

The following year at Daytona, Rob Dyson shared one of his cars with James Weaver, Price Cobb and Elliot Forbes-Robinson to come fifth (and was just one of four 962s in the race).

Five 962s took part at Le Mans in 1992, and there were seven the following year. Kremer's CK6 was the best-placed finisher with seventh in 1992 and Obermaier matched that as 'best Porsche' in 1993.

At a time when sports car racing was at its bleakest point, the old 962s were there doing what they had always done – providing a thoroughly good spectacle. Meanwhile, the continuous development had not stopped.

Around this time, Joest hired Ralf Juettner from the Weissach motorsport department to oversee the continuing development of the cars and manage the race team. Juettner recalls the continuous process of

Two seasons' development show on the Joest 962 at Road America in 1993. Note the low position of the double-element rear wing and the chisel-shaped nose. This photo also shows the extra vane placed in each radiator duct – the result of an FIA edict in 1989 that said no mechanical part of the car shall be visible when viewed from above. (Geoffrey Hewitt)

improvement that the ageing 962 received, even in the early 1990s. 'We were always making special things at that time. We did the new bodywork and the double rear wing just for Daytona. We changed the underbody for Daytona and Sebring and we always had a new package from season to season. A lot of work went into that cooling system, both oil and water.

'We changed the whole cooling system and in America, the difference was something like 10° or 15° lower. The good thing was that it was reliable, because we had been getting cracks in the hoses and so on. On those cars the biggest task was to decouple all the vibrations in the system. Porsche used this in the GT1 later on.

'We also thought a lot about the engine, particularly the bearings. For instance, the main crankshaft bearings were 'U'-shaped to prevent floating, and their shoulders usually fell off. That wasn't normally a problem, but every now and then part of the shell would go into the oil pump and cause a major problem. We did a lot of development with titanium con-rods with steel flanges to make it possible to run steel against steel [with oil in between]. That was no problem, but the titanium against steel – that was a problem. We also did gearbox oil pumps and hydraulic differentials, things like this.'

During this period, there was a strong feeling that sports car racing had to return to its traditional format of endurance, rather than sprint racing. Those with an interest also wanted to see the racing based on a production-derived grand touring category, rather than prototypes.

These were not good times for Porsche either, the company was weathering the worst business recession

A sight not to be seen again. The Joest 962 leads the field out of the tight left-hand bend after the Moraine Sweep towards Turn 6 at Road America in 1993. The car was driven by 'John Winter' (Louis Krages) and Manuel Reuter. Another Joest 962 (seen here in fourth place) and driven by John Paul Jnr, was second. (Geoffrey Hewitt)

in its history. There had been several changes of senior management and the company's reputation in motor racing was in tatters.

After Professor Bott had retired as research and development head in late 1988, he had been succeeded by Dr Ulrich Bez. As Reinhold Joest has recounted, Bez started then stopped a new sports car programme. He soon tired of the ongoing IndyCar project and by 1990 had cancelled that before any solid results had been achieved.

He embarked on the Formula One engine project and partnered with the journeyman Arrows team far too late for the engine design team to prepare an integrated design. That adventure ended in embarrassment after just half a season in 1991.

Bez had hired Max Welti from Sauber-Mercedes to run the motorsport programme and he then proceeded to dismantle the time-served structure that existed within the competition department. It appeared as if there was a systematic effort to remove the very individuals that had given the Porsche motorsport heritage such charisma. From a smooth-running and responsive organisation under Helmuth Bott, Porsche Motorsport went into a black hole.

Within Weissach, the public embarrassments and restructuring were too much for some to bear. Individuals that had contributed so much to Porsche over decades, left in frustration or facing an early retirement.

It was not until Dr Wendelin Wiedeking took over as spokesman for the Board in September 1992, that a sense of leadership – for the whole of Porsche – arrived.

The first priority was to salvage the production car business. Motorsport was on skeleton rations at this point, as evidenced by the single entry of a 911 Turbo GT at Le Mans in 1993. By 1994, the interim 993-bodied 911 Carrera was selling well, and the survivors in the motorsport department spotted an opportunity to scoop an inexpensive publicity bonanza.

When, in September 1993, the ACO published the regulations for the 1994 Le Mans 24 Hours, a class was added for the new generation of high technology grand touring cars – cars like the Jaguar XJ220 and the proposed McLaren F1.

The Weissach team agreed with the longer term aim to move towards grand touring cars, but they realised that Le Mans in 1994 was still likely to be won overall by a prototype. They decided to probe the edges of the envelope.

Norbert Singer spoke to the ACO's technical head Alain Bertaut about some ideas. Bertaut was flexible,

he wanted to see Porsche back at Le Mans, but as Singer recalls, 'he didn't want any more 'Moby Dicks'!'

Singer proposed moving in a very radical direction. He was aware how some of the customer race teams had adapted the 962C for road use. He began to consider how such road cars might then be adapted back to racing use – technically still within the definition of a production grand touring car!

Vern Schuppan was one who was known to be building a small series of road cars. By 1992, three prototypes were built and every detail was set for a production batch of 25, but his design had moved away from being a racing 962 on the road to a more luxury specification. Sadly, before this consideration progressed further, Schuppan's Japanese backer pulled out and the project folded.

Another option was Jochen Dauer. The German had competed in Supercup and Group C between 1987 and 1990, but had found his racing team redundant as the rules changed. He too had turned his attentions to building a road-going version of the 962.

'There was the Schuppan proposal,' says Singer, 'and later there was one guy in Cologne and maybe someone else, but Dauer said he wanted to use the original car.'

Dauer's prototype was displayed at the September 1993 Frankfurt Motor Show. With an attractive body by former Porsche design stylist Achim Storz, the drag coefficient was claimed as 0.31 (compared to a typical racer at 0.40).

There was no doubting the car's elegance. It weighed in at around 1,080kg (2,381lb) and was

The Dauer 962LM really was derived (sort of) from a road-going version – only the road version needed adapting slightly before its homologation, so that the racing version's aerodynamics were satisfactory.

powered by a twin-turbo flat-six that Dauer claimed was good for 730bhp.

The motorsport department studied the possibility of entering Dauer's car in the GT class at Le Mans, and put the proposal to the Porsche Board that winter.

'Dauer had started by saying he wanted the original 962 on the road,' continues Singer. 'There were some who put a normal road turbo in the car to avoid the noise and emissions, but Dauer said he wanted the race engine homologated. He wanted the original car.

'Dauer's car was a real 962 and we took this as our baseline when we started work in the wind tunnel,' says Singer, with not a little tongue in cheek, 'to make this road car into a racing car.'

By January, Singer had full approval and a budget to do the job properly.

Alain Bertaut of the ACO had meanwhile issued a revision of the regulations, banning ground-effects aerodynamics, but this was a small compromise to pay.

It's difficult not to smile when you listen to Singer describing the development of the Dauer 962LM, as the car became known.

'Mr Bertaut thought that a lot of the work and restriction for the car would be covered by the road homologation. For a road car you had to meet certain road criteria, so he felt it wasn't necessary to write a regulation.'

Porsche took on the responsibility of gaining that homologation for Dauer. 'I had a good connection

The winning Dauer 962LM in the pits at Le Mans in 1994. The Toyotas kept the Porsches on their toes throughout, but the Japanese cars failed to win because of their weak transmissions.

The Dauer 962LM cars at Le Mans were based on Dave Klym-built 962 monocoques. There was considerable extra reinforcement of the footbox area.

with some guys here in our company doing road homologation. When I talked to them, I realised that it was quite an open field!' Singer lets go one of his famous baritone laughs, 'and then I had a hard discussion with Mr Bertaut. I had to convince him that what he thought was really closed, was actually completely open.'

The project turned out to be not quite so simple as it appeared. The low-drag body shape and an absence of the underbody ground-effect ducts seriously compromised the planned racing car's stability. The result was a revised body and many parts taken from the motorsport department stores in Weissach.

The new car's type approval for a Le Mans entry that year was required by 31 March. The actual certificate from the German TüV authority was dated 15 March. A prototype was tested at Goodyear's Miréval facility and at the team's traditional test circuit at Paul Ricard, near Bandol in Southern France.

The initial reaction of the drivers – Hans-Joachim Stuck did much of the development driving – was that

the flat-bottomed car was a real handful compared with the old 962. With its full-house water-cooled flat-six, it was certainly quick enough, but with relatively little downforce, braking distances were longer.

The public, and the ACO, first saw the Dauer 962LM at the test weekend in early May. The car caused a sensation, with fellow GT competitors (including Porsche's own customers running Carrera RSRs in the same class) crying 'foul' and doing everything to have the Porsches excluded.

Alain Bertaut was far from impressed. He voiced his concern that the car was quite different to Singer's original proposal and as had been shown in Frankfurt.

The team's response was coldly pragmatic. They had their type approval certificate proving the Dauer 962LM was a roadworthy vehicle. Porsche had just interpreted the regulations more extensively than the rest. Singer's comment is given with a characteristic grin: 'We simply gave them a preview of the GT regulations'.

The test weekend showed the car, predictably, to be much faster than the other GT class competition, and

Kremer entered this K8 spyder at Le Mans in 1994. Derek Bell drove with maximum boost to lead the first lap of the race and with co-drivers Jürgen Lässig and Robin Donovan, the car finished sixth.

true to Singer's initial estimates, was in with a chance of overall victory. This was despite serious opposition in the Le Mans Prototype class from Toyota, Nissan, Courage and a lone Kremer K8 – itself an open-cockpit 962 derivative.

Nissan looked strong, the IMSA cars had won both Daytona and Sebring that year, but at Le Mans they were handicapped by a 200kg (441lb) weight penalty on the 1,000kg (2,205lb) Dauer. The Toyotas looked the most serious opposition. The highly developed Group C-derived cars had twin-turbo, 6-litre V8 engines. They were flat-bottomed and although they could use wider tyres and were 50kg (110lb) lighter,

were only permitted 80-litre (17.6gal) fuel tanks, compared with the Dauer's 120-litre (26.4gal) tank.

Norbert Singer calculated that the Toyotas could run two stints on their tyres. Porsche would have to change their narrow 12.5in rears every stop. But the upside was that the Dauer could go four more laps than the Toyota, so although the Porsche stops would be longer, they would be fewer, but unless your name was Falk or Singer, it wasn't easy to see who really had the advantage.

Porsche lined up a top driver team for the Dauer 962s. This included Stuck, Thierry Boutsen and Danny Sullivan in one car, with Hurley Haywood,

Yannick Dalmas and Mauro Baldi in the other. Hurley has good memories of the Dauer 962LM. 'That car was very enjoyable for me to drive because it reminded me a lot of the 936. It had that ability to drift through the corners. It didn't have the tremendous downforce of the regular 962 because of the flat bottom. But it was very familiar. You know, I enjoyed driving that car immensely. It was a 962 so when you were sitting in it, it was very comfortable.

'It was stable on the road, but in the corners you could kind of play with it and modulate the throttle . You could get the car going in and out of oversteer, and that was one of the few times that I drove at Le Mans with guys of my own size.

'Originally, I was scheduled to drive with Stuck and Boutsen. Sullivan, Dalmas and Baldi were going to be in the other car. They had done a pre-test at Magny Cours and everybody had been driving the same car. Then Baldi and Dalmas had gone to the factory and had had a seat made for them, so when Sullivan got to Le Mans there was no way he could get into their seat, and so they said for me to try the seat and it fitted perfectly. I said: "Yes, this is great". So the three of us drove in basically the same position and we didn't have to do anything – with no pillows or bolsters anywhere. In a 24-hour race it doesn't seem like that's all that important , but the seat support is crucial in a race that long, especially with those kind of corners.'

Derek Bell in the Kremer K8 led the first lap, but after this high-boost performance, he was overwhelmed by the other prototypes – and the Dauers. By the end of the second hour the two Porsches led.

In the early evening, Dalmas ran out of fuel just short of the pits and later Haywood had a drive-shaft fail. Both incidents dropped the FAT-International-supported car down the leaderboard. Then Danny Sullivan in the other car had a puncture at the second Mulsanne chicane. After a slow crawl round, he missed the pit entrance and after another very slow lap, he pitted. This placed the two Toyotas in first and second after just six hours, with Eddie Irvine proving to be a sensation in the SARD-run car.

The Toyotas ran into their own problems however. After a double stint by Irvine, his car needed new discs and pads, a time-consuming process that had to be repeated twice more in the race. Then the other Toyota (run by the Nisso organisation) broke its

differential. It took an hour to change and pushed the car back to fifth.

Meanwhile, the two Dauers were coming up the order after a long night. So hard were the two Porsches being driven that Stuck went off at one stage on Sunday morning, while Boutsen lost the nose section later. That car's hopes evaporated when it too suffered a drive-shaft failure.

It came down to Haywood, Dalmas and Baldi in the Dauer and the SARD Toyota of Mauro Martini, Jeff Krosnoff and Eddie Irvine. But after these two cars had traded the lead through Sunday, the Toyota ground to a halt just opposite the pits with just 90 minutes to go. Driver Krosnoff shouted to his pit crew that the gear linkage had broken. He found third gear, cruised around and it took 13 minutes to fix it in the pits.

The Dauer Porsche took the lead, but in the last hour, Eddie Irvine pulled out everything to try to catch up. Irvine's performance overhauled Thierry

After the factory withdrew their own entries in international sports car racing, Reinhold Joest received closest support from Weissach. The team pulled off a surprise win at Dijon in May 1989 and gave the Mercedes a fright at Le Mans that year. The following year, and with unsuitable Michelin tyres, the results were not quite so impressive.

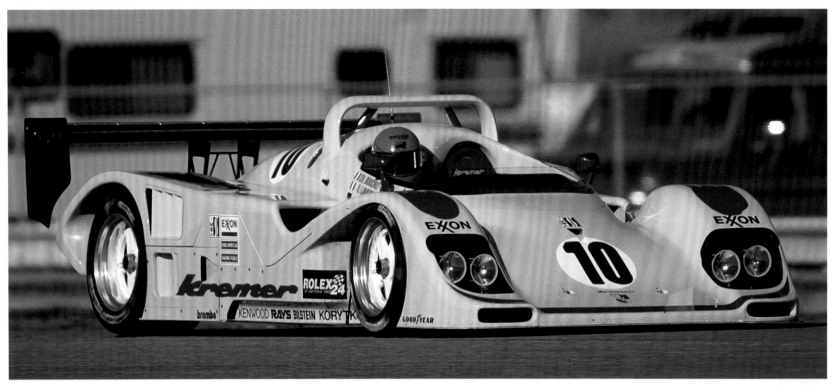

This Kremer K8 won the Daytona 24 Hours, driven by Giovanni Lavaggi, Jürgen Lässig, Christoph Bouchut and Marco Werner. As had happened so many time before, the Porsche-engined car's durability left the Ferrari opposition for dead. (Geoffrey Hewitt)

Boutsen in the other Dauer for second place, but he failed by a lap to catch the leader.

After a lean spell of seven years, the 962 had restored Porsche's pride.

It seemed that it was all over for the 962 though, as there was no chance that the car would be allowed to run again at Le Mans – the old stager was embarrassing all the modern prototypes and threatening to eclipse even the high-technology GT cars like the McLaren. But at Daytona in 1995, Kremer's K8 slipped through the restrictor net.

Despite the new factory WSC-95 being withdrawn after a last-minute rule change by IMSA governing turbo engine restrictors in the new World Sports Car class – two Kremer K8 Spyders did race.

The K8 could be described as a grandson of the 962, being an open-cockpit Thompson chassis using the 962 engine, transmission and corners. Derek Bell had shown the car's speed at Le Mans the year before, but at Daytona it flew. When all the exotic Ferrari 333SPs had retired, the K8 driven by Giovanni Lavaggi, Jürgen Lässig, Christoph Bouchut and Marco Werner won. And this really was the last time a 962-derived car won a major motor race – the authorities saw to that.

By 1994, Porsche had won Le Mans 13 times. No less than seven of those victories were achieved with the 956 or the 962, and if we include Kremer's victory in 1995, there were also six wins at Daytona. Sebring had fallen to the 962 no less than four times. This is a record of victories in the world's top international long distance races that is likely never to be repeated.

We tend to think of the 956 and 962 as only an endurance racer, but the real calibre of these cars was shown in their versatility to repeatedly come out on top in the sprint races of IMSA, the German Supercup and the European-based Interserie.

That these cars from Weissach crowned the careers of so many – those that top the list include Ickx, Bell, Wollek, Holbert, Haywood, Foyt, Rahal and Stuck – is just as important as the car's ability to turn 'gentlemen' drivers such as Louis Krages and Preston Henn into winners.

This wasn't a razor-edged instrument that only the best could master. It was a racing car for all seasons and all men – as much at home in the misty, night-time rain of the Mulsanne as the scorching pace of a street race in Miami.

Good cars come and go in racing, but only the truly great become enduring champions.

Appendix 1
RULES AND REGULATIONS

FIA Group C
World Endurance Championship for Manufacturers
Main elements of the 1982 FISA Group C regulations

The 1982 regulations defined the championship as comprising 1,000km distance or six-hour time events with a maximum fuel allowance per car of 600 litres. Each car could make no more than five refuelling stops per race. Refuelling was to be by gravity rig only, with a maximum fuel flow of 50 litres per minute.

For Le Mans, a fuel allowance of 2,600 litres was given with no more than 25 refuelling stops permitted.

The chassis regulations defined a two-seat sports car with a closed cockpit and closely defined dimensions. Ground-effect underbody venturis were permitted. The underside was to include a flat reference plane measuring 1,000mm by 800mm, starting just behind the front wheels. Excepting the wheels and tyres, no other part of the car was allowed to project below this plane (so preventing Formula One-style side skirts).

The cockpit was defined to have a width of not less than 1,300mm. The windshield was to have a convex outside profile with a width of not less than 900mm (measured at a point 300mm below the highest point of the cockpit).

Two cockpit doors were required with a minimum width at their lowest point to be 500mm. The door windows were to be 400mm long by 250mm high.

Other regulations limited cabin width and footwell size to improve driver safety.

For the same reasons, the fuel tank was to be placed within 650mm of the longitudinal centre line of the car and within the wheelbase. The fuel system capacity (not just the tank) could not exceed 100 litres.

The nose section should not extend forwards of the front axle line by more than 20 per cent of the wheelbase. This length determined the tail section dimension (measured back from the rear axle line), which could be different by no more than 15 per cent of the wheelbase dimension.

Normally-aspirated or forced induction engines were allowed with no limit on capacity, but they had to meet the fuel consumption requirements as specified. These amounted to placing a requirement to meet an average usage of no worse than 60 litres per 100km (or better than 4.7 miles to the imperial gallon). Engines were only permitted from manufacturers with existing homologated units.

Minimum weight (without fuel or driver):
    800kg (1,764lb)
Maximum length: 4,800mm (189in)
Maximum width: 2,000mm (78.75in)
Minimum height: 1,000mm (39.4in)
Maximum height: 1,100mm (43.3in)
Maximum wheel rim size: 16in (406mm)

Major Group C rules changes in following years:
1984: IMSA cars allowed to run at Le Mans. Minimum weight increased to 850kg. More than five refuelling stops permitted
1985: 15 per cent reduction in fuel allowance (equivalent to 51 litres/100km or 5.54 miles to the imperial gallon).
Cars manufactured after 1 January 1985 to have driver's feet located behind main axis of front axle. Light alloy roll-over cages replaced by steel.
1986: Gravity refuelling apparatus now permitted to deliver fuel at 60 litres per minute. Improvement in crash structure regulation at front of car

1987: Cars with driver's feet ahead of front axle main axis now excluded.

Commercial grade fuel only to be used (97 RON), supplied by organisers. Fuel additives excluded.

1988: Underbody mandatory flat area increased to full width of body (2,000mm) and 900mm length. Rear underbody duct exit height limited to 280mm above floor of car. Fuel octane number increased to 98.7 RON.

1989: Minimum weight increased to 900kg. 3.5-litre normally aspirated racing engine class created (with minimum weight of 760kg). All races 480km long.

1991: Turbocharged cars excluded from new Sportscar World Championship.

1992: Sportscar World Championship ceases.

IMSA Grand Touring Prototype
Main elements of championship regulations from 1982

IMSA race distances were not regulated. Excluding the Daytona 24 Hours and Sebring 12 Hours, typical IMSA races could be one or two-driver events of between 100 miles and 500 miles long. Time races were also included and these varied between three hours and six hours.

Chassis regulations as Group C except that driver's feet must be behind main axis of front axle, greater underbody duct parameters. All aerodynamic devices have to be within the planform of the bodywork.

The core of IMSA's regulations were the eight scales defining a car's weight relative to its engine type and capacity. By 1984, and in simple terms, these were categorised around whether the engine was a production-based unit with two valves per cylinder or a pure-bred racing engine with four valves per cylinder. The categories were further divided on whether these types were normally aspirated or had forced induction (turbocharging). For each engine type a graph of vehicle weight against engine capacity was drawn, which determined the minimum weight for that particular car/engine combination.

The Porsche 962 initially came within the requirements for the IMSA GTP Group 3: Production-based engine with two valves per cylinder and forced induction. This defined a maximum engine capacity of 3.57 litres and a minimum weight at that capacity of 900kg.

In the coming years, these engine/weight parameters changed as follows (plus other relevant rule changes):

1985: Maximum engine capacity reduced to 3.5 litres.

1986: Maximum engine capacity reduced to 3.2 litres and minimum weight at that capacity increased to 943kg.

1987: Maximum engine capacity reduced to 3 litres and minimum weight reduced to 930kg.

1988: Forced induction engines must be fitted with an inlet air restrictor of 57mm, positioned within 50mm of the turbocharger. Mid-season revision: air-cooled single-turbo Porsche engines allowed minimum weight concession to 924kg.

Porsche's four-valve, all water-cooled, twin-turbo engine allowed in IMSA GTP Group 4 class (maximum capacity of 3 litres, minimum weight 953kg and fitted with 36mm restrictor on each turbo).

1989: All water-cooled, twin-turbo engine to be fitted with 38mm restrictors.

1990: Air-cooled single-turbo Porsche engines to be fitted with 54mm restrictor and minimum weight increased to 953kg.

1993: IMSA GTP ceases.

Appendix 2
FACTS AND FIGURES

This data is intended for guidance only and may differ in detail from car to car

1982 Porsche 956 (956 001–005)

Engine: Type 935/76 (late season) flat six-cylinder engine with water-cooled four-valve cylinder heads and air-cooled (Nikasil-coated) alloy cylinder barrels. Vertical cooling fan located at front of engine. Cast-magnesium alloy crankcase with eight plain main bearings. Steel crankshaft with titanium alloy connecting rods and forged alloy pistons. Two gear-driven overhead camshafts per bank. Two KKK K26 turbochargers with twin, air-to-water intercoolers. Bosch Motronic 1.2 engine management with single spark plug per cylinder.

Capacity: 2,649cc

Bore/Stroke: 92.3mm/66mm

Maximum power: 620bhp at 8,200rpm (at 1.2bar boost)

Maximum torque: 630Nm at 5,400rpm

Compression ratio: 7.2:1

Transmission: Type 956 magnesium-case gearbox and aluminium clutch bellhousing. Five forward speeds with synchromesh and reverse. Single-plate Sachs clutch. Locked differential.

Chassis/Body: Aluminium monocoque tub with additional aluminium tube roll-over cage and rear steel sub-frames to carry engine/gearbox/rear suspension. Seven-piece Kevlar body reinforced with carbon-fibre. Laminated glass windshield with heating, clear plastic side windows. Low- and high-downforce tail options (with matching nose- and rear-underbody pieces). Underbody with suction-inducing longitudinal ducts each side of centre section. 99-litre rubber fuel cell located between the driver and engine bulkheads. Integrated compressed-air jacking system.

Suspension and steering: Rack-and-pinion steering. Front suspension by unequal-length wishbones and titanium rising-rate coil-springs over alloy Bilstein gas shock absorbers. Rear suspension by lower wishbone and parallel upper-links with inboard rising-rate titanium coil-springs over alloy Bilstein gas shock absorbers, operated by fabricated rocker arms pivoted at upper links.

Brakes: Dual-circuit braking system with all-round four-piston Porsche-designed alloy calipers on drilled, ventilated 30mm thickness, 325mm diameter steel discs.

Wheels and Tyres: 12in-wide front, 15in-wide rear centre-lock magnesium alloy 16in-diameter six-spoke Speedline wheels with Dunlop tyres (front: 16/600/280; Rear: 16/650/350).

Weight: 840kg (40% front/60% rear); 1983 customer 956: 820kg

Length: 4,770mm

Width: 1,990mm

Height: 1,080mm

Wheelbase: 2,650mm

Track (f/r): 1,648mm/1,548mm

Performance:

Acceleration: 0 to 62.5mph: N/A

Maximum speed: 217mph (349kph)

962 IMSA 1984 (962 101–104)

Engine: Type 962/70 flat six-cylinder engine with air-cooled cylinder heads and (Nikasil-coated) alloy cylinder barrels. Vertical cooling fan located at front of engine. Cast-magnesium alloy crankcase with eight plain main bearings. Steel crankshaft with titanium alloy connecting rods and forged alloy pistons. Two chain-driven overhead camshafts per bank. One inlet and one exhaust valve per cylinder. Single KKK K36 turbocharger with single air-to-air intercooler and exhaust taken out at rear. Bosch Motronic 1.2 engine management with single spark plug per cylinder.

Capacity: 2,869cc
Bore/Stroke: 93.0mm/70.4mm
Maximum power: 680bhp at 8,200rpm
Maximum torque: 660Nm at 5,800rpm
Compression ratio: 7.5:1
Transmission: Type 956/62 magnesium-case gearbox and aluminium clutch bellhousing. Five forward speeds with synchromesh and reverse. Single-plate Sachs clutch.
Chassis/Body: As 956 except: Lengthened (by 120mm) aluminium sheet monocoque with steel roll-over bar. Revised tail with aerofoil mounted over planform of rear body. 120-litre fuel cell.
Wheels and Tyres: 13in-wide front, 14.5in-wide rear centre-lock magnesium alloy 16in-diameter six-spoke Speedline wheels with Dunlop tyres.
Weight: 850kg
Length: 4,770mm
Track (f/r): 1,634mm/1,548mm
Wheelbase: 2,770mm (120mm longer than 956)

962 IMSA 1988 (Holbert Racing)

As 962 except:
Engine: Type 935/82 by Andial. Flat six-cylinder engine with air-cooled cylinder heads and (Nikasil-coated) alloy cylinder barrels. Vertical cooling fan located at front of engine. Cast-magnesium alloy crankcase with eight plain main bearings. Steel crankshaft with titanium alloy connecting rods and forged alloy pistons. Two chain-driven overhead camshafts per bank. One inlet, one exhaust valve

and two sparking plugs per cylinder. Single Garrett AiResearch turbocharger with single air-to-air intercooler and exhaust taken out at rear. Bosch Motronic MP1.7 engine management with electronic wastegate control. Single, 57mm induction air-inlet restrictor.

Capacity: 2,994cc
Bore/Stroke: 95.0mm/74.4mm
Maximum power: 700bhp at 8,200rpm
Maximum torque: 710Nm at 5,400rpm
Compression ratio: 9.0:1
Chassis/Body: Holbert Racing 962 HR1 aluminium-monocoque with billet aluminium front and rear bulkheads and improved front crash structure
Weight: 930kg

962C FIA Group C1 1990 (962 011–015)

As 962 except:
Engine: Type 935/86, flat six-cylinder engine with water-cooled four-valve cylinder heads and water-cooled (Nikasil-coated) alloy cylinder barrels. Cast-magnesium-alloy crankcase with eight plain main bearings. Steel crankshaft with titanium alloy connecting rods and forged alloy pistons. Two gear-driven overhead camshafts per bank. Two KKK K26 turbochargers with twin, air-to-water intercoolers. Bosch Motronic MP1.7 engine management with single spark plug per cylinder.

Capacity: 3,164cc
Bore/Stroke: 95.0mm/74.4mm
Maximum power: 750bhp at 8,200rpm
Maximum torque: 715Nm at 5,800rpm
Compression ratio: 9.5:1
Chassis/Body: As 962 except: revised nose section and tail with separate rear aerofoil mounted from transmission.
Weight: 900kg

Appendix 3
INTERNATIONAL CHAMPIONSHIP RACE WINS

Listing of major international championship and non-championship race victories

FIA World Endurance Championship (WEC) 1982–1985
FIA European Endurance Championship (EEC) for Drivers 1983

Race	Champ-ionship	Date	Team	Drivers	Car
1982					
Silverstone 6 Hours	WEC	18 May	Porsche AG	J. Ickx, D. Bell	956 001
Le Mans 24 Hours	WEC	19–20 June	Porsche AG	J. Ickx, D. Bell	956 002
Spa 1,000km	WEC	5 September	Porsche AG	J. Ickx, J. Mass	956 003
Fuji 6 Hours	WEC	3 October	Porsche AG	J. Ickx, J. Mass	956 003
Brands Hatch	EEC	17 October	Porsche AG	J. Ickx, D. Bell	956 003
Kyalami 9 Hours	NC	6 November	Porsche AG	J. Ickx, J. Mass	956 003

1982 World Endurance Championship: Makes – Porsche AG
1982 World Endurance Champion Driver – J. Ickx

Race	Champ-ionship	Date	Team	Drivers	Car
1983					
Monza 1,000km	WEC	10 April	Joest Racing	B. Wollek, T. Boutsen	956 104
Silverstone 1,000km	WEC	8 May	Porsche AG	D. Bell, S. Bellof	956 007
Nürburgring 1,000km	WEC	29 May	Porsche AG	J. Ickx, J. Mass	956 005
Le Mans 24 Hours	WEC	18–19 June	Porsche AG	A. Holbert, V. Schuppan, H. Haywood	956 003
Spa 1,000km	WEC	4 September	Porsche AG	J. Ickx, J. Mass	956 005
Brands Hatch 1,000km	EEC	18 September	John Fitzpatrick Racing	D. Warwick, J. Fitzpatrick	956 102
Fuji 1,000km	WEC	2 October	Porsche AG	D. Bell, S. Bellof	956 009
Mugello 1,000km	EEC	23 October	Joest Racing	B. Wollek, S. Johansson	956 104
Kyalami 1,000km	WEC	10 December	Porsche AG	D. Bell, S. Bellof	956 009

1983 World Endurance Championship: Makes – Porsche AG
1983 World Endurance Champion Driver – J. Ickx
1983 European Endurance Champion Driver – B. Wollek

Race	Champ-ionship	Date	Team	Drivers	Car
1984					
Monza 1,000km	WEC	23 April	Porsche AG	D. Bell, S. Bellof	956 009
Silverstone 1,000km	WEC	13 May	Porsche AG	J. Ickx, J. Mass	956 010
Le Mans 24 Hours	WEC	16–17 June	Joest Racing	K. Ludwig, H. Pescarolo	956 117
Nürburgring 1,000km	WEC	29 May	Porsche AG	D. Bell, S. Bellof	956 009
Brands Hatch 1,000km	WEC	18 September	Richard Lloyd Racing	J. Palmer, J. Lammers	956 106
Mosport Park 1,000km	WEC	5 August	Porsche AG	J. Ickx, J. Mass	956 010
Spa 1,000km	WEC	2 September	Porsche AG	D. Bell, S. Bellof	956 009
Imola 1,000km	WEC	16 September	Brun Motorsport	S. Bellof, H.-J. Stuck	956 116
Fuji 1,000km	WEC	30 September	Porsche AG	S. Bellof, J. Watson	956 009
Kyalami 1,000km	WEC	3 November	Joest Racing	L. Krages, D. Schornstein, H. Pescarolo	956 105
Sandown Park 1,000km	WEC	2 December	Porsche AG	D. Bell, S. Bellof	956 009

1984 World Endurance Championship: Makes – Porsche AG
1984 World Endurance Champion Driver – S. Bellof

1985

Mugello 1,000km	WEC	14 April	Porsche AG	J. Ickx, J. Mass	962 002
Monza 1,000km	WEC	28 April	Kremer Racing	M. Winkelhock, M. Surer	962 110
Silverstone 1,000km	WEC	12 May	Porsche AG	J. Ickx, J. Mass	962 002
Le Mans 24 Hours	WEC	17–18 June	Joest Racing	K. Ludwig, P. Barilla, L. Krages	956 117
Hockenheim 1,000km	WEC	14 July	Porsche AG	D. Bell, H.-J. Stuck	962 003
Mosport Park 1,000km	WEC	11 August	Porsche AG	D. Bell, H.-J. Stuck	962 003
Spa 1,000km	WEC	1 September	Porsche AG	D. Bell, H.-J. Stuck	962 003
Brands Hatch 1,000km	WEC	22 September	Porsche AG	D. Bell, H.-J. Stuck	962 003
Shah Alam 800km	WEC	1 December	Porsche AG	J. Ickx, J. Mass	962 002

1985 World Endurance Championship: Teams – Porsche AG
1985 World Endurance Champion Driver – D. Bell

FIA World Sports Prototype Championship (WSPC) for Teams and Drivers
1986

Monza 1,000km	WSPC	20 April	Porsche AG	D. Bell, H.-J. Stuck	962 003
Silverstone 1,000km	WSPC	5 May	Porsche AG	D. Bell, H.-J. Stuck	962 003
Le Mans 24 Hours	WSPC	31 May–1 June	Porsche AG	D. Bell, H.-J. Stuck, A. Holbert	962 003
Norisring 100 Miles	WSPC	29 June	Joest Racing	K. Ludwig	956 117
Brands Hatch 1,000km	WSPC	20 July	Richard Lloyd Racing	B. Wollek, M. Baldi	956 106b
Jerez	WSPC	3 August	Brun Motorsport	O. Larrauri, J. Pareja	962 115
Spa 1,000km	WSPC	15 September	Brun Motorsort	T. Boutsen, F. Jelinski	962 117
Fuji 1,000km	WSPC	6 October	Joest Racing	P. Barilla, P. Ghinzhani	956 117
Kyalami 500km	NC	22 November	Joest Racing	P. Ghinzhani	956 117

1986 World Sports Prototype Championship: Teams – Brun Motorsport
1986 World Sports Prototype Champion Drivers – D. Bell, H.-J. Stuck

1987

Le Mans 24 Hours	WSPC	13–14 June	Porsche AG	D. Bell, H.-J. Stuck, A. Holbert	962 006
Norisring 200 Miles	WSPC	28 June	Britten-Lloyd Racing	M. Baldi, J. Palmer	962 106b
Kyalami 500km	NC	28 November	Britten-Lloyd Racing	J. Mass	962 106b

1987 World Sports Prototype Championship: Teams – Brun Motorsport
1987 World Sports Prototype Champion Drivers – D. Bell, H.-J. Stuck

1988

Kyalami 500km	NC	26 November	Joest Racing	B. Wollek, F. Jelinski, W. Taylor	962 129

1989

Dijon	WSPC	21 May	Joest Racing	B. Wollek, F. Jelinski	962 011

Endurance Triple Crown (ETC)
1994

Le Mans 24 Hours	ETC	18–19 June	Porsche AG	M. Baldi, Y. Dalmas, H. Haywood	962 GT003

Sports Car Club of America (SCCA), Canadian-American Challenge
1983

Road America	Can-Am	17 July	John Fitzpatrick Racing	J. Fitzpatrick	956 102

International Motor Sports Association (IMSA) Camel GTP Championship
1984

Mid Ohio 500km	IMSA	10 June	Holbert Racing	A. Holbert, D. Bell	962 103
Watkins Glen 6 Hours	IMSA	8 July	Holbert Racing	A. Holbert, D. Bell	962 103
Road America 500 Miles	IMSA	26 August	Holbert Racing	A. Holbert, D. Bell	962 103
Pocono 500km	IMSA	9 September	Holbert Racing	A. Holbert, D. Bell	962 103
Daytona 3 Hours	IMSA	25 November	Holbert Racing	A. Holbert, D. Bell	962 103

1985

Daytona 24 Hours	IMSA	3–4 February	Preston Henn	A. J. Foyt, B. Wollek Al Unser Snr, T. Boutsen	962 104
Miami GP	IMSA	24 February	Holbert Racing	A. Holbert, D. Bell	962 103
Sebring 12 Hours	IMSA	23 March	Preston Henn	B. Wollek, A. J. Foyt	962 104
Riverside 600km	IMSA	28 April	Jim Busby	P. Halsmer, J. Morton	962 105
Laguna Seca 225 Miles	IMSA	5 May	Holbert Racing	A. Holbert	962 103
Charlotte 500km	IMSA	19 May	Holbert Racing	A. Holbert, D. Bell	962 103
Lime Rock	IMSA	27 May	Rob Dyson	D. Olsen	962 101
Mid Ohio 500km	IMSA	9 June	Holbert Racing	A. Holbert	962 103
Watkins Glen 3 Hours	IMSA	7 July	Holbert Racing	A. Holbert, D. Bell	962 103
Portland 300km	IMSA	28 July	Holbert Racing	A. Holbert	962 HR1
Sears Point 300km	IMSA	4 August	Bruce Leven	B. Wollek	962 109
Road America 500 Miles	IMSA	25 August	Rob Dyson	D. Olsen, B. Rahal	962 101
Pocono 500km	IMSA	8 September	Holbert Racing	A. Holbert, D. Bell	962 HR1
Watkins Glen 500 Miles	IMSA	29 September	Holbert Racing	A. Holbert, D. Bell	962 HR1
Columbus 500km	IMSA	6 October	Rob Dyson	D. Olsen, P. Cobb	962 101
Daytona 3 Hours	IMSA	1 December	Holbert Racing	A. Holbert, D. Bell	962 HR1

1985 IMSA Camel GTP Championship: Manufacturers – Porsche
1985 IMSA Camel GTP Champion Driver – A. Holbert

1986

Daytona 24 Hours	IMSA	1–2 February	Holbert Racing	A. Holbert, D. Bell, A. Unser Jnr	962 103
Miami GP	IMSA	2 March	Bruce Leven	B. Wollek, P. Barilla	962 109
Sebring 12 Hours	IMSA	22 March	Bob Akin	B. Akin, H.-J. Stuck, J. Gartner	962 113
Riverside 6 Hours	IMSA	27 April	Rob Dyson	R. Dyson, P. Cobb	962 120
Charlotte 500km	IMSA	18 May	Rob Dyson	P. Cobb, D. Olsen	962 120
Lime Rock	IMSA	26 May	Holbert Racing	A. Holbert	962 HR1
Mid Ohio 500km	IMSA	8 June	Holbert Racing	A. Holbert, D. Bell	962 HR1
Watkins Glen 500 Miles	IMSA	6 July	Holbert Racing	A. Holbert, D. Bell	962 103
Portland 300km	IMSA	27 July	Holbert Racing	A. Holbert	962 HR1
Sears Point 300km	IMSA	3 August	Rob Dyson	R. Dyson, P. Cobb	962 122
Road America 500 Miles	IMSA	24 August	Holbert Racing	A. Holbert, D. Bell	962 103
Watkins Glen 500km	IMSA	21 September	Holbert Racing	A. Holbert, D. Bell	962 HR1
Columbus 500km	IMSA	5 October	Bruce Leven	B. Wollek, S. Pruett	962 HR2
Daytona 3 Hours	IMSA	26 October	Rob Dyson	R. Dyson, P. Cobb	962 122

1986 IMSA Camel GTP Championship: Manufacturers – Porsche
1986 IMSA Camel GTP Champion Driver – A. Holbert

1987

Daytona 24 Hours	IMSA	31 Jan–1 Feb	Holbert Racing	A. Holbert, C. Robinson, D. Bell, Al Unser Jnr	962 103
Miami 3 Hours	IMSA	1 March	Bruce Leven	J. Mass, B. Rahal	962 121
Sebring 12 Hours	IMSA	21 March	Bruce Leven	J. Mass, B. Rahal	962 121
Road Atlanta 500km	IMSA	12 April	Rob Dyson	P. Cobb, J. Weaver	962 122
Laguna Seca 300km	IMSA	3 May	Bruce Leven	K. Ludwig	962 121
Lime Rock	IMSA	25 May	Holbert Racing	A. Holbert	962 103
Mid Ohio 500km	IMSA	7 June	Bruce Leven	J. Mass, B. Rahal	962 121
Watkins Glen 500km	IMSA	5 July	Rob Dyson	P. Cobb, V. Schuppan	962 122
Portland 300km	IMSA	26 July	Holbert Racing	C. Robinson	962 HR1
Sears Point 300km	IMSA	2 August	Bruce Leven	J. Mass	962 121
Road America 500 Miles	IMSA	16 August	Rob Dyson	P. Cobb, J. Dumfries	962 122
San Antonio	IMSA	6 September	Holbert Racing	D. Bell, C. Robinson	962 HR1
Columbus 300km	IMSA	4 October	Bruce Leven	B. Rahal	962 121
Del Mar 2 Hours	IMSA	25 October	Bruce Leven	J. Mass	962 121

1987 IMSA Camel GTP Championship: Manufacturers – Porsche
1987 IMSA Camel GTP Champion Driver – C. Robinson

1988

Miami 3 Hours	IMSA	28 February	Rob Dyson	P. Cobb, J. Weaver	962 120
Sebring 12 Hours	IMSA	20 March	Bruce Leven	K. Ludwig, H.-J. Stuck	962 121
San Antonio 3 Hours	IMSA	4 September	Rob Dyson	P. Cobb, J. Weaver	962 DR1
Tampa	NC	27 November	Brun Motorsport	O. Larrauri, M. Sigala	962 BM002

1988 IMSA Camel GTP Championship: Manufacturers – Porsche

1989

Daytona 24 Hours	IMSA	4–5 February	Jim Busby	D. Bell, B. Wollek, J. Andretti	962 C02
W. Palm Beach 3 Hours	IMSA	23 April	Jim Busby	J. Andretti, B. Wollek	962 C02

1990

Tampa	IMSA	30 September	Rob Dyson	J. Weaver	962 148

1991

Daytona 24 Hours	IMSA	2–3 February	Joest Racing	L. Krages, F. Jelinski H. Pescarolo, H. Haywood, B. Wollek	962 129

1993

Road America 500km	IMSA	11 July	Joest Racing	L. Krages, M. Reuter	962 016

1995

Daytona 24 Hours	IMSA-WSC		Kremer	G. Lavaggi, J. Lässig, C. Bouchut, M. Werner	Kremer-Porsche K8

Japanese Sportscar Championship (JSC)

1983

Suzuka 500km	JSC	3 April	Nova Engineering	V. Schuppan, N. Fujita	956 108
Fuji 500km	JSC	5 June	Nova Engineering	V. Schuppan, N. Fujita	956 108
Fuji 1,000km	JSC	24 July	Nova Engineering	V. Schuppan, N. Fujita	956 108
Suzuka 1,000km	JSC	28 August	Nova Engineering	V. Schuppan, N. Fujita	956 108
Fuji 500 Miles	JSC	27 November	Nova Engineering	V. Schuppan, N. Fujita	956 108

1983 Japanese Sportscar Champion Drivers: V. Schuppan, N. Fujita

1984

Suzuka 500km	JSC	1 April	Nova Engineering	V. Schuppan, Y. Katayama	956 108
Fuji 500km	JSC	3 June	Nova Engineering	Ku. Takahashi, Ke. Takahashi	956 113
Suzuka 1,000km	JSC	26 August	Nova Engineering	Ku. Takahashi, Ke. Takahashi G. Lees	956 113
Fuji 500 Miles	JSC	25 November	Nova Engineering	V. Schuppan, Y. Katayama	956 118

1985

Fuji 1,000km	JSC	5 May	Trust Engineering	V. Schuppan, K. Suzuki	956 118
Fuji 500 Miles	JSC	28 July	Nova Engineering	Ku. Takahashi, Ke. Takahashi	962 111
Suzuka 1,000km	JSC	25 August	Nova Engineering	Ku. Takahashi, Ke. Takahashi	962 111
Fuji 500km	JSC	24 November	Nova Engineering	Ku. Takahashi, Ke. Takahashi	962 111

1985 Japanese Sportscar Champion: Manufacturers – Porsche
1985 Japanese Sportscar Champion Drivers – Ku. Takahashi, Ke. Takahashi

1986

Suzuka 500km	JSC	6 April	Nova Engineering	Ku. Takahashi, Ke. Takahashi	962 111
Fuji 1,000km	JSC	4 May	Nova Engineering	Ku. Takahashi, Ke. Takahashi	962 111
Fuji 500 Miles	JSC	20 July	Trust Engineering	V. Schuppan, K. Suzuki, G. Fouche	956 111
Suzuka 1,000km	JSC	24 August	Nova Engineering	J. Yoneyama, H. Okada, T. Asai	956 101
Fuji 500km	JSC	23 November	Trust Engineering	V. Schuppan, K. Suzuki	956 111

1986 Japanese Sportscar Championship: Manufacturers – Porsche
1986 Japanese Sportscar Champion Drivers – Ku. Takahashi, Ke. Takahashi

1987

Suzuka 500km	JSC	12 April	Nova Engineering	M. Thackwell, H. Okada	962 111
Fuji 500 Miles	JSC	19 July	Nova Engineering	Ku. Takahashi, K. Acheson, K. Mogi	962 126
Fuji 500km	JSC	24 November	Nova Engineering	Ku. Takahashi, K. Acheson, K. Mogi	962 126

1987 Japanese Sportscar Championship: Manufacturers – Porsche
1987 Japanese Sportscar Champion Drivers – Ku. Takahashi, K. Acheson

1988

Fuji 500km	JSC	6 March	Nova Engineering	H. Okada, S. Dickens	962 132
Suzuka 500km	JSC	10 April	Vern Schuppan	E. Elgh, M.-S. Sala	962 003
Fuji 1,000km	JSC	1 May	Kremer Racing	K. Nissen, B. Giacomelli	962 CK6-88
Fuji 500 Miles	JSC	24 July	Nova Engineering	H. Okada, S. Dickens	962 132
Suzuka 1,000km	JSC	28 August	Nova Engineering	H. Okada, S. Dickens	962 132

1988 Japanese Sportscar Championship: Manufacturers – Porsche
1988 Japanese Sportscar Champion Drivers – H. Okada, S. Dickens

All Japan Sportscar Championship (AJSC)

1989

Fuji 500km	AJSC	12 march	Nova Engineering	H. Grohs, A. Nakaja	962 132
Fuji 1,000km	AJSC	30 April	Vern Schuppan	V. Schuppan, E. Elgh	962 008
Fuji 500 Miles	AJSC	23 July	Kremer Racing	M. Sekiya, H. Okada	962 CK6/1
Suzuka 1,000km	AJSC	3 December	Alpha Construction	Ku. Takahashi, S. Dickens	962 134

1989 All Japan Sportscar Championshipship: Manufacturers – Porsche
1989 All Japan Sportscar Champion Drivers – Ku. Takahashi, S. Dickens

Races in which the Porsche Doppel-Kupplung (PDK) transmission was used

1984
Imola DNF (transmission)

1985
Brands Hatch 5th
Malaysia DNF (driveshaft)

1986
Monza (WEC) 1st and 6th
Nürburgring (Supercup) 1st
Silverstone (WEC) 2nd
Le Mans test day races 1st
Le Mans DNF (transmission)
Hockenheim (Supercup) 1st
Norisring (WEC and Supercup) 15th
Nürburgring (WEC) DNF (accident)
Spa (WEC) 2nd and 7th
Nürburgring (Supercup) 2nd
Fuji (WEC) 25th (driveshaft) and DNF (transmission)

1987
Jarama (WEC) 2nd
Jerez (WEC) 2nd
Monza (WEC) 6th (defective turbo)
Nürburgring (Supercup) 1st
Silverstone (WEC) 3rd
Norisring (Supercup) 3rd (DNF from WEC race)
Hockenheim (Supercup) 1st
Diepholz (Supercup) 2nd
Nürburgring (Supercup) 2nd

1988
Nürburgring (Supercup) 2nd
Hockenheim (Supercup) 11th
Norisring (Supercup) 2nd
Diepholz (Supercup) DNF (transmission)
Nürburgring (Supercup) 1st

Appendix 4
CHASSIS NUMBERS

This is all known 956s and 962s built, with first owners and showing first race (and finishing position), subsequent wins in either the WEC (or WSPC), IMSA and JSC (or AJSPC), and other comments. This is not intended to be a complete history of each car, but a preliminary guide.

The list is based on the best information available to the author at the time of writing, but no guarantee can be given for accuracy or comprehensiveness. Racing is racing and cars get crashed, monocoques get replaced and in some cases the original tubs were repaired. In my researches it has become clear that the term 'written off' doesn't really apply to a racing car, it only opens up the possibility of two new cars emerging from one original! As Kevin Jeanette has always stressed, there are a lot of 're's involved in racing – rebuilt, re-chassised, restored, rebodied and replaced. Identifying what 're-' applies to any car is a vital aspect of determining its history, so I have deliberately avoided going too deeply into the detail life adventures of every car. If this information sets you up with a string of questions about a certain car, then it has achieved its aim! My thanks to Jürgen Barth, Bob Carlson, Jim Busby and Kevin Jeannette for their contributions to this list

Chassis number	Class	Year of build	First owner	Debut (and first race position); subsequent international race wins; other comments
Factory chassis (10 cars)				
956 001	C	1982	Porsche	First prototype, Silverstone (2nd)
956 002	C	1982	Porsche	Le Mans (1st)
956 003	C	1982	Porsche	Le Mans (2nd); Spa, Fuji, Brands Hatch Le Mans 83 (1st)
956 004	C	1982	Porsche	Le Mans (3rd)
956 005	C	1983	Porsche	Monza (2nd); Nürburgring, Le Mans (2nd), Spa Later damaged Weissach, given to Porsche museum
956 006	C	1983	Porsche	Monza (7th)
956 007	C	1983	Porsche	Silverstone (1st). Crashed Nürburgring
956 008	C	1983	Porsche	Damaged Weissach. Rebuilt for Trust/Rothmans
956 009	C	1983	Porsche	Fuji, Oct 83 (1st) 84: Monza, Nürburging, Spa, Fuji, Sept. Sandown Park
956 010	C	1984	Porsche	Monza (2nd) Silverstone, Mosport 85: achieved first PDK finish at Brands Hatch
1983 customer build (12 cars)				
956 101	C	1983	Kremer Racing	Silverstone (5th) First ordered by de Cadenet 85: run by Nova in 86: Suzuka (Aug)
956 102	C	1983	John Fitzpatrick Racing	Zolder (2nd)

956 103	C	1983	T-Bird Racing (Preston Henn)	Le Mans (10th)
956 104	C	1983	Joest Racing	Zolder (1st), Monza
956 105	C	1983	Dieter Schornstein	Zolder (6th)
956 106	C	1983	Richard Lloyd Racing	Monza (6th)
956 107	C	1983	Porsche	Test bed for F1 engine, Frankfurt IAA car; Porsche museum
956 108	C	1983	Nova Engineering	Suzuka, April 83 (1st). Crashed Fuji
956 109	C	1983	Obermaier	Zolder (DNF) (Laessig/Plankenhorn)
956 110	C	1983	John Fitzpatrick Racing	Le Mans (DNF), Brands Hatch (1st)
956 111	C	1983	Brun Motorsport	Norisring (DNF) 85: sold to Trust Engineering
956 112	C	1983	Matsuda collection	Fuji, Oct 83 (4th)

1984-onwards factory build (19 cars)

962 001	IMSA	1984	Porsche	Daytona (DNF)
962 002	C	1985	Porsche	Mugello (1st), Selangor
962 003	C	1985	Porsche	Mugello (NC), Hockenheim, Mosport Brands Hatch 86: Monza, Le Mans
962 004	C	1985	Porsche	Le Mans (DNF)
962 005	C	1986	Porsche	Norisring (15th) Lightweight Supercup car
962 006	C	1986	Porsche	Spa (7th) 87: Le Mans
962 007	C	1987	Porsche	Jerez (DNF)
962 008	C	1987	Porsche	Jarama (2nd)
962 009	C	1987	Porsche	Norisring (DNF) Sold to Tim Lee-Davey (Nürburgring 89, DNF)
962 010	C	1988	Porsche	Le Mans (2nd)
962 011	C	1989	Joest Racing	See 962 142 90: changed to IMSA GTP
962 012	C	1990	Joest Racing	Suzuka (DNF)
962 013	C	1990	Joest Racing	Le Mans (Written off in practice)
962 014	C	1990	Joest Racing	Suzuka (11th)
962 015	C	1990	Joest Racing	Le Mans (4th)
962 016	IMSA	1993	Joest Racing	Daytona (DNF), Road America
962 GT001	GT1	1994	Porsche	Prototype: not raced; monocoque
962 GT002	GT1	1994	Porsche/Joest Racing	Le Mans (3rd) Used monocoque 962 173
962 GT003	GT1	1994	Porsche/Joest Racing	Le Mans (1st) Used monocoque 962 176

1984-onwards customer build (83 cars)

956B 113	C	1984	Nova Engineering	Fuji, June (1st); Suzuka (Aug)
956B 114	C	1984	John Fitzpatrick Racing	Silverstone (8th)
956B 115	C	1984	Kremer Racing	Le Mans (6th) Sold to Alpha Cubic (Japan)
956B 116	C	1984	Brun Motorsport	Le Mans (4th), Imola
956B 117	C	1984	Joest Racing	Le Mans (1st) 86: Fuji
956B 118	C	1984	Nova Engineering	Fuji, (July, 2nd); Fuji (Nov) 85: Fuji (May). Repl. monocoque for 956 108

962 101	IMSA	1984	Bayside Disposal (Bruce Leven)	Riverside (2nd, Holbert) 85: Sold to Dyson Lime Rock, Road America, Columbus
962 102	IMSA	1984	Bob Akin	Charlotte (DNF)
962 103	IMSA	1984	Al Holbert	Charlotte (DNF); Mid-Ohio, Watkins Glen, Road America, Pocono, Daytona (Nov) 85: Miami, Laguna Seca, Charlotte, Mid-Ohio, Watkins Glen (July) 86: Daytona; Road America (NV) 87: Daytona, Lime Rock (NV)
962 104	IMSA	1984	T-Bird Racing (Preston Henn)	Daytona, Nov (3rd 85: Daytona 24, Sebring
962 105	C	1984	John Fitzpatrick Racing	Brands Hatch (3rd) Sold to Jim Busby 85: crashed at Daytona, believed not repaired
962 106	IMSA	1985	BF Goodrich (Jim Busby)	Daytona 24 (3rd)
962 107	C	1985	Brun Motorsport	Mugello (3rd) 86: converted to IMSA Believed reshelled to Thompson monocoque Later sold to Shelton brothers
962 108	IMSA	1985	BF Goodrich (Jim Busby)	Daytona (DNF) Chassis was replaced with Chapman 02C monocoque and known as 108B. 87: crashed again at Sears Point and rebuilt again with Chapman monocoque (03C)
962 109	C	1985	Bayside Disposal (Bruce Leven)	Road Atlanta (3rd), Sears Point 86: Miami
962 110	C	1985	Kremer Racing	Mugello (2nd), Monza 87: rebuilt with Thompson monocoque
962 111	C	1985	Trust Engineering	Suzuka, April (3rd), Fuji (July and Nov), Suzuka 86: Suzuka, Fuji (May, July and Nov) 87: Suzuka (Apr and Aug) Repl. monocoque for 956 113
962 112	C	1986	John Fitzpatrick Racing	Le Mans (10th) Repl. monocoque for 956 102
962 113	IMSA	1985	Bob Akin	Portland (DNF) 86: Sebring Repl. monocoque for 962 102 87: crashed, parts used to build new car with Chapman honeycomb (04C, NV) monocoque
962 114	C	1985	Kremer Racing	Monza (8th). Repl. monocoque for 956 110 86: given Thompson monocoque for Nürburgring
962 115	C	1985	Brun Motorsport	Monza (4th). Repl. monocoque for 956 116
962 116	IMSA	1986	Joest Racing	Daytona (Oct) 87: after Sebring, run in Group C with Thompson monocoque (known as 116IM) Believed to have received steel floor to improve stiffness
962 117	C	1986	Brun Motorsport	Monza (5th), Spa Repl. monocoque for 962 107
962 118	C	1986	Kremer Racing	Le Mans (DNF); Repl. monocoque for 962 110 87: rebuilt with Thompson monocoque
962 119	IMSA	1986	BF Goodrich	Daytona (DNF), West Palm Beach Repl. monocoque for 962 105 Disliked by drivers Painted as Rothmans car for promotion work

962 120	IMSA	1986	Rob Dyson	Miami (DNF). Riverside, Laguna Seca, Charlotte
962 121	IMSA	1986	Bayside Motorsports (Bruce Leven)	West Palm Beach (DNF) 87: Miami, Sebring, Laguna Seca, Mid Ohio, Sears Point, Del Mar
962 122	IMSA	1986	Rob Dyson	Watkins Glen (DNF), Sears Point, Daytona (Oct) 87: Road Atlanta, Watkins Glen, Road America
962 123	IMSA	1987	Primus Motorsport (Preston Henn)	Daytona (DNF). See Holbert HR6
962 124	C	1986	Porsche	Renumbered 962 006
962 125	C	1986	Porsche	Not registered, used as crash-test car
962 126	C	1986	Nova Engineering	Suzuka (Apr, 2nd); Fuji (July and Nov); Repl. monocoque for 956 115
962 127	C	1986	Trust Engineering	Suzuka (10th), Fuji (May) Repl. monocoque for 956 118
962 128	IMSA	1986	Brun Motorsport	Daytona (DNF)
962 129	C	1986	Joest Racing	Monza (DNF) Repl. monocoque for 956 117 91: Daytona
962 130	C	1987	Obermaier Racing	Le Mans (2nd) Repl. monocoque for 956 109
962 131	C	1988	Team Salamin	Jerez (9th)
962 132	C	1988	Nova Engineering	Fuji (Mar, 1st)
962 133	C	1988	Jochen Dauer	Nürburgring (DNF)
962 134	C	1988	Nova Engineering	Fuji (Mar, 6th)
962 135	C	1988	Porsche	Renumbered 962 007
962 136	C	1988	Porsche	Renumbered 962 008
962 137	C	1988	Porsche	Renumbered 962 009
962 138	C	1988	Tim Lee-Davey	Nürburgring (DNF)
962 139	IMSA	1988	Bayside Motorsports (Bruce Leven)	Daytona (4th)
962 140	C	1988	Porsche	Renumbered 962 010
962 141	C	1989	Porsche	Assigned for 8-cylinder prototype: 962/8-001 Later sold to Dauer, Nürburgring (DNF)
962 142	C	1989	Joest Racing	Dijon (1st). Run as 962 011
962 143	C	1989	Vern Schuppan	Fuji (Oct, 6th)
962 144	C	1990	Jochen Dauer	Monza (DNF). Later run by Joest
962 145	C	1989	Joest Racing	Le Mans (3rd)
962 146	C	1990	Vern Schuppan	Le Mans (12th)
962 147	C	1990	Nova Engineering	Suzuka (14th)
962 148	C	1989	Dyson Racing	Lime Rock (6th) 90: Tampa (NV, see 962 DR2)
962 149	C	1989	Joest Racing	Repl. monocoque for 962 012
962 150	C	1989	Brun Motorsport	Brands Hatch (6th)
962 151	C	1990	Nova Engineering	Suzuka (10th)
962 152	C	1990	Walter Lechner	Budapest (Interserie, 10th)
962 153	C	1990	Trust Engineering	Le Mans (13th)
962 154	C	1990	Alpha racing Team	Suzuka (8th) Monocoque built by Stickel, Germany
962 155	C	1990	Obermaier Racing	Suzuka (DNF). Monocoque by Fabcar
962 156	C	1990	Joest Racing	Repl. monocoque for 962 014. Stickel
962 157	C	1990	Team Salamin	Monza (16th). Fabcar
962 158	C	1990	Joest Racing	Repl. monocoque for 962 015; Stickel
962 159	C	1990	Trust Engineering	Le Mans (13th). Fabcar
962 160	C	1990	Brun Motorsport	Dijon (12th). Fabcar
962 161	C	1990	Richard Lloyd Racing/ Nick Mason	Le Mans (11th). Stickel

962 162	C	1990	Bo Strandell/ Convector Racing	Dijon (18th). Fabcar
962 163	C	1990	Brun Motorsport	Montreal (DNF). Fabcar
962 164	C	1990	Nova Engineering	Fuji (Mar, 10th). Fabcar
962 165	C	1990	Team Salamin	Nürburgring (4th). Stickel
962 166	C	1990	Trust Engineering	91: Fuji (Apr, 5th). Stickel
962 167	C	1990	Nova Engineering	91: Fuji (Mar, 5th). Fabcar
962 168	C	1990	Alpha Racing Team	91: Fuji (Mar, 8th). Fabcar
962 169	C	1990	Jochen Dauer	Believed to be Le Mans GT 1994 prototype LM GT001. Fabcar
962 170	C	1990	Trust Engineering	Spare monocoque. Fabcar
962 171	C	1990	Nova Engineering	Spare monocoque. Fabcar
962 172	IMSA	1990	Jochen Dauer	91: Daytona (DNF). Fabcar
962 173	C	1990	Jochen Dauer	94: basis for Le Mans car, LM GT002 Le Mans 1994 (3rd). Fabcar
962 174	C	1990	Bo Strandell	Use unknown. Fabcar
962 175	IMSA	1990	Jochen Dauer	91: Daytona (DNF)
962 176	C	1990	Jochen Dauer	94: basis for Le Mans car, LM GT003 Le Mans 1994 (1st). Fabcar
962 177	C	1991	Brun Motorsport	91: Daytona (DNS). Fabcar

Other 956/962 chassis

Richard Lloyd Racing (7 cars)

956 106b	C	1984	Richard Lloyd Racing	Spa (DNF)
956 106b2	C	1986	Richard Lloyd Racing	Silverstone (4th)
962 106b	C	1987	Britten-Lloyd Racing	Jarama (8th), Norisring
962 200	C	1988	Britten-Lloyd Racing	Jerez (4th)
962 201	C	1989	Lloyd-Porsche GB	Nürburgring (11th)
962 202	IMSA	1988	Dyson Racing	See Rob Dyson DR1
962 203	C	1989	Trust Engineering	Fuji (Mar, DNF) Later run by ADA Engineering

Holbert Racing (7 cars)

962 HR1	IMSA	1985	Al Holbert	Portland (1st), Pocono, Watkins Glen (Sept) Daytona (Dec) 86: Lime Rock, Mid-Ohio, Watkins Glen (July), Portland; Road America (NV, see 962 103) 87: Lime Rock (NV, see 962 103) Portland, San Antonio Holbert monocoque
962 HR2	IMSA	1986	Bayside Motorsport (Bruce Leven)	Daytona (DNF), Columbus 87: Columbus Holbert monocoque
962 HR3	IMSA	1986	Hotchkiss Wynns	Watkins Glen (8th) Fabcar monocoque F01
962 HR4	IMSA	1987	A. J. Foyt	Daytona (4th) Fabcar monocoque
962 HR5	IMSA	1987	Hotchkiss Wynns	Road America (6th) Repl. monocoque for HR3 Believed this chassis also known later as F02
962 HR6	IMSA	1987	Primus Motorsport	Believed to be factory monocoque 962 123
962 HR7	IMSA	1987	Holbert Racing	Chapman monocoque 01C (NV)

Kremer Racing (14 cars)

962 CK6C		1987	Kremer Racing	Fuji (Mar, 2nd)
				Used Thompson monocoque
962 CK6-88 C		1988	Kremer Racing	Fuji (Oct, 16th)
				Used Thompson monocoque
962 CK6/01 C		1989	Kremer Racing	Fuji (Mar, 4th)
				Used Thompson monocoque
962 CK6/02 C		1989	Kremer Racing	Budapest (Interserie, 1st)
				Carbon-fibre monocoque
				Leased to Strandell in 1990
962 CK6/03 C1		1989	Kremer Racing	Le Mans (9th)
				Carbon-fibre monocoque
962 CK6/04 C1		1990	Kremer Racing	Budapest (Interserie, 1st)
				Interserie champion.
				Carbon-fibre monocoque
962 CK6/05-2		1990	Kremer Racing	Suzuka (13th)
				Carbon-fibre monocoque
962 CK6/06-2		1990	Kremer Racing	Monza (9th)
				Used Thompson monocoque
962 CK6/07-2		1990	Kremer Racing	Le Mans (24th)
				Used Thompson monocoque
962 CK6/08 C1		1991	Kremer Racing	Nürburgring (3rd)
				Carbon-fibre monocoque
962 CK6/09 C1		1991	Kremer Racing	Le Mans (DNF)
				Used Thompson monocoque
962 CK7/01		1992	Kremer Racing	Interserie Spyder
962 CK7/02		1993	Kremer Racing	Interserie Spyder
962 CK8	WSC	1994	Kremer Racing	Le Mans (6th)
				95: Daytona
				Used Thompson monocoque

Brun Motorsport (8 cars)

962 001BM C		1987	Brun Motorsport	Jarama (7th)
				Thompson monocoque
962 002BM C		1987	Brun Motorsport	Brands Hatch (5th)
				Thompson monocoque
962 003BM	IMSA	1988	Gebhardt/Moretti	Sears Point (14th)
				Used Thompson monocoque
				Believed this was rebuilt by John Shapiro and was
				known from 1989 as 001GS
962 004BM C		1989	Brun Motorsport	Fuji (Mar, 3rd)
				Used Thompson monocoque
962 005BM C		1989	Brun Motorsport	Suzuka (Apr, 8th)
962 006BM C		1989	Brun Motorsport	Dijon (DNF)
962 007BM C		1990	Brun Motorsport	Suzuka (6th)
				Used Thompson monocoque
962 008BM C		1990	Brun Motorsport	Silverstone (8th)

Jim Busby (3 cars)

962 02C	IMSA	1986	BF Goodrich	Replacement Chapman monocoque
				for 108; also known as 108B.
				87: crashed at Sears Point
962 03C	IMSA	1989	BF Goodrich/Miller	Daytona (1st); West Palm Beach
				Also known as 962 108C
				Chapman monocoque
962 07C	IMSA	1990		Kevin Jeannette Spare Chapman monocoque
				Sold to Jeannette and built as Gunnar 966

Rene Herzog (2 cars)

962 05C	IMSA	1989	Rene Herzog	Sears Point (14th) Chapman monocoque Built by John Shapiro
962 06C	IMSA	1990	Rene Herzog	Chapman monocoque Built by Shapiro Later sold to Kevin Jeannette

Vern Schuppan (5 cars)

962 138/01	C	1989	Tim Lee-Davey	Le Mans (26th) Also known as SH962-89/01
962 138/02	C	1990	Tim Lee-Davey	Le Mans (19th)
962 TS/01C	C	1990	Vern Schuppan	Suzuka (Apr, 9th)
962 TS/02C	C2	1991	Vern Schuppan	Le Mans (DNF)
962 TS/03C	C2	1991	Vern Schuppan	Le Mans (DNF)

Rob Dyson (2 cars)

962 DR1	IMSA	1988	Dyson Racing	West Palm Beach (3rd) Is RLR 962 202
962 DR2	IMSA	1990	DSR Motorsport	Road Atlanta (5th) Tampa (NV, see 962 148) Used Fabcar honeycomb-monocoque

Gunnar Racing (1 car)

966 001	IMSA	1991	Gunnar Racing (Kevin Jeannette)	Daytona (NC) Used last Chapman 962 monocoque (C07) but was never built as 962 Used carbon-fibre dash panel

Walter Lechner (2 cars)

962 WLM01 C	1989		Walter Lechner (Salamin)	Nürburgring (German Supercup, 4th) Used Thompson monocoque
962 WLM02	C	1987	Walter Lechner	Nürburgring (German Supercup, 6th) Used Thompson monocoque

Franz Konrad (1 car)

962 001K	C	1990	Franz Konrad	Budapest (Interserie 11th) Believed Kremer Thompson monocoque (CK6/01?)

Heinz-Jürgen Dahmen (1 car)

962C

009/88	C	1988	Heinz-Jürgen Dahmen	Wunsdorf (Interserie, DNF)

Hans Obermaier (2 cars)

962 901	C	1990	Obermaier Racing	Suzuka (Apr, DNF) Used Thompson monocoque
962 902	C	1990	Obermaier Racing	Silverstone (10th) Used Thompson monocoque

Almeras Frères (1 car)

962 EAF/1	C	1990	Alemeras Frères	Monza (DNF) Used Thompson monocoque

Abbreviations: DNS = Did not start; DNF = Did not finish; NC = Not classified; NV = Entry not validated

BIBLIOGRAPHY

Porsche Racing Cars of the '70s by Paul Frère
Porsche in Motorsport by Peter Morgan
Porsche 917 by Peter Morgan
Classic Porsche Racing Cars by Michael Cotton
Porsche au Mans by Dominique Pascal
Endurance Racing 1982-1991 by Ian Briggs
Porsche 956-962 by John Allen
Porsche 956-962 – the most successful sports cars from Weissach by Ulrich Upietz
Porsche in Le Mans by Ulrich Upietz
Porsche Turbo Racing Cars by Ian Bamsey
The World's Greatest Motor Competitions: Le Mans by Ian Bamsey
Jaguar V12 Race Cars by Ian Bamsey and Joe Saward
Jaguar vs. Porsche by Ken Wells
Der Porsche 956/962 Lothar Boschen and Gustav Büsing
Time and Two Seats by János L. Wimpffen
Le Mans: The Porsche Years: 1975-1982 Compilation by R. M. Clarke

Le Mans: The Porsche and Jaguar Years: 1983-1991 Compilation by R. M. Clarke
1992 Le Mans 24 Hours by Jean-Marc Teissèdre and Christian Moity
1993 Le Mans 24 Hours by Jean-Marc Teissèdre and Christian Moity
Autocourse 1987-88 Hazleton Publishing
Autocourse 1988-89 Hazleton Publishing
Porsche Sport '93 by Ulrich Upietz
Porsche Sieg '94 24 Heures du Mans by Ulrich Upietz
Grand Prix Databook 1997
Porsche *Panorama* magazine (1982–1995) Porsche Club of America (in particular the Porsche Sport column by Bill Oursler)
Motor Sport magazine (1982–1993)
Autosport magazine (1981–1993)
Christophorus magazine (1986–1993)
Derek Bell by Derek Bell and Alan Henry
Porsche chassis numbers (web listing by Martin Krejci) www.962.com

INDEX